SHAKESPEARE AND THE NATURAL WORLD

Exploring the rich range of meanings that Shakespeare finds in the natural world, this book fuses ecocritical approaches to Renaissance literature with recent thinking about the significance of religion in Shakespeare's plays. MacFaul offers a clear introduction to some of the key problems in Renaissance natural philosophy and their relationship to Reformation theology, with individual chapters focusing on the role of animals in Shakespeare's universe, the representation of rural life, and the way in which humans' consumption of natural materials transforms their destinies. These discussions enable powerful new readings of Shakespeare's plays, including *A Midsummer Night's Dream*, *As You Like It*, *King Lear*, *Macbeth*, *The Tempest*, *The Winter's Tale*, and the history plays. Proposing that Shakespeare's representation of the relationship between man and nature anticipated that of the Romantics, this volume will interest scholars of Shakespeare studies, Renaissance drama and literature, and ecocritical studies of Shakespeare.

TOM MACFAUL is Lecturer in English at St Edmund Hall, University of Oxford. He is the author of many books and articles, including *Problem Fathers in Shakespeare and Renaissance Drama* (Cambridge, 2012), *Poetry and Paternity in Renaissance England* (Cambridge, 2010), and *Male Friendship in Shakespeare and his Contemporaries* (Cambridge, 2007).

SHAKESPEARE AND THE NATURAL WORLD

TOM MACFAUL

CAMBRIDGE
UNIVERSITY PRESS

CAMBRIDGE
UNIVERSITY PRESS

University Printing House, Cambridge CB2 8BS, United Kingdom

One Liberty Plaza, 20th Floor, New York, NY 10006, USA

477 Williamstown Road, Port Melbourne, VIC 3207, Australia

314-321, 3rd Floor, Plot 3, Splendor Forum, Jasola District Centre, New Delhi - 110025, India

79 Anson Road, #06-04/06, Singapore 079906

Cambridge University Press is part of the University of Cambridge.

It furthers the University's mission by disseminating knowledge in the pursuit of education, learning and research at the highest international levels of excellence.

www.cambridge.org
Information on this title: www.cambridge.org/9781107543577

First published 2015
First paperback edition 2018

A catalogue record for this publication is available from the British Library

Library of Congress Cataloging in Publication data
MacFaul, Tom.
Shakespeare and the natural world / Tom MacFaul.
pages cm
Includes bibliographical references and index.
ISBN 978-1-107-11793-8 (hardback)
1. Shakespeare, William, 1564–1616 – Knowledge – Natural history. 2. Shakespeare, William, 1564–1616 – Religion. 3. Nature in literature. 4. Animals in literature. 5. Country life in literature. 6. Human ecology in literature. 7. Ecocriticism I. Title.
PR3039.M34 2015
822.3′3 – dc23 2015014535

ISBN 978-1-107-11793-8 Hardback
ISBN 978-1-107-54357-7 Paperback

For Simon Dennis and Jonathan Holt,
and in memory of Daniel Webster (1972-2015)

Contents

Acknowledgements

This book has been a pleasure to write. My first note of gratitude goes to Merton College, Oxford, which provided me with a congenial and stimulating environment in which to work for three years. I am particularly grateful to my students there, some of whose questions prompted the project, on whom I tried out many of my initial ideas, and whose intelligent scepticism has helped me develop my thinking on a range of subjects, and I'm glad to take this opportunity to thank a few of them by name: Sanders Bernstein, Clio Doyle, Alex Grafen, Sarah Jones, Lucy Pinching, Cathy Scott and John Warriner. My new college, St Edmund Hall, Oxford, has been very welcoming, and I'm grateful to the college and to the English Faculty of Oxford University for help with research costs. I'm also grateful to various friends and colleagues for one reason or another: Sally Bayley, Aisling Byrne, Steven Gunn, Richard McCabe, Ben Morgan, Lucy Newlyn, Jenni Nuttall, Emma Smith, Tiffany Stern and Michael Whitworth.

I am very grateful to Sarah Stanton, of Cambridge University Press, for her faith in the project, and to the Press's readers for their invaluable suggestions about tightening up the argument. Courtney Lee Adams has copy-edited the text efficiently, and Micah Coston has prepared the index, and has also helped to check quotations. I thank them both warmly. I take full responsibility for any remaining errors.

As the work on this book was coming to a close, I was deeply saddened by the death of my friend Dan Webster. The book is dedicated to his memory. He shares this dedication with Simon and Jonny because I know he would have liked that, and for other very good reasons.

Introduction
Broken knowledge

The natural world in Shakespeare's time was conceived as a complex and tangled system of sympathies and antipathies, and man's place in it was highly questionable; everything in life was seen as connected, but this was the source of worry and wonder rather than of complacency.[1] New religious, philosophical and scientific ideas created uncertainty about how the natural world worked, and about its relationship to the divine. Those ideas created anxiety: as we'll see, there was even a worry that how people thought about nature might have an effect on how the world really worked. The sense of order in the natural world was becoming increasingly provisional, slippery and complex, having to accommodate more and more strange phenomena, which challenged the belief in man's centrality and his ability to comprehend and master the world. In Shakespeare's plays, those people who try to master nature in an individualistic way tend to be doomed, but that those who adopt a give-and-take attitude to the relationship between people and nature may find some chance of moving towards some kind of salvation, finding a form of grace. Recognizing the compromised and compromising quality of the natural world enables Shakespeare's characters to be happy in this world, and possibly points towards the more permanent happiness of the afterlife.

Hamlet famously tells Horatio that there are 'more things in heaven and earth . . . Than are dreamt of in your philosophy' (I. v. 166–7).[2] He believes that the common natural philosophy of his time is an inadequate dream, and expresses a certain taunting delight at his friend's discomfiture. He

[1] I use the phrase 'Shakespeare's time' (or some variation thereof), rather than 'Renaissance', 'Early Modern' or 'Reformation', as the phrase is more neutral: I simply want to focus on the intellectual atmosphere of Shakespeare's working life (from the late 1580s to around 1613), without pressing on any of the ideological triggers that the other terms involve.

[2] All references to Shakespeare's works are to *The Riverside Shakespeare*, ed. G. Blakemore Evans et al. (Boston: Houghton Mifflin, 1997), though I have frequently consulted the most recent Arden, Oxford and Cambridge editions, and have adopted some of their readings, as well as making minor orthographical changes of my own.

welcomes the ghost on account of it being 'a stranger' (line 165), something that doesn't fit into the commonplace order of things. Yet its strangeness is paradoxical: it is at least the likeness of his own father, the former king of this country, not an intruder. Its presence makes Hamlet inclined to become 'strange or odd' (line 170) in his antic disposition, and makes 'time... out of joint' (line 188). The order of things is subverted, but precisely by a representative of an old order. In the face of such a strange phenomenon, Hamlet and his companions are struck with wonder as their system of knowledge is broken, and they are revealed as being 'fools of nature' (I. iv. 54). That phrase is complex: the main sense is that they are fools because they only believe in natural phenomena when there are supernatural things too; yet they are also like 'natural' fools in being born stupid, and such fools were often considered strangely wise; finally, they are fooled *by* Nature, who has tricked them into believing that the natural world is limited and comprehensible.

Nature, for Shakespeare, always has tricks up its sleeve; there is always something more. King Lear declares that if we 'Allow not nature more than nature needs, / Man's life is cheap as beast's' (II. iv. 266–7). Nature is excessive, particularly in the way it links person to person, often grotesquely: Lear has just called Goneril 'a bile, / A plague-sore, or embossed carbuncle, / In my corrupted blood', but this is not a radical repudiation of her – indeed, it is rather an inverted recognition of their ineradicable connection, for he 'must needs call [her] mine' (lines 223–5). Organic connectedness is all, and the sense of connection involved is always related to and mediated through something excessive and supplementary, like a boil or Hamlet's 'vicious mole of nature' (I. iv. 24), a mark of inborn sin, which is both part of natural wholeness and a subterranean supplement which disfigures even as it gives character.[3]

That sense of excess, of the irreducible untidiness and slipperiness of the natural world, is a central subject of this book. While some of Shakespeare's contemporaries – and some of his characters – believed that man could stand in a special place outside nature and could therefore master it (as Archimedes had famously imagined),[4] Shakespeare repeatedly shows the dangerous folly of that presumption. The natural world, in all its complexity, is used to channel and compromise human motives, challenging the

[3] As the Ghost soon manifests itself under the stage, it becomes punningly connected to this mole (I. v. 170). On Shakespeare's sense of beauty being characterized by such flaws, see Stephen Greenblatt, *Shakespeare's Freedom* (Chicago: The University of Chicago Press, 2010), chapter 2.

[4] He claimed, according to Pappus of Alexandria, that if he had a big enough lever, and a place to stand, he could move the whole world.

vain notion of what Macbeth calls the 'single state of man' (I. iii. 140) – whether that notion is driven by ideas of religious transcendence, political power, or scientific knowledge. Those who accept the limitation of human wisdom, however, may have more hope, and may even find a strange kind of grace in doing so.

A central argument of this book is that Shakespeare anticipates the Romantics in finding hints of something unfallen, and even potentially redemptive, in the natural world. Raymond Williams sees a decisive shift in attitudes towards nature during the eighteenth century, between Addison and Wordsworth:

> Two principles of Nature can . . . be seen simultaneously. There is nature as a principle of order, of which the ordering mind is part, and which human activity, by regulating principles, may then rearrange and control. But there is also nature as a principle of creation, of which the creative mind is part, and from which we may learn the truths of our own sympathetic nature.[5]

I want to argue that these principles can be found, at least in embryo, in the works of Shakespeare and some of his contemporaries, and that they are even more significantly and productively entangled there. Whereas the Romantics have to make a leap of faith in order to appropriate nature's validation of human creativity, for Shakespeare nature is a creative principle both within and outside man, one which he must acknowledge he can never master. While many of his contemporaries were increasingly insisting on man's capacity to master nature, Shakespeare sees a certain wise passivity as the prerequisite for accessing grace through nature. It is important, though, to recognize that Shakespeare's natural world was not the same thing as Wordsworth's: the orthodox religious thinking of his time made it clear that nature was fallen, 'cursed in the curse of man', as John Donne puts it.[6] Yet intimations of redemption could be found in other forms of thinking that cut across and complicated religious orthodoxy.

The orderly medieval worldview, in which nature was organized on the basis of a clear, hierarchical set of connections between orders of being, was on the brink of abandonment, and would be decisively relinquished as a result of Descartes' and Newton's mechanistic ideas; yet, even while the older view of nature was becoming obsolete, some tried to rescue it by conceiving of it as even more organically and mysteriously interconnected

[5] Raymond Williams, *The Country and the City* (London: Chatto & Windus, 1973), p. 127.

[6] 'The First Anniversary: An Anatomy of the World' (1611), line 200. References to *The Poems of John Donne*, ed. Robin Robbins, 2 vols. (Harlow: Longman, 2008).

than earlier ages had argued. Such thinkers, whether influenced by Stoicism, Epicureanism, or Neoplatonism, or by an eclectic mix of those lines of ancient thought, often believed that the natural world was self-sufficient, unfallen, or even itself divine.

Another key aspect of the times' intellectual ferment emerged as a consequence of such controversies about the operation of the natural world: an increasing sense that one's beliefs or opinions about how the world worked might actually change the nature of the phenomena; as Hamlet puts it, 'there is nothing either good or bad, but thinking makes it so' (II. ii. 249–50). This had an effect on both natural and religious thinking, for the Reformation had already shown people the relativism and provisionality of the most important aspects of belief. Whereas political authority was marshalled to ensure at least outward conformity on matters of religious belief, a great deal more freedom was allowed in people's thinking about the natural world, and that freedom of thought could in turn affect people's understanding of religious questions, most notably the relations of humans to grace.

The primary purpose of grace is, of course, to bring about salvation. Yet it is also clear that the language of grace is frequently used to refer to more mundane forms of redemption: the reconciliation of lovers and family members, the resolution of political conflict, and, more generally, the finding of earthly happiness. When the language of grace and redemption is used in such contexts, it is at one level a figure of speech, but it may also be a prefiguration. Earthly happiness may be an outward and visible sign of inward and spiritual redemption. Correspondingly, the Book of Nature, if read aright, may give signs of divine approval. In addition, the Reformation's detachment of good works from grace, though downgrading the value of good works and earthly happiness, may have enabled the natural world to stand as a relatively autonomous sphere of satisfaction for human beings who can't do anything about their ultimate fate. Happiness on earth may not necessarily prefigure salvation, but it is still happiness, and it is something we can work to achieve. It may at least set one on the road to grace, or prepare one for it.

How far one could actively prepare oneself for grace was a highly controversial matter. The Reformation was particularly keen to convict the Roman Catholic Church of the Pelagian heresy – the idea that humans could bring about their own salvation by good deeds – but Pelagianism has a tendency to creep in by the back door, even when the orthodox are on the lookout for it.[7] Many orthodox Protestants, while insisting that faith is

[7] See Alison Shell, *Shakespeare and Religion* (London: Methuen, 2010), p. 166.

the only route to salvation, allow that the human will at least participates in the process of arriving at faith – voluntarism.[8] The orthodox may also insist that good works are not necessary to salvation, but they are an *appropriate* response to an inward conviction of divine favour, and evidence of sanctification.[9] This idea almost aestheticizes morality, making it something pleasing to God but ultimately inconsequential for one's salvation.[10] Good works become a separate sphere of meaning in this world, even if they don't affect the next one.

The tendency to separate spheres of meaning chimes with new approaches to studying nature. Those who focus on a study of the natural world (e.g., Francis Bacon) often bracket off matters of salvation as being already settled by an inscrutable divine providence. In doing so, however, they often import categories of good and bad from religious thinking, with the result that a natural world studied on its own terms starts to have its own apparent capacity to validate human action. This approach, along with the separation of good works from salvation, together helps motivate human responses to the natural world which are unanchored to theology even as they are structured by habits of religious responsiveness. These attitudes allow for the validation – up to a point – of human art, while requiring that art to be rooted in the natural world. Both may derive some of their force from Stoicism.

Stoics argue that humans must make their will conform with nature, and that the virtue that arises from such conformity is its own reward. *Arete* (virtue/excellence) leads to *eudaimonia* (happiness/flourishing). This view is in itself compatible with Calvinism (indeed Calvin himself was much influenced by Stoicism), in that it provides a basis for morality while leaving salvation out of the issue.[11] Renaissance Stoics – most notably Lipsius –

8 See R. T. Kendall, *Calvin and English Calvinism to 1649* (Oxford: Oxford University Press, 1979), pp. 33–4, 59–61.

9 See William J. Bouwsma, *John Calvin: A Sixteenth-Century Portrait* (New York: Oxford University Press, 1988), pp. 88, 180–1, 199. See also Kendall, *Calvin and English Calvinism*, pp. 25, 75, 87, 91.

10 The preacher narrator of Marilynne Robinson's *Gilead* (London: Virago, 2005), pp. 141–2 comments: 'Calvin says somewhere that each of us is an actor on a stage and God is the audience. That metaphor has always interested me, because it makes us artists of our own behaviour, and the reaction of God to us might be thought of as aesthetic rather than morally judgmental in the ordinary sense'. For Calvin's use of theatrical metaphors, and the idea of the natural world as a participative theatre of God's glory, see Belden C. Lane, 'Spirituality as the Performance of Desire: Calvin on the World as the Theatre of God's Glory', *Spiritus* 1 (2001): 1–30.

11 On Calvin and Stoicism, see John Sellars, *Stoicism* (Durham: Acumen, 2006), p. 142, and Bouwsma, *John Calvin*, for a fuller account of Calvin's own struggles with Stoicism. Reid Barbour, in *English Stoics and Epicureans: Ancient Legacies in Early Stuart Culture* (Amherst: University of Massachusetts Press, 1998), pp. 94–105, sees an alliance between Stoicism and Calvinism that answered a corresponding alliance between Epicureanism and Arminianism, even though Calvinists tried to deny this (pp. 204–8).

attempted to accommodate Christianity with their philosophy, and though Stoicism is not on its own terms genuinely compatible with Christianity, as it is a wholly materialist (or pantheist) philosophy, its very incompatibility enables its understanding of the natural world to operate in parallel with Christian thinking, separating the orders of nature and grace.[12] English Stoicism attempts a balance between 'free will and submissive holism' that resonates in Shakespeare.[13] Renaissance Neostoicism offers a grounding for the idea of natural virtue, then, one which chimes with the Protestant anxiety about preparation for grace. For Stoics, if one cannot become the ideally constant Sage, one can at least *prepare* oneself in the direction of the ideal: the process is as valuable as the end product.[14] The analogies with Protestant thinking are clear (one can't earn grace, but one can be ready for it).[15] If humans are to fit their will to that of nature, they need to recognize the limitations of their own capacities – and this, I think, is the central way in which Shakespeare presents the natural world: as a means of mediating our relation to others, as a source of happiness, as a way of limiting the exercise of our will, and – at least potentially – as a means of salvation.

I do not, it must be stressed, mean to argue that Shakespeare *is* a Stoic, any more than he is a Calvinist, a Catholic or a Platonist.[16] What I mean to show is that there was an extraordinary range of thinkable ideas about nature in his time, and that he was able, with the unique eclecticism of the dramatist, to make suggestive imaginative patterns out of mixtures of those ideas, however heterodox, such mixing might be considered. 'Thought is free,' sings Stephano in *The Tempest*, but he's soon frightened out of that liberal view by the invisible Ariel's music, and prays for 'Mercy' (III. ii. 123, 131) before being consoled by Caliban. This is a highly characteristic movement: an expansion of thought is reined in by recalcitrant reality, but the free play of beliefs and opinions is not wholly or finally stifled.

[12] Stoicism's sense of the cosmos as a living being, organically interconnected in all sorts of ways, is in turn compatible with much modern thinking about nature, such as James Lovelock's Gaia hypothesis; see Sellars, *Stoicism*, pp. 93, 103, 95.

[13] Barbour, *English Stoics*, p. 214.

[14] See Barbour, *English Stoics*, pp. 116–7.

[15] See Bouwsma, *John Calvin*, p. 187. The question of preparation for faith is controversial: according to Calvin, there is no such thing, but there is rather preparation *of* faith, which is God's business rather than man's. However, Calvin's followers tended to slip into more voluntaristic positions. See Kendall, *Calvin and English Calvinism*, pp. 19–20, 64.

[16] See T. S. Eliot, 'Shakespeare and the Stoicism of Seneca', in *Selected Essays*, 3rd ed. (London: Faber and Faber, 1951), pp. 126–40. Eliot's point that Shakespeare 'needed less contact' with an idea 'in order to absorb all that he required' is a crucial one for my argument: the availability of an idea in his time is enough for us to be reasonably confident that he could make imaginative use of it.

Thinking has an active, imaginatively transitive power in Shakespeare's plays, transforming the world, even if only for a moment.[17]

Opinion, belief and point of view therefore have considerable traction. Leonard Barkan points out that in Nicholas of Cusa's account the scholastic model of proportional relationships breaks down 'because everything within the creation depends upon point of view, i.e. these familiar proportions represent only our limited point of view'.[18] Whether our limited point of view is responsible or whether, as in later thinkers, the sense of harmony in nature is fractured by human interference, there is no stability. Opinion has power. Sixteenth-century English people had grown used to sudden changes of religious position, and anticipated the possibility of more changes, with the result that their deepest religious beliefs had become privatized, provisional, equivocal.[19] Though questions of natural philosophy were not so subject to official changes of belief system, an open-minded, ironically distanced attitude to religion could easily spill over into other spheres of belief, particularly when they were not crisply distinguished from each other. Alison Shell shows that while Shakespeare's work is 'saturated in religious discourse', 'the Judaeo-Christian story is something less than a master narrative' for Shakespeare (unlike most of his contemporaries).[20] Likewise, Shakespeare is uniquely capable of saturating his works with doctrines of the natural world, without getting tied down by any one master narrative. Shell further argues that many of Shakespeare's plays exist in a *gentile* world, that is, a world in which the grand narratives of the Judaeo-Christian tradition don't quite apply; yet she is clear that such a fictional world was an uneasy one for Shakespeare's audience.[21] These gentile worlds open space for experiment: Sarah Beckwith has suggested that Reformed belief opened the door for a certain bewildering sense that subjective attitudes could transform the objective reality of the world; as she puts it,

> Reformed sacramental theology . . . situates the efficacy of the sacrament in the transformation of the one receiving communion, in the subjective faith – and knowledge – of the worshipper rather than the objective

[17] E.g. in *Henry V*, where we are invited to 'Think, when we talk of horses, that you see them / Printing their proud hooves i' th' receiving earth' (Prologue 26–7), and Troilus's insistence that he will 'Think' Diomedes' hand an altar of sacrifice for Cressida (*Troilus and Cressida*, IV. iii. 8).

[18] Leonard Barkan, *Nature's Work of Art: The Human Body as Image of the World* (New Haven: Yale University Press, 1975), p. 9.

[19] For a good discussion of this topic, see Lena Cowen Orlin, *Locating Privacy in Tudor London* (Oxford: Oxford University Press, 2007), p. 10.

[20] *Shakespeare and Religion*, p. 3.

[21] *Shakespeare and Religion*, pp. 205, 216.

(*ex opere operato*) work of the priest. 'You will receive so much as you believe you receive,' proclaims Luther.[22]

Queen Elizabeth seems to have believed in an opposite but correlated position, writing of the Eucharist,

> 'Twas Christ the Word that spake it.
> The same took bread and brake it,
> And as the Word did make it,
> So I believe and take it.[23]

A variant version makes the point of the last two lines even clearer: 'And what the Lord did make it, / That I believe and take it'. For Luther, whatever one believes can perhaps alter the nature of reality; but Elizabeth suggests that the objective nature of the world as made by God can affect one's belief – one therefore has to accept a rather peculiar position, believing in something without knowing what it is. There is considerable give and take between mind and world, which are in a mutually dynamic relation. If human opinion could change the nature of such pivotal phenomena as the Eucharist, surely it had an analogous power to change more trivial, secondary aspects of the natural world.

Before we look further at the ideas available, though, it is important to set out the problems in writing about such a complex concept as 'nature'. What we mean by nature has been a key issue in recent ecocriticism. Timothy Morton warns us that the very idea of 'Nature' tends to take us too far into the realm of metaphysics,[24] but if we are alert to the concept's slipperiness, it can remain helpful; as Mary Midgley has pointed out, 'if you try to sling Nature – or indeed the whole idea of Nature – out through the door, she always comes quietly back down the chimney'.[25]

C. S. Lewis's careful study of the word's implications is a valuable starting-point: he shows that 'nature' first means the characteristic properties of any given thing, then comes to mean the characteristic properties of everything, then everything (what Lewis calls the 'dangerous sense'); the crucial turn comes when what Lewis calls the 'demoted sense' of the word emerges, meaning everything but the God who created it. But nature can then be demoted – or promoted – in opposition to man's activity: when

[22] Sarah Beckwith, *Shakespeare and the Grammar of Forgiveness* (Ithaca: Cornell University Press, 2011), p. 27.

[23] Elizabeth I, *Collected Works*, ed. Leah S. Marcus, Janel Mueller and Mary Beth Rose (Chicago: The University of Chicago Press, 2000), p. 47.

[24] Timothy Morton, *Ecology without Nature: Rethinking Environmental Aesthetics* (Cambridge, MA: Harvard University Press, 2009).

[25] Mary Midgley, *Are You an Illusion?* (Durham: Acumen, 2014), p. 83.

we want to praise man's creativity or rationality, nature is something to rise above, but when we want to condemn man's interference, that interference is called 'unnatural'.[26] Though his whole reading of the term's development is a salutary corrective against Romantic conceptions of nature, Lewis also acknowledges that our sense of relief at our escape from obviously man-made worlds has some claim to be called *natural*: when natural forces are more visible and human activity less salient, we instinctively feel ourselves to be entering the natural world; however, much that world may in fact be altered by human action.[27]

This idea has been developed by Kate Soper: admitting like Lewis that our commonplace talk about nature is loose, she insists (following Wittgenstein) that the ordinary (what she calls the 'lay') meanings of the term make desirable discriminations about our uses of the world.[28] Less philological and historical than Lewis, and inflected by more recent modes of thinking, Soper has updated his warnings about the potential confusions in the idea of nature. She shows that ecopolitical appeals to nature are in tension with a postmodern identity politics which rejects any appeal to the natural. Soper deftly finds a middle ground, acknowledging the discursive dangers of lazy appeals to nature's authority, while recognizing that a realist approach to the natural is needed to set the basis for any legitimate activist thinking, or indeed any kind of 'explanatory and prescriptive force' for one's arguments.[29]

Between Lewis and Soper, Raymond Williams famously warned that nature is 'perhaps the most complex word in the language', but he also provides a clear potted history of that complexity, with more political implications than are present in Lewis. Williams shows that the dominant medieval–Renaissance concept was the idea of Nature as a deity, subordinate only to the Christian God, and sometimes His competitor as an 'absolute monarch', replaced in the seventeenth century by the more comprehensible, negotiable sense of Nature as a 'constitutional monarch, with a new emphasis on natural laws', into which men could (and indeed should) enquire.[30] Shakespeare's age, one might say, was trying to preserve a mixed constitution, rather like Queen Elizabeth's famous 'monarchical

[26] C. S. Lewis, *Studies in Words*, 2nd edition (Cambridge: Cambridge University Press, 1967), pp. 24–64.

[27] *Studies in Words*, p. 74.

[28] Kate Soper, *What Is Nature? Culture, Politics and the Non-Human* (Oxford: Blackwell, 1995), pp. 20, 182–4.

[29] *What Is Nature?*, p. 133.

[30] Raymond Williams, *Keywords: A Vocabulary of Culture and Society*, revised ed. (London: Flamingo, 1983), pp. 219–24.

republic';[31] the paradoxes involved had deep political, scientific and imaginative implications which will be central to this book.

Recent ecocriticism of Renaissance literature has admirably developed from the conceptual groundwork we find in Lewis, Soper and Williams. Gabriel Egan has convincingly argued that the organic and often holistic thinking which permeates Shakespeare's plays need not be seen as politically conservative, but in fact frequently provides opportunities for real competition over political matters.[32] We do not need to return to the outdated – though sometimes unfairly maligned – concept of the Great Chain of Being, which Tillyard saw as central to Elizabethan and Jacobean culture;[33] rather, we might see a system of order that is much more complex and tangled, and which enabled (though also continually put in question) relations between humans and their environment. Todd Borlik, developing from Egan, has shown that an alert reading of the meanings of nature in the period can help us recognize the limitations of human political power, and emphasizes how a 'green' version of the Great Chain roots human subjectivity in non-human nature.[34]

Others have taken more pessimistic views: Bruce Boehrer shows how the drama of Shakespeare's times responded to ecological challenges, and to fears about the changing natural environment;[35] Charlotte Scott has argued that Shakespeare's plays are informed by early modern discourses of husbandry, and that those discourses, like the plays (and the Sonnets), emphasize an ongoing transition to human mastery of the natural environment.[36] The present book takes rather a different line: while Boehrer argues that Shakespeare becomes more pessimistic about the natural world as his work develops, I argue that he shows a continuing – if increasingly

[31] See Patrick Collinson, 'The Monarchical Republic of Queen Elizabeth I', in *Elizabethan Essays* (London: Hambledon Press, 1994), pp. 31–57.

[32] Gabriel Egan, *Green Shakespeare: From Ecopolitics to Ecocriticism* (Abingdon: Routledge, 2006), p. 4 and *passim*. Human activity since the Industrial Revolution has undoubtedly changed our planet's ecosystems so radically that catastrophe is probably imminent, and perhaps unavoidable. Enlightenment universalism was right insofar as it's true that fossil fuels burned in Accrington affect the climate of the Antarctic, which in turn makes seas rise in Sri Lanka. As Timothy Morton points out, 'everything is connected. And it sucks'. – Timothy Morton, *The Ecological Thought* (Cambridge, MA: Harvard University Press, 2010), p. 33.

[33] E. M. W. Tillyard, *The Elizabethan World Picture* (London: Chatto & Windus, 1943), A.O. Lovejoy, *The Great Chain of Being* (Cambridge, MA: Harvard University Press, 1964).

[34] Todd A. Borlik, *Ecocriticism and Early Modern English Literature: Green Pastures* (New York: Routledge, 2011).

[35] Bruce Boehrer, *Environmental Degradation in Jacobean Drama* (Cambridge: Cambridge University Press, 2013).

[36] Charlotte Scott, *Shakespeare's Nature: From Cultivation to Culture* (Oxford: Oxford University Press, 2014).

complicated – hope that nature may have redemptive properties, if one takes the right stance towards it.[37] Scott's sense of human mastery has a distinctly moral element: husbandry of the environment is an external expression of self-cultivation. While I agree with Scott's view that the environment enables 'an affective relationship between the individual and their social world', this book differs from Scott in emphasizing Shakespeare's sense of the need for a certain wise passivity in such engagements.[38] Human thought and human will may be able to change the world, for better or worse, but the natural world tends to react dynamically to such changes, in turn altering the range of what is thinkable and willable. When men – and it is mostly men – try to master nature and insist on their standing outside it, they tend to be destroyed; when people – often women – accept the mystery of nature and our complex embeddedness in it, they may find a way towards grace.

Attitudes to nature cannot be detached from religious questions in the period. Consequently, in addition to ecocritical thinking, this book is informed by the 'religious turn' in Renaissance/ Reformation studies: that is, the increasing desire to take seriously the religious beliefs of the time on their own terms, rather than as the mere instruments of power.[39] As David Scott Kastan puts it, religion was the 'epistemological ground organizing the fundamental categories of thought' in the period, and Shakespeare's plays 'assume a world in which God is immanent, even if that immanence is not their subject'.[40] I want to develop from this approach, by focussing on matters which a modern audience might not see as religious, but which always tended, in the mindset of the period, to bring religious matters into play. The invocation of nature was not a way of escaping from a religious perspective, but rather enabled a broadening of religious questions, and

[37] See especially *Environmental Degradation*, p. 78, where Boehrer argues that 'after *As You Like It*, no Shakespearean character ever again discovers in nature the antidote to urban or courtly ills'. As I show in the chapters below, such antidotes can be found in plays as various as *All's Well That Ends Well*, *Cymbeline*, *The Winter's Tale*, and even provisionally in *Timon of Athens* and *King Lear*; it is true, though, that if there are antidotes they tend not to be discovered by individuals, emerging rather as aspects of the community, or, more broadly, the shape of the play's imaginative world.

[38] Simon C. Estok, *Ecocriticism and Shakespeare: Reading Ecophobia* (New York: Palgrave Macmillan, 2011), p. 89, meanwhile, is committed to seeing the connections between 'ecophobia' and other kinds of habits of 'homocentric' thinking in Shakespeare's time. But, as Timothy Morton points out, 'the position of hunting for anthropocentrism *is anthropocentrism*' – *The Ecological Thought*, p. 76. My position, like Shakespeare's, starts from an unapologetically anthropocentric focus, but I believe that Shakespeare's anthropocentrism is ultimately sufficiently decentring to avoid ecophobia.

[39] See Ken Jackson and Arthur F. Marotti, 'The Turn to Religion in Early Modern English Studies', *Criticism* 46 (2004): 167–90.

[40] David Scott Kastan, *A Will to Believe: Shakespeare and Religion* (Oxford: Oxford University Press, 2014), pp. 3, 6.

perhaps offered ways of solving them. The order of nature may have been increasingly separated from (though dependent on) the order of grace, but people remained deeply inquisitive as to how the two might be connected. As we shall see, Shakespeare's plays are preoccupied, in various fascinating ways, with working this problem out. Before we address these issues further, though, we need a firmer grasp on the changing models of the natural world in Shakespeare's time.

Changing models

Shakespeare stood on the cusp of the most momentous change in the conception of the natural world, identified by R.G. Collingwood as a change from the ancient 'view of nature as an intelligent organism' to a new view of 'nature as a machine'. For the Greeks and – mostly – for medieval and early Renaissance thinkers there was a clear 'analogy between the world of nature and the individual human being', so that man 'comes to think of himself as a body whose parts are in constant rhythmic motion, these motions being delicately adjusted to each other so as to preserve the vitality of the whole', and to think of the natural world in a similar way.[41] Though this view had not decisively been replaced in Shakespeare's day, it was under considerable pressure, leaving room for other emergent ways of thinking, but without a definite turn to post-Cartesian mechanism.[42] 'In ancient and medieval cosmology the ideas of matter, life and mind were so fused together as to be hardly distinguishable; the world, *qua* extended, was regarded as material; *qua* moving, as alive; *qua* orderly, as intelligent'.[43] Collingwood's picture is clear and mostly convincing, but it is rather too general in its assessment of early Renaissance thinking on nature, particularly failing to take account of the extremely subtle and complicated thinking of Neoplatonic writers on the relationship of mind

41 R. G. Collingwood, *The Idea of Nature* (London: Oxford University Press, 1945), p. 8. Collingwood confusingly describes the mechanistic vision of nature as a 'Renaissance' view, but given that its decisive expounders were Galileo and Descartes, it might be better to think of this as a proto-Enlightenment view. For a more recent account, see Soper, *What is Nature?*, and for a concise and telling development of ideas, see Midgley, *Are You an Illusion?*, chapter 3 and *passim*.

42 Jean-Pierre Maquerlot, *Shakespeare and the Mannerist Tradition: A Reading of Five Problem Plays* (Cambridge: Cambridge University Press, 1995), pp. 50–1, argues that Shakespeare's generation 'still saw the world as ultimately bound up with the divine scheme of things even if the ways of God were becoming more and more difficult to scan . . . They were imbued with a sense of the contingency of earthly things and of the relativity of opinion and knowledge: hence a frame of mind prone to doubt and questioning, but also to an unquestioning surrender to dogma in everything outside the scope of natural philosophy and secondary causes.'

43 *The Idea of Nature*, p. 133.

to the natural world – those strains of thought that did not ultimately go forward into the modern conception of nature. In fact, in certain crucial ways, the late Renaissance was a peak period for imagining the whole of nature as alive: we see this, for instance in both Neoplatonism and Neostoicism, philosophical positions which strained to make ancient thought compatible with Christianity.

The general picture of Renaissance thought has recently been considerably refined by Stephen Gaukroger.[44] Gaukroger's work offers a compelling and complex larger narrative, but a few key points need to be picked out for our purposes: modern natural science does not emerge fully formed like Athena/Minerva, as a form of objective wisdom, but as an alternative to a number of failed traditions of knowledge, particularly Aristotelianism, Christianized Platonic naturalism, and the kinds of historical investigation that were prompted by the Reformation. Gaukroger argues that no new system decisively emerged in the late Renaissance, but that it was rather a time when 'Reconciliation of doctrines is paramount, or where this is not possible, gathering of arguments for competing opinions'.[45] Those competing opinions often took on a life of their own, and those who did push forward systems, such as Telesio and Bruno, tended to blur the distinction between natural and supernatural,[46] more firmly tying human psychology to the natural world. These Italian thinkers, though they were heavily influenced by Plato, refused to accept his sense that the soul's main purpose was to escape the material world (a doctrine most powerfully articulated in the *Phaedrus*): they saw the human soul as embedded in the soul of the world as a whole, engaged in mutual – though often antagonistic – relations with it. For Bruno, nature – the material universe – is God, utterly imbued with World Soul, with individuals being mere ripples or accidents in the Oneness.[47] For Telesio, by contrast, there are spiritual souls beyond the material universe, which act as its guarantee; on the other hand, Telesio sees nature as wholly alive, if dedicated only to self-preservation, rather than higher ends.[48] Even for the more decisively transcendentalist Ficino, the natural function of the mind is transcendental, but it must nonetheless attend to the material world, and in doing so it becomes

[44] Stephen Gaukroger, *The Emergence of a Scientific Culture: Science and the Shaping of Modernity 1210–1685* (Oxford: Oxford University Press, 2006).

[45] *The Emergence of a Scientific Culture*, p. 126.

[46] *The Emergence of a Scientific Culture*, p. 110.

[47] For a clear account of these philosophies, see Brian P. Copenhaver and Charles B. Schmitt, *Renaissance Philosophy* (Oxford: Oxford University Press, 1992), pp. 303–317.

[48] See Bernadino Telesio, *La Natura Secondo i suoi Princìpi*, ed. R. Bondì (Milan: Bompiani, 2009).

embedded – however temporarily – in nature.[49] Regardless of the distinctions between these thinkers, a mutual dynamic between human thought and the natural world was enabled by their attitudes. The result of these competing, often tangled and self-contradictory positions was philosophical confusion but creative ferment. As Alisdair MacIntyre puts it, this epistemological crisis broke down people's 'accustomed ways of relating *seems* and *is*', forcing an urgent but impossible project of rethinking the world, which was 'of central importance to the culture', and not merely an academic enterprise.[50] The imagination was set free, but also set adrift. William Bouwsma describes Calvin's attitude to natural knowledge in terms that might apply to Shakespeare:

> There might still be order among things; but this had now to be understood not as *the* order of things, which was God's affair, but *an* order imposed on a few things by some human beings for their own human, limited, and transient purposes. Such a conception opened up the possibility of many orders of things, as many as might be useful.[51]

This sense of contingency and relativism was best worked through in the multidimensional, dynamic world of drama, rather than in dogmatic philosophy or theology. Shakespeare's generation was lucky or unlucky enough to stand at the point when the richest variety of perspectives on the world were available, before some of these perspectives were rejected in the emergence of a new synthesis associated with Bacon, Descartes and Newton.[52]

Francis Bacon is often taken as the major forerunner of modern attempts to master nature, yet even his work is continually suffused with older attitudes, particularly in its earlier phases (i.e. before the *New Organon* (1620)).[53] In the *Advancement of Learning* (1605), he writes that

[49] Drawing on Ficino, in fact, Mary Midgley has recently argued that the pre-mechanistic philosophy of the Renaissance can be useful to us as we struggle to reimagine our relationship to and embeddedness in an environment in crisis. See Mary Midgley, 'Introduction: The Not-So-Simple Earth', in *Earthy Realism: The Meaning of Gaia*, ed. Mary Midgley (Exeter: Societas, 2007), pp. 4–6. Simon Palfrey argues that in Bruno, Campanella, Telesio and other sixteenth-century thinkers, 'Each particle of matter possesses the power to reproduce, with a viscosity allowing it to adhere to different bodies. Certainly there are suggestions here of a kind of poetics of nature, whereby almost-intangible matter can reproduce, and where affects are carried on the air, like music or metaphor' – *Shakespeare's Possible Worlds* (Cambridge: Cambridge University Press, 2014), p. 219.

[50] Alisdair McIntyre, 'Epistemological Crises, Dramatic Narrative and the Philosophy of Science', in *The Tasks of Philosophy: Selected Essays Volume 1* (Cambridge: Cambridge University Press, 2006), pp. 3–23, 9–10.

[51] *John Calvin*, pp. 152–3.

[52] Peter Coates, *Nature: Western Attitudes since Ancient Times* (Cambridge: Polity, 1998).

[53] In *The New Organon*, p. 81, he goes so far as to suggest that man needs to 'harass' nature in order to get it to give up its secrets – references to Francis Bacon, *The New Organon*, trans. Michael Silverthorne, ed. Lisa Jardine (Cambridge: Cambridge University Press, 2000).

> There is fourmed in every thing a double Nature of Good; the one, as every thing is, a Totall or substantive in it selfe; the other, as it is a parte or Member of a greater Bodye; whereof the later is in degree the greater, and the worthier, because it tendeth to the conservation of a more generall fourme. Therefore we see, the Iron in particuler simpathye mooveth to the Loadstone; But yet if it exceede a certayne quantity, it forsaketh the affection to the *Loadstone* and like a good patriot mooveth to the *Earth* which is the Region and Countrye of Massie Bodyes; so may we go forward, and see that *Water* and *Massy bodyes* move to the *Center of the earth*; but rather then to suffer a divulsion in the continuance of Nature they wil moove upwards from the Center of the Earth: forsaking their duty to the *Earth* in regard of their duty to the *World*. This double nature of Good & the comparative thereof is much more engraven upon Man, if he degenerate not: unto whom the Conservation of duty to the publique ought to be more precious then the Conservation of life and being.[54]

The sense of nature's holistic connectedness here is strong, but there is also a (politicized) division of duties, a centrifugal sense of higher purposes that pulls man out of his natural condition, good though that might be. The doubleness of nature is very firmly emphasized here, as is the precariousness of man's place in it.

Nature, then, was treated with extraordinary ambivalence. It was considered the ground of all that was good, but at the same time the basis of all bad.[55] A. P. Rossiter formulates the useful idea of 'an *under-nature*' that undermines attempts to rely on nature as the source of goodness and (hierarchical) value.[56] This is complementary to but rather different from the doubleness of nature identified by John F. Danby, who sees a conflict between old notions of a harmonious, kind nature and a proto-Hobbesian selfishness in Shakespeare's work.[57] Danby's idea of doubleness is attractive but oversimplified, avoiding the sense of real uncertainty that pervades Shakespeare's age; the sense that nature's two sides operated simultaneously. The doubleness extended to human nature, which was considered to be both a crucial part of nature and detached from it.[58] The detachment

54 Francis Bacon, *The Advancement of Learning*, ed. Michael Kiernan, in *The Oxford Francis Bacon* (Oxford: Clarendon Press, 2000), IV: 136–7.

55 Robert Pogue Harrison, *Forests: The Shadow of Civilization* (Chicago: The University of Chicago Press, 1992), p. 101, argues that nature 'becomes an ambiguous word' in Shakespeare, because 'On the one hand it means the presocial or prelawful state of anarchy; on the other, it means the "natural", that is, nonconventional basis of human law itself'.

56 A.P. Rossiter, *Angel with Horns: Fifteen Lectures on Shakespeare* (1961; Harlow: Longman, 1989), p. 305.

57 John F. Danby, Shakespeare's Doctrine of Nature: A Study of *King Lear* (London: Faber and Faber, 1949).

58 For further thoughts on nature's doubleness, see Graham Bradshaw, *Shakespeare's Scepticism* (Brighton: Harvester, 1987), p. 5.

from nature, in turn, was double: on the one hand, it was a mark of man's superiority; on the other, it bespoke a painful alienation. There was, then, no one orthodox method of reading nature: man was free to read nature in his own way, to engage in a heuristic exploration with no pre-set answers.

The freedom of these thoughts demonstrates discontent with an older Aristotelian 'system straining under its own excesses and elaborations'.[59] The results of this strain are attempts to simplify which actually tend to complicate things, but which generally push in the direction of finding life everywhere – hylozoism, to use the technical term. The next century would mechanize nature, but the sixteenth tended to organicize it: as Allen Debus puts it 'it is misleading to separate the study of inorganic from that of organic nature in the Renaissance. For Aristotelians, Platonists, and Paracelsians alike in the sixteenth century the world was conceived to be alive – and at all levels'.[60] Life is everywhere; the world bristles with intentions and emotions.

Indeed, one of the most potent ideas that pervades thinking about nature in Shakespeare's time is the notion that everything is connected by natural *sympathy*. Feelings of love resonate between people, mediated by the material universe, which is taken to be alive. The idea goes back to Plato: the titular speaker of Plato's *Timaeus*, perhaps the most abidingly influential work of ancient philosophy, argues that the Universe is a 'single living thing', containing all living things (69c).[61] This idea was revived, refined and developed in the Renaissance. Ficino explains:

> Why do we think that Love is a *magician?* Because the whole power of magic consists in love. The work of magic is the attraction of one thing because of a certain affinity of nature. But the parts of this world, like the parts of a single animal, all deriving from a single author, are joined to each other by the communion of a single nature. Therefore just as in us the brain, lungs, heart, liver, and the rest of the parts draw something from each other, and help each other, and sympathize with any one of them when it suffers, so the parts of this great animal, that is all the bodies of the world, similarly joined together, borrow and lend natures to and from each other. From this common relationship is born a common love; from love, a common attraction. And this is the true magic.[62]

59 Copenhaver and Schmitt, *Renaissance Philosophy*, p. 305.
60 Allen G. Debus, *Man and Nature in the Renaissance* (Cambridge: Cambridge University Press, 1978), p. 34.
61 References to Plato, *The Complete Works*, ed. John M. Cooper (Indianapolis: Hackett Publishing, 1997).
62 Marsilio Ficino, *Commentary on Plato's Symposium on Love*, trans. Sears Jayne (Woodstock, CT: Spring Publications, 1985), p. 127.

Powerful as they are, such ideas were not swallowed as incontestable truths; rather, they were treated as probable arguments,[63] unlike the necessary revealed truths of the Christian Bible. As such, they were taken as mere opinions, available for rhetorical deployment, their truth and virtue being dependent on the context and purpose of their use – uses which might have a real effect on the world.

For instance, John Ford's *The Lover's Melancholy* offers some rather contradictory images of human love as connected to ideas of natural sympathy. Thamasta, who is in love with 'Parthenophill' (really the maiden Eroclea in disguise), gives the examples of a 'league' between 'The constant lodestone and the steel', a 'secret / Of sympathy' between 'The gentle myrtle' and the olive tree (as well as the ivy and the oak) in order to justify her strange love, arguing from natural examples that 'in all actions, nature yields to fate' (III. ii. 77–93).[64] Thamasta invokes the idea of secret sympathies here for persuasive purposes, as a way to show that apparently unnatural, 'ungrounded' love for a stranger may really be natural as a result of fate. She suggests that natural connections, which may be mysterious in themselves, are trumped by other circumstantial connections, which may involve a higher form of natural sympathy. But she is stretching the point here, showing how such language could be used to justify any kind of feeling, and her point is invalidated by the fact of Eroclea's sex (or is it? is nature a bit queer?). As in Fletcher's *The Captain*, where similar images of nature are used to justify illegitimate passion (in that case, incest), we have to be suspicious of such rhetorical resources.[65] Yet those resources can also be used to ground more legitimate love. Palador, contemplating the oddity of his feeling for Parthenophill, argues (apparently to himself, but overheard by Eroclea-Parthenophill)

> As there is in nature
> In everything created, contrariety,
> So likewise is there unity and league
> Between them in their kind; but man, the abstract
> Of all perfection, which the workmanship
> Of heaven hath modelled, in himself contains

[63] Indeed, Plato's speakers often present their arguments in these terms: e.g. Timaeus, and Socrates himself in *Phaedrus*.

[64] References to John Ford, *'Tis Pity She's a Whore and Other Plays*, ed. Marion Lomax (Oxford: Oxford University Press, 1995).

[65] Richard A. McCabe, in *Incest, Drama and Nature's Law, 1550–1700* (Cambridge: Cambridge University Press, 1993), p. 215, points out that such deployments of the idea of nature for libertine purposes were given licence by the sense that the law of nature had become the law of corrupt nature.

Passions of several quality; the music
Of man's fair composition best accords
When 'tis in consort, not in single strains.
My heart has been untuned these many months
Wanting her presence, in whose equal love
True harmony consisted. Living here
We are heaven's bounty all, but fortune's exercise.
(IV. ii. 43–55)

The differences from Thamasta's speech are subtle but significant: Palador is not trying to persuade anyone, arguing with himself rather than with someone else; he does not deploy copious examples of natural connectedness to make his point; he gives due credit to heaven as the validator of natural connections; and his invocation of the idea of music presents a harmonious and balanced vision of those connections rather than displaying a delight in oddity and discord as Thamasta does. Above all, he gives himself up to natural process rather than trying to master it.

The desire to master the natural world, then, tends to fail, but the world may be partly made to do one good by an acceptance of one's limited place in it. As we shall see throughout this book, a wise acceptance of nature's mysterious qualities – a kind of Keatsian 'negative capability' – is required for Shakespeare's characters successfully to manage their relationships with one another and with the world. By contrast, those who attempt to appropriate and transcend nature, to become free artists of themselves, are those whom nature tends to bite back.

C.S. Lewis's account of the imaginative satisfactions of the medieval model of the universe is powerful and convincing: he argues that medieval artists loved to dwell on the coherence of that model *as a system*.[66] But – and this is crucial to my argument here – by Shakespeare's time that system no longer seemed intellectually convincing, even if it still seemed imaginatively satisfying. To use Lewis's own terms, it was in the process of being discarded, but there were no comparably satisfying alternatives. In fact, I would turn around Lewis's formulation: he argues that '[t]he achieved perfection was already there. The only difficulty was to make an adequate response';[67] I would rather suggest that in Shakespeare's time the adequate response was already there, but the difficulty was believing in the achieved perfection on which it supposedly relied. Leonard Barkan argues that 'the poets of the time are reacting less to the advent of the new

[66] C.S. Lewis, *The Discarded Image: An Introduction to Medieval and Renaissance Literature* (Cambridge: Cambridge University Press, 1964), pp. 202–4.
[67] *The Discarded Image*, p. 204.

than to the last exaggerated gasps of the old';[68] in order to rescue the old, coherent, organic system, writers of Shakespeare's time seem to need to exaggerate it, but in doing so, I think, they recognize that it is no longer wholly satisfying, that it is a set of provisional or arbitrary fictions rather than an orderly system, and as such it becomes profoundly precarious. That precariousness is partly the result of boundary problems: how is the natural world to be divided up? And, once it is divided, how are its various parts to interact?

Uncertain boundaries

When the idea of nature is invoked in the literature of the period, some attempt to create a division is usually in train. The Renaissance attitude to nature was characterized by a search for the crucial dividing line between nature and that which defines nature by being beyond it, but no one could quite agree where that line lay: man and nature, God and Nature, nothingness and nature, lifelessness and nature, the sublunary and the world above – all were proposed as crucial divides, but none were finally convincing.

Laurie Shannon argues that the key – or at least the least contested – divide in Renaissance thinking was not that between man and the natural world, but that between animals (including man) and plants.[69] This is a productive and useful idea, as we shall see in Chapter 2, but we should be wary of the idea that there is only one division at work. Instead, there is a set of overlapping concepts, in which man is implicated, and from which he can only for a moment, and with difficulty, separate himself.[70] Keith Thomas is right to suggest that the dominant strain of thinking about nature in the sixteenth and seventeenth centuries was one in which all of creation was designed to serve man,[71] but it is easy to simplify a dominant view into an ideology. As Thomas demonstrates, the devil is in the details: a slow process of change was underway, in which created beings – particularly

68 Barkan, *Nature's Work of Art*, p. 48.

69 Laurie Shannon, *The Accommodated Animal: Cosmopolity in Shakespearean Locales* (Chicago: The University of Chicago Press, 2013), p. 99.

70 As Simon Palfrey argues, *Late Shakespeare: A New World of Words* (Oxford: Oxford University Press, 1997), p. 15, 'Shakespeare fully exploits the paradox of wilderness, as an environment equally of purification, punishment and recapitulation. Romance's poetic geography is therefore not prelapsarian. Each evocation of origin is highly contested, shadowed by intimations both of ending and perhaps delusion, and counterpointed always with its symbiotic cause and consequence: the court-cum-city, never truly left behind'. Chapter 1 develops on this thinking.

71 Keith Thomas, *Man and the Natural World: Changing Attitudes in England 1500–1800* (London: Allen Lane, 1983).

animals – were gradually being recategorized, becoming unsettled and uncanny as the boundaries moved.[72] Jeanne Addison Roberts usefully presents the idea of *wildness* as a Venn diagram, in which the normative, tame, comprehensible spheres of masculine, human, civilized modes of being overlap uncomfortably with more unspeakable spheres; she focuses on how images of the Wild adumbrate the limitations of civilized human maleness, which is defined in opposition to the 'Wilds of female, animal, barbarian and even the semivisible male Wild'.[73] It is in the areas of overlap in such a model that the most powerful modes of natural connection can be found.

Boundaries, then, are in some ways less important than overlaps. Bruce Boehrer comments on 'the startling ease and unexpectedness with which the early modern discourse of nature could transform itself in response to individual situations', and how the 'superficially unified system of meaning involved' could become radically contested as a result.[74] Man's opinions, as we have seen, could change the phenomena. As in modern understandings of the uncertainty principle, there is no neutral observer. Man, whose actions had after all caused the Fall of nature in the first place, could continue to influence the natural world, for good or ill. Kristen Poole describes a 'crisis of cosmic geography' in the Renaissance, showing that there were 'diametrically opposed notions of space' in the period, one involving 'an understanding of space as mathematical and geometric' and another, older model persisting in which space was seen as 'metamorphic and fluid'.[75] That fluidity was a two-way process, in which humans and nature could change one another.

In contrast to the dualism that characterizes post-Cartesian thinking, a key feature of the Renaissance representation of nature is that it has no obvious gaps. For example, Renaissance paintings of the countryside are not like later landscapes, full of open spaces, because the links between things need to be emphasized rather than their differences. Similarly, Renaissance representations of people emphasize the links between individuals rather than opening up spaces between them. This is partly to do with the idea

72 By the later seventeenth century, the organic model had decisively broken down: as Barkan points out, Hobbes's model of the state as a body is definitely *not* an organic one; Marvell, in turn, is sceptical about man's ability to perceive any kind of wholeness, and Milton takes the universe 'as a thing in itself', not dependent on man's perceptions. *Nature's Work of Art*, pp. 113–4, 280–1.

73 Jeanne Addison Roberts, *The Shakespearean Wild: Geography, Genus, and Gender* (Lincoln, NE: University of Nebraska Press, 1991), p. 5.

74 Bruce Boehrer, *Shakespeare among the Animals: Nature and Society in the Drama of Early Modern England* (New York: Palgrave, 2002), p. 36.

75 Kristen Poole, *Supernatural Environments in Shakespeare's England: Spaces of Demonism, Divinity and Drama* (Cambridge: Cambridge University Press, 2011), pp. 5, 10.

that nature abhors a vacuum, but also with the idea that everything is subtly connected, that overlapping zones enable transitions between one mode of being and another.[76] Yet there are other kinds of subtler gaps in Renaissance painting, pressed upon us by the sense that there is often no unified perspective. As Alastair Fowler shows, the persistence of multiple perspective involves a refusal of the unified, single-point perspective that was gradually emerging in Renaissance painting: a unified perspective implies a disinterested, transcendent observer, whereas multiple perspective reminds us of our entanglement in the world's moral complexities.[77] The transitions in such painting become mediating spaces (never empty, never considered as pure space), whose unity is guaranteed by something other than our own eye or the painter's: that other may be an unknowable deity, but it is just as likely to be a mysterious idea of nature. Fowler also emphasizes the way in which Renaissance mimesis characteristically *involves* the spectator, encouraging empathy: he calls this 'participatory realism', which involves 'empathy with the outer world'.[78] Though I would be suspicious of the idea of *empathy* (a word and idea not really available in the Renaissance), preferring the more mediated and partial concept of sympathy, we need to be constantly aware that we never stand outside nature in Shakespeare's vision, that our emotional engagement is constantly passing *through* the plays' worlds.

The key reason to feel a sense of connection to the natural world and of overlaps between its spheres was the widespread belief that the human soul had something radically in common with animal and even plant souls. Man was thought to have three souls: the vegetable soul or soul of growth he shared with plants and non-human animals; the sensitive and mobility-enabling soul he shared with animals; finally, the spiritual or intellectual soul transcended these others, and was unique to man.[79] This powerful idea had classical origins but could be accommodated within a Christian framework. For Christian thinkers, only the highest form of the soul was to be saved.

The idea of the tripartite soul has its some of its origins in Plato's *Timaeus* (e.g. 77a–c), and the idea is refined at the end of that dialogue, with a half-ironic narrative of the transmigration of souls between the

[76] Angus Fletcher, *Time, Space, and Motion in the Age of Shakespeare* (Cambridge, MA: Harvard University Press, 2007).
[77] Alastair Fowler, *Renaissance Realism: Narrative Images in Literature and Art* (Oxford: Oxford University Press, 2003).
[78] *Renaissance Realism*, pp. 79, 122. On the absence of the concept of empty space, see p. 4.
[79] For a clear delineation of the issues involved here, see Hiram Haydn, *The Counter-Renaissance* (1950; New York: Grove Press, 1960), p. 318.

various levels of creation. Men who are cowardly or unjust become women 'in the second generation', the innocent but simple-minded become birds, non-philosophical men become land-animals, and so forth (91a–92c). This obviously makes man *prior* to the beasts, as well as to women, and it offers a reason for despising both, even as it links privileged mankind to those wilder beings. If this passage is in the way of being a cautionary tale, it reminds us of the precariousness of masculine, intellectual humanity.

The idea of the transmigration of souls is also stated in *Phaedo* (81a–82c), as Socrates' own position: there, for example, bad people of various sorts become appropriate kinds of beasts in the next life, whereas just but non-philosophical types become bees, characterized by their social virtue. It is clear that for Plato there were souls in plants and animals (*Phaedo*, 70e). In the *Republic*, Plato gives a mainly political picture of the tripartite soul, and it takes Aristotle to develop a full theory of souls which takes account of plants and animals on their own terms. In *On the Soul*, he argues that plants have a nutritive, reproductive soul, a soul of growth as Donne would put it; non-human animals have a sensitive soul (with varying degrees of sensations), which has the power of voluntary movement; and man alone has an intellectual soul, and this is the only one that can be separated from the body.[80] This idea embeds man firmly in nature because he has something fundamental in common with plants and animals. His desires, and his emotions more generally, are shared with other natural beings. His intellect may ultimately separate him, making him transcend materiality, but most human preoccupations are not separate. Indeed Aristotle argues that animals have something very close to thought: namely imagination, which motivates them ($433^{a}1$), just not as rationally as in man. Some animals may even have 'deliberative' as well as sensitive imaginations. The key boundary is a fuzzy one.[81]

Indeed, any attempt to understand any aspect of nature involves the acceptance of overlaps. Bacon argues that 'there is no nature which can be regarded as simple; every one is seeming to be compounded of two. Man has something of the brute; the brute has something of the vegetable; the vegetable something of the inanimate body; and so all things are in truth biformed and made up of a higher species and a lower'.[82] Any definition is double, and though Bacon here goes some way to making things a bit

80 *On the Soul*, $413^{b}1$–$415^{a}1$, $432^{a}1$, in *The Complete Works of Aristotle: The Revised Oxford Translation*, ed. Jonathan Barnes, 2 vols. (Princeton: Princeton University Press, 1984).

81 The final line of the treatise, which may be spurious, suggests that animals can talk to one another.

82 *de Sapientia Veterum*, in *The Works of Francis Bacon*, ed. J. Spedding, R. L. Ellis, and D. D. Heath, 7 vols. (London: Longman's, 1857–74), VI: 710–1.

neater than Aristotle did, he has a logical problem in relying on the concept of 'the brute' (i.e. animal), for instance, while admitting that the brute itself is double. Humanity's position in the creation is made dependent on lower categories that are not themselves simple. The result is that, for Bacon, 'mans bodie is the most extreamly compounded' thing in nature;[83] if man isn't quite a *microcosm* of the natural world as a whole, he is still its most variform being.

Human variousness and unfixity was accounted for by a stream of Platonic and Neoplatonic narratives, which both involve humanity in nature and pull us out of it. Plato's fable of man's creation in *Protagoras* has the Titan Epimetheus hand out all the blessings of powers and abilities onto the natural world, forgetting to keep something particular in reserve for man; this forces his brother Prometheus to give man fire (along with art and technology) as his particular – but perhaps unnatural, supplementary – gift (321c–322a). The Promethean idea alienates humanity from nature. As this is so obviously a fable, though, it has no absolute authority, and indeed could inspire other analogous but subtly different fables. In the Renaissance, Pico della Mirandola gives a crucially revised account of man's position in the natural world. He is unsatisfied by accounts of man as 'the intermediary between creatures, the king of the lower beings, by the acuteness of his senses, by the discernment of his reason, and by the light of his intelligence the interpreter of nature, the interval between fixed eternity and fleeting time.' Instead, he gives an alternative account of man's creation that emphasizes human *flexibility*: in Pico's story, God had already created 'this cosmic home', and placed the angels and the animals in their proper places,

> But, when the work was finished, the Craftsman kept wishing that there were someone to ponder the plan of so great a work, to love its beauty, and to wonder at its vastness. Therefore . . . He finally took thought concerning the creation of man. But there was not among His archetypes that from which He could fashion a new offspring, nor was there in His treasure-houses anything which he might bestow on His new son as an inheritance, nor was there in the seats of the world a place where the latter might sit to contemplate the universe. All was now complete; all things had been assigned to the highest, the middle, and the lowest orders. But in the final creation it was not the part of the Father's power to fail as though exhausted . . .

[83] *The Advancement of Learning*, IV: 96–7. He goes on to say that the soul is the simplest of things, and that music is necessary to harmonize the variable composition of man's body. Man still shares things with the natural world on this account, if only on the level of the body rather than the soul. Yet that compounded quality of the human body still has an effect on his psychology.

> At last the best of artisans ordained that that creature to whom He had been able to give nothing proper to himself should have joint possession of whatever had been peculiar to each of the different kinds of being. He therefore took man as a creature of indeterminate nature and, assigning him a place in the middle of the world, addressed him thus: 'Neither a fixed abode nor a form that is thine alone nor any function peculiar to thyself have we given thee, Adam, to the end that according to thy longing and according to thy judgement thou mayest have and possess what abode, what form, and what functions thou thyself shalt desire. The nature of all other beings is limited and constrained within the bounds of laws prescribed by Us. Thou, constrained by no limits, in accordance with thine own free will, in whose hand We have placed thee, shalt ordain for thyself the limits of thy nature. We have set thee at the world's centre that thou mayest from thence more easily observe whatever is in the world. We have made thee neither of heaven nor of earth, neither mortal nor immortal, so that with freedom of choice and with honour, as though the maker and moulder of thyself, thou mayest fashion thyself in whatever shape thou shalt prefer. Thou shalt have the power to degenerate into the lower forms of life, which are brutish. Thou shalt have the power, out of thy soul's judgement, to be reborn into the higher forms, which are divine.'[84]

This is one of the most important developments in the history of thought about humanity's place in the order of the universe. Pico follows the Bible in making man the last part of creation, rather than giving him priority as Plato does.[85] Man is still crucial, but he is no longer central. He is fundamentally alienated, having no particular role of his own: he is a spectator on nature. Yet he also, crucially, has choice: the natural world is all laid out before him, and it is for him to choose whereabouts he enters it. Pico wants man to choose angelic options, to rise above nature as Plato urges, but he gives no compelling reason why man has to do so: opting to stay in the natural world may be legitimate according to this myth. Leonard Barkan comments that this passage involves 'at once a celebration of man's multiplicity . . . and a frightening view of man's need to unify his own multiplicity, for it is clear from God's speech to Adam that if man does not choose or does not act he is nothing'.[86] Barkan is right to suggest that man is under pressure here, but one might wonder if the option of

84 Trans. Elizabeth Livermore Forbes, in *The Renaissance Philosophy of Man*, ed. Ernst Cassirer, Paul Oscar Kristeller and John Herman Randall, Jr. (Chicago: The University of Chicago Press, 1948), pp. 223–5.

85 The Judaeo-Christian tradition would see man as the last, best work – but given that woman was really the last creation in Genesis's narrative, there was a twist in the tail of this reasoning.

86 Barkan, *Nature's Work of Art*, p. 32. For further commentary on Pico's importance, see Giorgio Agamben, *The Open: Man and Animal*, trans. Kevin Attell (Stanford: Stanford University Press, 2004).

purely null spectatorship is as enticing as it is alarming. Man's ability to fashion himself is not absolutely free: if he wants to remodel himself, he needs to take account of the existing natural models. He can be a tree or a tortoise (or an angel), but he cannot change himself into anything that does not yet exist.

George Herbert, in 'The Pulley', offers his own version of a creation myth:

> When God at first made man,
> Having a glasse of blessings standing by;
> Let us (said he) poure on him all we can:
> Let the worlds riches, which dispersed lie,
> Contract into a span.
>
> So strength first made a way;
> Then beautie flow'd, then wisdome, honour, pleasure:
> When almost all was out, God made a stay,
> Perceiving that alone of all his treasure
> Rest in the bottome lay.
>
> For if I should (said he)
> Bestow this jewell also on my creature,
> He would adore my gifts instead of me,
> And rest in Nature, not the God of Nature:
> So both should losers be.
>
> Yet let him keep the rest,
> But keep them with repining restlessnesse:
> Let him be rich and wearie, that at least,
> If goodnesse leade him not, yet wearinesse
> May tosse him to my breast.[87]

This God resembles Pico's, in that He changes His mind and improvises halfway through His Creation. Nature here is absolutely filled with 'blessings', and is only insufficient to man because it lacks 'rest'. What Herbert means by this is a little obscure: his punning on the balance between 'the rest' (all of Nature's blessings) and 'rest' (the one thing that's missing) may further blur the issue, but it also forces us to see that the only true rest, that which makes all perfect, is to be found in God's 'breast'. God, not feminine Nature, is that which is finally satisfying, but Herbert suggests that the difference between the God of Nature and Nature itself, though crucial, is also infinitesimal, a matter of one key word.

[87] References to *The English Poems of George Herbert*, ed. Helen Wilcox (Cambridge: Cambridge University Press, 2007).

Herbert himself is tempted to rest in Nature: in 'Affliction' (I), he wishes that he were a tree, 'For sure then I should grow / To fruit or shade: at least some bird would trust / Her household to me, and I should be just' (lines 58–60). The lovely, humble desire to be of *use* here reflects a sense of humanity's (or at least unredeemed humanity's) position as a spare part in the natural world, an unnecessary supplement, a whoreson Zed.[88] It may pick up on Pico's sense of human flexibility, but it also recognizes that the natural, non-human world is not subject to potential damnation. As he is about to be taken off to hell, Marlowe's Faustus expresses a similar sentiment, wishing that he might be changed into 'some brutish beast' (A Text, V. ii. 109), so that he could avoid going to hell.[89] In these conceptions, driven by Calvinist anxieties that the majority of people will be damned and can't do anything about it, we also see an emergent sense that nature is *nearly* self-sufficient and perfect. So close, yet so far. The natural world therefore becomes the site of yearning. Something like this yearning may motivate Sidney's belief that poets can 'deliver' forth a 'golden' world that repairs the imperfections of 'brazen' Nature.[90] In turn, that rehabilitated nature might help man to his salvation.

Grace in nature?

In the Christian view, nature is fallen, infected by Original Sin as man is: man will be saved from Sin, restored by God's grace to his original unfallen state, but nature in most views will not be so restored, despite the fact that it was not responsible for the Fall.[91] This paradox had been an aspect of Christianity from the first, but in the Renaissance new theories of nature and of human reason complicated matters. For Stoics, for example, reason was simply conformity to nature, and therefore nature, considered holistically, could be seen as unfallen. Reason and nature were supposed to be perfectly fitted to one another, so that rational thought was perfectly able to comprehend the natural world. Even Christian views could chime

88 There's an analogy here with Derrida's notion of 'that dangerous supplement' – see Jacques Derrida, *Of Grammatology*, trans. Gayatri Spivak (Baltimore: Johns Hopkins University Press, 1976), pp. 141–64 – but I don't want to insist too much on that.

89 References to Christopher Marlowe, *Doctor Faustus: A- and B-Texts (1604, 1616)*, ed. David Bevington and Eric Rasmussen (Manchester: Manchester University Press, 1993); for more on this see Chapter 2, below.

90 Sir Philip Sidney, *An Apology for Poetry, or The Defence of Poesy*, ed. Geoffrey Shepherd (Manchester: Manchester University Press, 1965), p. 101.

91 Shannon, in *The Accommodated Animal*, pp. 51, 56–7 points out that the injustice of the natural world being tainted by man's sin was a problem that exercised both John Donne and Calvin.

with this. Reason is, according to the standard scholastic account, unfallen, though man's *access* to it may be dimmed or weakened. Richard Hooker, the most moderate of Elizabethan thinkers, thought that almost every aspect of the natural world could be grasped by reason, because its laws were fixed.[92] William Perkins, the most influential Reformed writer of Shakespeare's lifetime, even argued that the seat of faith was in the intellect.[93] Philip Sidney believed that 'our erected wit maketh us know what perfection is' – that is, our reason is capable of complete insight, even if 'our infected will' prevents us from acting on it.[94] Gaining perfect access to reason might undo the Fall at least in some respects: to understand nature, then, might be to approach grace. Yet this was controversial: even to say it might be hubristic. In any case, it would only be undoing part of the damage caused by the Fall: the intellectual but not the spiritual side, one might say. Calvin's attitude to reason was rather self-contradictory, sometimes emphasizing that our reason could understand the natural world, sometimes that our reason was hopelessly blinded.[95] Part of the problem for Calvin was that he believed God, who was constantly intervening in the world, could arbitrarily change the laws of nature at any moment.[96] Human reason therefore needed to be flexible, and modest, recognizing the limits of one's insight into God's plans. The fit between reason and the natural world had become slippery.

Man's defining capacity, then, his reason, enabled partial insight but also put him at a distance from the natural world. Whereas humanity

[92] Richard Hooker, *Of the Laws of Ecclesiastical Polity: Preface, Book I, Book VIII*, ed. Arthur Stephen McGrade (Cambridge: Cambridge University Press, 1989), p. 77: 'The rule of natural agents that work by simple necessity, is the determination of the wisdom of God, known to God himself the principal director of them, but not unto them that are directed to execute the same. The rule of natural agents which work after their own accord, as the beasts do, is the judgement of common sense or fancy concerning the sensible goodness of those objects wherewith they are moved. The rule of ghostly or immaterial natures, as spirits and Angels, is their intuitive intellectual judgement concerning the amiable beauty and high goodness of that object, which with unspeakable joy and delight, doth set them on work. The rule of voluntary agents on earth is the sentence that reason giveth concerning the goodness of those things which they are to do. And the sentences which reason giveth are some more, some less general, before it come to define in particular actions what is good.' Also, p. 81: 'the law of reason or human nature is that which men by discourse of natural reason have rightly found out for themselves to be all forever bound unto in their actions. Laws of reason have these marks to be known by. Such as keep them, resemble most lively in their voluntary actions, that very manner of working which nature herself doth necessarily observe in the course of the whole world. The works of nature are all behoveful, beautiful, without superfluity or defect; even so theirs, if they be framed according to that which the law of reason teacheth.' The influence of Stoicism here is evident.

[93] See Kendall, *Calvin and English Calvinism*, p. 56.

[94] *An Apology for Poetry*, p. 102.

[95] Bouwsma, *John Calvin*, pp. 88, 133, 139, 142, gives a complex and nuanced account of Calvin's struggle with the problem of how far reason is affected by the Fall.

[96] Bouwsma, *John Calvin*, pp. 33, 166–7.

had been considered as deeply embedded in the order of nature in the medieval period, we have seen that Pico regarded man as fundamentally separated from or supplementary to the order of nature; this had the effect of removing some of the taint of Original Sin from nature, enabling it to be a fuller force for good on its own account. Indeed, once humanity came to be seen as alienated from nature, the idea of our reintegration into nature could be seen as a model for redemption. Ficino argued that the Mind, though its proper occupation was the contemplation of heaven, needed to look down from its proper sphere into Nature, because it needed to help the human Spirit, which was embedded within Nature;[97] the Mind therefore needed to adjust its categories to those of Nature, to seek out those aspects of Nature that were, however secretly, unfallen. The search for the redemptive aspects of Nature became a way for the human Mind and Spirit to gain the necessary purchase to lift themselves back to heaven. This process does not necessarily entail a proto-Romantic pantheism (though it can do in Bruno and in Neostoicism), but it does mean that thinkers of Shakespeare's time were much happier than their predecessors to take nature on its own terms, rather than to look through it towards the divine.

The need for natural purposes to be meaningful became more acute as a result of the Reformation's deprecation of good works: after Luther, and particularly after Calvin, no longer could good actions be treated as treasures laid up in heaven. Salvation was to be by faith alone.[98] That left a problem: how was one to motivate good actions? Reading the Book of Nature alongside the Bible was one possibility: if the Bible offered a single route to salvation, nature might offer a set of alternative routes; those routes might be less salvifically consequential, but they nonetheless might have underlying divine sanction, offering one a hedge, as it were, against too unitary a conception of value. Even if those routes did not work to save one's soul (and who knows if they might?), they might be conceived as having some autonomous value, enabling meaningful connections between people, and avoiding the self-centred and otherworldly focus of fideism.[99]

[97] Marsilio Ficino, *Platonic Theology*, trans. Michael J. B. Allen with John Warden, ed. James Hankins with William Bowen, 6 vols. (Cambridge, MA: Harvard University Press, 2001), book XVI. The clearest account of this line of thought can be found in Erwin Panofsky, *Studies in Iconology: Humanistic Themes in the Art of the Renaissance* (New York: Oxford University Press, 1939), pp. 131–4.

[98] See Diarmaid McCulloch, *The Reformation* (London: Viking, 2004).

[99] See R. H. Tawney, *Religion and the Rise of Capitalism: A Historical Study* (London: John Murray, 1926), pp. 96–8, 109–10, 229–31.

Human art might be able to resolve the problems involved here. Norman Rabkin argues that there is in most of Shakespeare's works a real anxiety about the relationship of art to nature; that Shakespeare offers us patterns (whether providential or nihilistic) for understanding the world and refuses to let human experience be reduced to such patterns, even as he accepts the tragic nature of human need for such patterns; in the late plays, though, 'he asks us to accept an overlay of patterns, paradoxically embracing the contradictory gestalts of art and nature.'[100] Neither art nor nature is sufficient on its own: there must be a dynamic relationship between them. Edward Tayler gives a good, clear summary of the main issues involved in the art-nature debate: for post-medieval Christians, the division between the orders of nature and grace was a crucial way of organizing experience, and within the supposedly lower order of nature there was a further division, the more ambiguous division between nature and art. But this division was by no means rigid: 'As a way of organizing and labelling aspects of moral experience, the division remained so infinitely flexible that it could be used entirely differently in different contexts'; this flexibility is due to the idea that 'Art, the product of human "wit", may either perfect or pervert Nature'.[101] But, crucially, as we have seen, Philip Sidney believed that 'our erected wit maketh us know what perfection is, and yet our infected will keepeth us from reaching unto it'; man's wit, at least at its 'highest point', is equal with 'the efficacy of Nature'.[102] It might, then, have some salvific power.

The power of human art, then, in dynamic, flexible conformity to natural processes, might be considerable. This opens up the most radical possibility, that man's own efforts might affect the order of grace. This, of course is the Pelagian heresy, an idea condemned throughout Christian history, but one that was a particular bugbear of the Reformation. However, traces of that kind of thinking permeate a good deal of Renaissance literature, acting as a powerful counterforce to the dominant predestinarian thinking of Reformed religion.[103] One way of resolving this crucial tension might be to argue for the finding of grace in nature, allowing a certain wise passivity to bring about grace, but without an emphasis on human effort. Influential Calvinists such as William Perkins rather tortuously argue that the will to

100 Norman Rabkin, *Shakespeare and the Problem of Meaning* (Chicago: The University of Chicago Press, 1981), p. 140.

101 Edward William Tayler, *Nature and Art in Renaissance Literature* (New York: Columbia University Press, 1964), pp. 30–1.

102 *An Apology for Poetry*, p. 102.

103 On Pelagian tendencies in Renaissance Humanism, see Haydn, *The Counter-Renaissance*, pp. 58–62, see also Shell, *Shakespeare and Religion*, p. 166.

believe is faith, but that that will is not *active*, at least in the first instance.[104] Indeed, as I will show throughout this book, I think we can see a sense – heterodox as it might seem – that grace (or the road to it) might be found in nature; that there might be surprising discoveries of relative unfallenness in that complex, tangled world, which could help man to redemption, or a foreshadowing of it. 'Then is there mirth in heaven, / When earthly things made even / Atone together', sings Hymen as she enters in *As You Like It* (V. iv. 108–10). The idea of oneness implicit in 'atone' balances with the idea of evenness, which surely derives from the dual pairings of the play's lovers and reconciled brothers. The passive voice here – '*made* even' – quietly elides the question of agency; these earthly things delight the heavens so much that it seems hard to believe that the heavens do much more than spectate: if people have not brought about the happy endings, the natural world, the earth itself, may have done so. The *even*-ness of heaven may be imposed on earth, but decidedly earthly mirth (which word after all contains the sound of *earth*) is transferred to heaven. John Donne argues, in similarly gnomic terms, that 'In our selves we may finde things in heaven, and things on earth to reconcile', quietly suggesting that our reconcilement with God starts with earthly reconcilement to others.[105] Such thinking tends to be subterranean, not fully articulated, modestly hinted at in poetic passing rather than stated explicitly because to state it explicitly might be to damage the efficacy of the movement towards grace.[106] By accepting a certain passivity in the face of nature, one can avoid explicit Pelagianism, while giving humanity's position in the fallen world some form and meaning. God can be given ultimate agency, but by allowing Him to work through secondary causes in the natural world,[107] His providential purposes are allowed to come closer to man, not held at an impossible distance. His ways may remain mysterious, but they are not ineffably transcendent.

104 See Kendall, *Calvin and English Calvinism*, pp. 59–65.

105 Sermon Preached at St. Paul's, Christmas Day, 1622, in *The Sermons of John Donne*, ed. George R. Potter and Evelyn Simpson, 10 vols. (Berkeley: University of California Press, 1953–62), IV: 301.

106 Sarah Beckwith's study of ideas of forgiveness in Shakespeare also hints at the finding of grace in nature; see *Shakespeare and the Grammar of Forgiveness*, p. 94. This is only a minor aspect of Beckwith's argument, picked up in passing in a discussion of *Pericles*, as Beckwith is more interested in the redemptive possibilities of speech acts, but the finding of grace in nature would certainly help buttress and mediate such possibilities.

107 Alison Shell points out that there was considerable controversy in Shakespeare's time as to whether providence operated directly, or through 'secondary agents such as nature' – *Shakespeare and Religion*, p. 178.

The natural world, particularly the countryside, can be used as an image of paradise. For example, Thomas Campion's portrayal of God's creation is not as firmly insistent on the Fall as those of his contemporaries:

> Most sweet and pleasing are thy wayes, O God,
> Like Meadowes deckt with Christall streames and flowers:
> Thy paths no foote prophane hath ever trod,
> Nor hath the proud man rested in thy Bowers.
> There lives no Vultur, no devouring Beare,
> But onely Doves and Lambs are harbor'd there.
>
> The Wolfe his young ones to their prey doth guide;
> The Foxe his Cubbs with false deceit endues;
> The Lyons Whelpe suckes from his Damme his pride;
> In hers the Serpent malice doth infuse:
> The darksome Desart all such beasts contaynes,
> Not one of them in Paradice remaynes.[108]

This is a picture of a better world than ours, but it is not wholly transcendent, not a distant city on a hill. It is a pastoral landscape, fitted for man, and apprehensible to the human intellect and senses. Campion starts off by presenting God's ways as *like* meadows etc., but soon abandons the use of simile for more direct statement: doves and lambs are literally present in paradise; though they may represent the Holy Ghost and Christ respectively, their plurality weakens the force of the allegory. Paradise is a natural place, but one purged of the worst parts of nature, excluding the natural sins of the predators. A principle of careful division between the good and bad parts of the natural world can redeem it, and make it at least potentially redemptive for man.

Other thinkers of the time suggest that there may be unfallenness in the natural world. Giordano Bruno argues that '[t]he universal intellect is the innermost, most real and proper faculty or potential part of the world soul. It is that one and the same thing that fills everything, illuminates the universe and directs nature to produce her various species suitably.'[109] This creative intellect is in us all, in everything. One of Bruno's key points is a denial that the superlunary spheres operate by different rules from the sublunary; later scientists would also agree with this unification of the rules of nature, but Bruno's unification works in the opposite direction to theirs: where they would remove the idea of perfection from the higher spheres, Bruno emphasizes the possibility of perfection in the lower ones.

108 *The Works of Thomas Campion*, ed. Walter R. Davis (New York: Norton, 1970), p. 68.

109 Giordano Bruno, *Cause, Principle and Unity; And Essays on Magic*, ed. and trans. Robert de Lucca and Richard J. Blackwell (Cambridge: Cambridge University Press, 1998), p. 37.

The question of how such redemptive nature might be mediated to man is particularly puzzling. Lewis points out that medieval thought was addicted to the idea of intermediate beings: angels mediating between God and man; spirits mediating between body and soul.[110] But if angels are in short supply, such mediation may take place most profitably through pondering the relationship of people and *things*; as Katharine Eisaman Maus argues, 'property relations are not merely ways of attaching "persons" to "things", but are a careful distribution of rights and obligations among persons. The study of the way property is deployed in Shakespeare's plays turns out to be a study less of things than of relationships mediated by things: between prince and subject, master and servant, parent and child, siblings, friends, and enemies'.[111] This attitude, refusing to accept either simple objectification or solipsistic subjectivity, can be applied to Shakespeare's representation of nature, something that is less obviously *owned* than the kinds of property Maus discusses. Living things, perhaps, have the greatest power to enable this mediation: Aquinas argued that the 'plurality and inequality' of living beings was created in order that they might act *for* one another; the goodness of each being was manifested in its ability to act 'for the advantage' of another type of being; the imperfection and difference of modes of being, though it may have made creatures less like God, enabled them to be godlike at least in the sense of acting for the good of others.[112] As Philip Davis puts it, discussing the interplay of differentiated relationships in *As You Like It*, 'What is opened here within the self and between selves is exactly a space of thought, with the formal relationship between the self-estrangement of self-reflection and the leap of both empathy and envy left undecided but available for thinking'.[113] Knowing that people do not have simple access to one another's thoughts and feelings, Shakespeare uses the natural world as a place or trope of mediation, suspending the human tendency to solipsism but without becoming radically anthropocentric. Nature is other to man, but is also part of him. Since the Enlightenment, the sphere of nature has often been treated as utterly separate and autonomous from the human – valued as a world of objective reality that cannot change, and devalued as a mere resource for humanity. In our present crisis, it is therefore salutary to return to a mode of thinking which not only saw nature and human concerns as mutually

110 *The Discarded Image*, pp. 42–4 and *passim*.
111 Katherine Eisaman Maus, *Being and Having in Shakespeare* (Oxford: Oxford University Press, 2013), pp. 15–16.
112 Aquinas, *Summa Contra Gentiles*, cit. Haydn, *The Counter-Renaissance*, p. 313.
113 Philip Davis, *Shakespeare Thinking* (London: Continuum, 2007), p. 15.

embedded, but also considered nature as constantly changing its terms of engagement with us.[114]

Richard Mabey has recently argued that our need to change our stance towards nature may be best effected by reconsidering our idea of selfhood, suggesting that 'mind is a much broader entity than consciousness, and not necessarily confined in individual packages. It's a function of all life, the learned-from, responsive record that experience makes in living tissue. It can be cultural, co-operative, perhaps even communal. And maybe in keeping with our new understanding of the unity of physical life, we should try viewing mind not as *possessed* by individuals, but shared between them, as a kind of field.'[115] That attitude, I would suggest, was already available in Shakespeare's time. Bruno Latour argues that the modern 'Constitution' (in place from around the mid-seventeenth century) involves an effort to believe that humans and the objective world of nature are fundamentally separate, and a willed refusal to acknowledge anything which mediates between the two, even as such mediating things proliferate.[116] Shakespeare, this book will argue, is constantly interested in mediating things, things that are neither one thing or another and which enable translations between people and between people and the natural world: the countryside, animals, food and medicine, the central subjects of the chapters that follow.

Nature in decline?

Yet, if nature could be taken as a model or source of redemption, there was also a worrying sense that nature was in decline, and a controversy over the causes of this – as well as a controversy over whether it was happening at all. As we will see, some people even wondered whether the *belief* in nature's decline actually caused that decline. Victor Harris's magisterial work on the idea of nature's decay remains the most compelling analysis of certain key ideas: he shows that between 1570 and 1630, culminating in the work of Godfrey Goodman in 1616, there was a peak preoccupation with the idea that the natural world, including the heavens, were decaying as a result of man's Fall, and heading inexorably towards its final doom.[117] For Goodman, nature's decay had a clear divine purpose: to remind man of his fallen state

114 See Midgley, *Are You an Illusion?*, chapter 10.

115 Richard Mabey, *Nature Cure* (London: Chatto and Windus, 2005).

116 Bruno Latour, *We Have Never Been Modern*, trans. Catherine Porter (Cambridge, MA: Harvard University Press, 1993).

117 Victor Harris, *All Coherence Gone: A Study of the Seventeenth-Century Controversy over Disorder and Decay in the Universe* (London: Frank Cass, 1949).

and to encourage him to repent before it was too late. Even before the Fall, according to Goodman, nature had the propensity to decay, needing only the push of man's Original Sin to lead it into privation of its good qualities.[118] Yet Harris also makes it clear that Goodman's position was not an orthodoxy: the very insistence of his writing suggests that he expected people to disagree with him. Goodman's opponents were insistent that nature was fundamentally inviolable, and could not be tainted by man's Fall; they also thought that too great an emphasis on decay in nature would lead man to despair.[119] In other words, there was a fear that fear itself might make the natural world worse.

Donne's 'The First Anniversarie: An Anatomy of the World' (1611) is the most famous articulation of the idea of discord in the natural world affecting man, and vice versa. He presents the world, as Hamlet does, as being 'Quite out of joint', because the world took a 'fall' in its 'cradle' (lines 191, 196), the Fall of the angels happening even before the natural Creation took place:

> The noblest part, man, felt it first, and then
> Both beasts and plants, cursed in the curse of man.
> So did the world from the first hour decay,
> That evening was beginning of the day;
> And now the springs and summers that we see
> Like sons of women after fifty be;
> And new philosophy calls all in doubt:
> The element of fire is quite put out,
> The Sun is lost, and th'Earth, and no man's wit
> Can well direct him where to look for it;
> And freely men confess that this world's spent,
> When in the planets and the firmament
> They seek so many new; they see that this
> Is crumbled out again t'his atomies.
> 'Tis all in pieces, all coherence gone,
> All just supply, and all relation:
> Prince, subject, father, son, are things forgot,
> For every man alone thinks he hath got
> To be a phoenix, and that there can be
> None of that kind of which he is, but he.
> (lines 199–218)

Donne here attacks the idea of human uniqueness developing into an overvaluation of singularity; everyone thinks he has to be (or, indeed, already is)

118 *All Coherence Gone*, pp. 30–1. 119 *All Coherence Gone*, pp. 63, 129–30, 6, 52.

a phoenix, an immortal, regal, self-sufficient being. He is attacking the kind of deludedly self-sufficient, self-making characters whom Shakespeare would present as fundamentally unnatural, such as Richard III and Edmund in *King Lear*. Furthermore, at the centre of Donne's thinking, as in many other authors of the time, is the half-buried thought that changing opinions of natural phenomena may actually change the nature of the phenomena: for instance, that thinking there is no element of fire somehow puts that element out. Though this thought may be treated ironically, there's an uneasy sense behind the irony that it might be so.[120] Bacon argues that 'the cogitations of Man, doe fayne unto them *Relatives*, *Paralleles*, and *Conjugates*, whereas no such thinge is; as they have fayned an Element of Fire to keepe square with Earth, Water, and Ayre'.[121] Does this *opinion*, in Donne's terms, put out the element of fire? Bacon thinks it away; nature is not only in decline, but is being pushed further downhill by man's inquisitiveness and lack of belief.

By contrast, Ben Jonson took a more sanguine view of the issue:

> I cannot think Nature is so spent and decayed that she can bring forth nothing worth her former years. She is always the same, like herself: and when she collects her strength, is abler still. Men are decayed, and studies: she is not.[122]

At the heart of this is the question of whether nature is to be blamed or man. Donne's poem offers a brilliant challenge, but he is not stating an orthodoxy. What is most important for my purposes is the fact of the controversy: the fact that there was an intense preoccupation with such theologico-physical matters without a clear sense of orthodoxy. Nature could therefore be taken as a register of man's fall, or as an unfallen reminder of what man had lost, or as a potential source and model for grace and salvation. Crucially, Harris quotes Jean Francis Senault's view that 'Nature repaires the havock made by death'.[123] Does that mean that nature can undo the consequences of the Fall? Will thinking that make it so?

The key to the problem was that God's relationship to nature was at least as mysterious and controversial as man's to nature or man's to God. As Kristen Poole points out, 'Calvin presents a deity that is still very much engaged with his creation', whereas Richard Hooker emphasizes a more

120 Calvin worried that those who argued for a heliocentric universe were aiming to 'pervert the order of nature', devilishly changing the world by their opinions: see Bouwsma, *John Calvin*, p. 72.
121 *The Advancement of Learning*, IV: 116.
122 *Discoveries* 89–91, cit. Ian Donaldson, *Ben Jonson: A Life* (Oxford: Oxford University Press, 2011), p. 386.
123 *All Coherence Gone*, p. 151.

rule-governed universe.[124] She also argues that 'Contradictory, overlapping conceptions of the macro and the micro worlds could make their relationship discordant and confusing'.[125] There was, then, a controversy as to whether the natural world was in decline, but a further controversy as to whether the sense of its decline was caused by man's confused understanding of it.

In these circumstances, a new, exploratory approach was required. One key result was a new attention to the aberrant: to the monstrous and marvellous things that don't fit into the pattern – the things that Aristotle had thought we could safely ignore. Aristotle had emphasized the need to discover general laws, but Bacon suggests that we could find out more from those things which don't fit into the established scheme of things. Wonders might be meaningful and illuminating. Bacon praises the exploration of the irregularities of nature:

> The use of this worke, honoured with a president in *Aristotle*, is nothing lesse, then to give contentment to the appetite of Curious and vaine wittes, as the manner of MIRABILARIES is to doe: But for two Reasons, both of greate waight: The one to correct the parcialitie of Axiomes, and Opinions: which are commonly framed onely uppon common and familiar examples: The other, becaues from the Wonders of Nature, is the neerest Intelligence and passage towardes the Wonders of Arte: For it is no more, but by following, and as it were, hounding Nature in her wandrings, to bee able to leade her afterwardes to the same place againe. Neyther am I of opinion in this HISTORY of MARVAILES, that superstitious Narrations of Sorceries, Witchecraftes, Dreames, Divinations, and the like, where there is an assurance, and cleere evidence of the fact, be altogether excluded. For it is not yet knowne in what cases, and how farre, effectes attributed to superstition, do participate of Naturall causes: and therefore how-soever the practise of such things is to bee condemned, yet from the Speculation and consideration of them, light may be taken, not onely for the discerning of the offences, but for the further disclosing of Nature.[126]

If nature is to be disclosed, we must avoid trying to impose simple patterns on it. This open-minded attitude of course is of the utmost importance in the development of the modern scientific mindset, but it also opens the mind in other ways, to the rich and strange possibilities of the natural world, which may include redemption, or at least a sense of wonder that anticipates redemption.

124 *Supernatural Environments*, pp. 145, 153. 125 *Supernatural Environments*, p. 15.
126 *The Advancement of Learning*, IV: 63. See also *New Organon*, p. 42.

In Renaissance thinking, man and nature are in a productive, gamelike conflict; Bacon cites Solomon as saying

> *The glorie of God is to conceale a thing, But the glorie of the King is to find it out*, as if according to the innocent play of Children the divine Majestie tooke delight to hide his workes, to the end to have them found out, and as if Kinges could not obtaine a greater honour, than to bee Gods play-fellowes in that game, considering the great commaundement of wits and meanes, whereby nothing needeth to be hidden from them.[127]

Nature is a game of hide-and-seek, and we are God's playfellows as much as we are fools of Nature; taken in the right spirit, the game is pleasurable for its own sake, and a source of honour, even if we can't quite win. Bacon famously attempts to separate divine and natural enquiry, arguing that 'the contemplation of Gods Creatures and works produceth (hauing regard to the works and creatures themselues) knowledge, but hauing regard to God, no perfect knowledg, but wonder, which is broken knowledge'.[128] Yet it is possible that this wonder, this broken knowledge, is just as strong an aspect of humanity's relation to nature as it is of the relation to God. As we have seen, Bacon and others frequently invoke the idea of wonder in dealing with nature, and Calvin concluded that the best we can do in relation to the order of nature is to be ravished with astonishment.[129] This attitude is taken partly because the idea that the Infinite, once exclusively appropriated to God, could be an aspect of nature, and of man himself.[130] As this quality of the infinite enters the world, so does wonder, particularly when the old system of knowledge, whether theological or natural, was becoming broken. The epilogue to Marlowe's *Doctor Faustus* argues that the play's protagonist's 'fiendful fortune may exhort the wise / Only to wonder at unlawful things' (lines 5–6). Drama allows us the opportunity to *wonder* at those things that do not conform to the orthodox natural scheme, without committing ourselves to a rigid belief structure. Unlawful things, be they the supernatural, or just anomalies that don't fit into the older order of nature, strike us with the recognition of nature's infinite variety. Part of the wonder is that humans *can* apprehend these things, in however limited a way: lamenting the death of Antony, whom she sees as the only 'remarkable' thing in the world, Cleopatra says 'Nature wants stuff / To vie strange forms with fancy; yet t' imagine / An Antony were nature's

127 *The Advancement of Learning*, IV: 36. Bacon twice cites the same passage in the *New Organon*, pp. 12, 100.

128 *The Advancement of Learning*, IV: 8.

129 See Bouwsma, *John Calvin*, pp. 154–5.

130 See William Kerrigan and Gordon Braden, *The Idea of the Renaissance* (Baltimore: Johns Hopkins University Press, 1989).

piece 'gainst fancy' (IV. xv. 67, V. ii., 97–9). Nature, set alongside fancy, is lacking, but once one *imagines* an Antony, that is a natural wonder, even if the real Antony cannot live up to Cleopatra's imagination of him. The fact that Nature can produce such exceptions, such excessive supplements, is a cause for celebration; indeed, it may be the ultimate reason to celebrate being human, for without humans there would be no audience for such wonders. The participation of human thought and imagination is needed here to help make Nature's masterpieces. Cleopatra says that she is 'No more but e'en a woman, and commanded / By such poor passion as the maid that milks / And does the meanest chares' (IV. xv. 73–5). Yet she speaks these lines as she appears to be resurrected,[131] her servants thinking her dead. Resurrection turns her into a mere woman; she is not transfigured, she is just, disappointingly, *there*. She cannot will herself to die: but does this make her more or less of a goddess?

Her faint was prompted by the death of Antony, which provoked the extraordinary lament:

> The soldier's pole is fall'n! Young boys and girls
> Are level now with men; the odds is gone,
> And there is nothing left remarkable
> Beneath the visiting moon.
>
> (lines 65–8)

Antony's death won't quite bear the weight of these lines, which lament the passing of the heroic, romantic way of looking at the world, the loss of specialness in general, the loss of radical difference.[132] Here is a lament for the emergence of modernity, for a world in which there are no enchanted lands, no anointed kings, no exceptions to the rules. From such a world the moon thinks it well to withdraw. The reign of wonder is over. And yet drama will, again and again, restore it, however temporarily.

Embodied Nature in *Venus and Adonis*

I want to conclude this introduction by applying some of the ideas I have set up to *Venus and Adonis*. While the imaginative possibilities of the flexible, tangled, multi-perspectival models of nature are best exploited in the dialogical world of plays, particularly Shakespeare's, they may be

[131] Cf. Falstaff's resurrection in *Henry IV Part One*.

[132] It is experienced, of course, as a kind of castration: a loss of the logos-phallus that gives order to the universe.

more readily grasped and grounded in narrative verse, where authorial commentary on incidents and relationships gives a clearer indication of the philosophical positions being (tentatively) taken.

Venus and Adonis gives us a picture of 'Nature . . . herself at strife' (line 11) in her creation of the titular hero, who is a 'wonder' (line 13). The sense of strife in Nature's creation of Adonis may be mainly a matter of her trying to outdo herself, but there is also something self-thwarting in the idea of Nature creating something that so wonderfully transcends the natural. So perfect is Adonis that the world 'hath ending' with the end of his life, at least in Nature's view (line 12). The world, though, does not end when Adonis dies, so Nature is wrong about this. Perhaps Adonis is a type of Christ, whose death brings an end to the providential narrative of world history, while leaving that history to play out as an inconsequential epilogue. Or perhaps this is simply an overstatement, giving emotional weight to Adonis's loss, giving us a sense that the promised end and the image of that horror (to use the language of *King Lear*) are emotively immanent in history. Shakespeare seems concerned to point up the paradoxes and conflicts involved when something beyond the order of nature enters into the natural world. Whether that transcendent thing be God's grace, the order of providential history, or merely the intrusion of alienated human consciousness, the apparent simplicity of nature is radically challenged by its emergence, bringing a sense of wonder.

Venus, being a goddess, clearly ought to transcend the natural world. Her lap is a type of paradise, 'where never serpent hisses' (line 17). Yet she needs the earthily natural world: even Adonis's sweat is 'Earth's sovereign salve to do a goddess good' (line 28). When she feeds on his steaming breath, meanwhile, she 'calls it heavenly moisture, air of grace' (line 64); moist earthliness is tied up with a divine, salvific spirit – at least in her way of *naming* things, with perhaps a Catholic sense of transubstantiation. His lips are still another matter, Venus wishing that 'their verdure still endure, / To drive infection from the dangerous year' (lines 507–8); he is a potential cure for all mortality, but is not in the end transcendent, being embedded in nature, as the word *verdure* implies, and that makes him paradoxically mortal. Venus herself must descend into the order of nature, making herself a 'park' for Adonis (line 231). Though this is a protected natural landscape (described at some length), its protection is only nominal or rhetorical. As Adonis is set on his fatal hunt, Venus is left to run about in a landscape that tangles her up and makes her like a 'milch doe' (lines 871–6); her love, far from pulling him out of natural entanglement, has taken her (rather like Cleopatra) into a natural world over which she does not have a transcendent perspective; the process is similar to that sketched out by Ficino (see above). Taken allegorically, this suggests that love pulls one down *into* the natural world, rather than enabling Platonic transcendence. If love does have any redeeming power, it is tied up with mortality rather than being an escape from it.

Read in such a way, the poem constitutes a reflection on the issue of incarnation. That is not to say that it is exactly an allegory of Christ's incarnation, but that it has analogies and parallels with the Christian narrative. Both may be taken as ways of understanding how the transcendent (Ficino's Mind) may become a part of the natural world. That, in itself, is a complicated enough issue. But it can be simplified by assuming that nature is fallen, and therefore that the transcendent or heavenly is definitively better. What, though, if nature gives some evidence that it is not completely fallen? That is, if nature shows signs of redeeming itself, or even if it just contributes to that redemption, does that not compromise the supposed radical superiority of the heavenly? This, I think, is Shakespeare's subtlest point: if incarnation involves some fundamental fusion between the heavenly and the natural, the latter may be as necessary for redemption as the former, and must therefore have always had something unfallen in it.

Venus tries to explain the darkness of the night she spends not quite seducing Adonis in these terms:

> 'Now of the dark night I perceive the reason:
> Cynthia for shame obscures her silver shine
> Till forging Nature be condemned of treason
> For stealing moulds from heaven that were divine;
>   Wherein she framed thee, in high heaven's despite,
>   To shame the sun by day, and her by night.
>
> (lines 727–32)

It couldn't be clearer that Adonis is a symbol of something *unnatural* precisely and paradoxically in his quality of being Nature's most perfect product. From the perspective of heaven, he is a forgery, but in so being he is a perfect copy of a heavenly Idea, and one which invalidates the claim that only heavenly ideas are of true value. Put another way, such perfect forgery proves that the distinction between the transcendent world and the mundane is arbitrary, and heaven's response to this is accordingly arbitrary and spiteful.

Venus goes on to claim that Cynthia has

> bribed the Destinies
> To cross the curious workmanship of Nature,
> To mingle beauty with infirmities,
> And pure perfection with impure defeature,
> Making it subject to the tyranny
> Of mad mischances and much misery.
> (lines 733–8)

This mingling of infirmities is not, I would suggest, a *corruption* of Nature's work, such as is supposed to have occurred in the biblical Fall; the morally neutral verb 'mingle' makes sure of that, as does the plural of 'infirmities', which makes them less of a moralizing abstraction. The idea of 'defeature' may hint at ugliness, but its primary tendency is tragic and ironic: beautiful features are doomed to be defeated; do we think less of them for that? Surely, rather, it is the supernatural forces whose madness and tyranny oppress and kill Adonis that are the objects of condemnation, and not just from Venus's perspective. Love has descended into nature, and has not only found it better than the sterile world of the immortals, but has found that its superiority is a standing rebuke to the heavenly and transcendent world, whose unappealing resentment is provoked by it. Shakespeare's plays are full of figures who seem to come from some radically other world, to transform or redeem the natural world in the manner of a classical deus ex machina: but such figures either turn out to be ineffectual, or to be radically implicated in the natural world themselves. The appeal of the transcendent is recognized, but the limits of its powers are firmly indicated.

Adonis himself wants to stand outside natural processes. Venus accuses him of narcissism (line 161), of wanting to be wholly self-reliant. She warns him that he can't escape a debt to nature, asking 'Upon the earth's increase why shouldst thou feed, / Unless the earth with thy increase be fed?' (lines 169–70); but he refuses to 'borrow' anything from natural love, saying 'I will not owe it'. His thrift, though, is fruitless: just because he refuses to borrow from love does not mean that he avoids owing God a death.

Animals offer him an example of how he should act. His horse is much less sexually farouche than its master, breaking its bridle and rushing off after a 'breeding jennet' (line 260). But this horse is in some ways like Adonis himself, a perfect example of Nature's artistry:

> Look when a painter would surpass the life
> In limning out a well-proportioned steed,
> His art with nature's workmanship at strife,

As if the dead the living should exceed;
So did this horse excel a common one
In shape, in courage, colour, pace, and bone.
(lines 289–94)

These lines consciously echo the initial description nature's 'strife' in the creation of Adonis. The invocation here of the visual arts may hint at their redemptive potential, their ability to transcend death. The horse may be like a painting because its willingness to breed gives it a kind of immortality.

Adonis himself only gets a very limited immortality, preserved as a flower.[133] His death is the result of his own foolhardiness and perhaps of his own refusal to engage with life as represented by Venus, but it is not directly represented. Instead, Shakespeare focuses on Venus's fears for him. As a result, her fears seem almost to cause his death: she calls out 'woe' (line 833), and the caves around her echo her, like flattering 'parasites' (line 847): 'She says, "'Tis so", they answer all, "'Tis so", / And would say after her, if she said "No."' (lines 851). Her feelings are translated into the landscape, bringing death into the world. When she finds Adonis's body, it has merged into the countryside: 'No flower was nigh, no grass, herb, leaf, or weed / But stole his blood, and seemed with him to bleed (lines 1055–6). This 'solemn sympathy' of nature (line 1057) is rather more vivid than a mere pathetic fallacy. Something of Adonis's special character is forever part of nature, just as Christ's incarnation blesses the natural world. The flower into which Venus transforms her dead beloved is initially described as purple 'chequered with white', but then is immediately re-described as 'Resembling well his pale cheeks, and the blood / Which in round drops upon their whiteness stood' (lines 1168–70). We are left in doubt as to which colour is the ground and which the figure: is the whiteness of his innocence primary or the bloody tainting of mortality? Has the natural world corrupted innocence, or has the shedding of innocent blood brought a blessing? In the end, it is a matter of perspective: how we look at the image changes its meaning.

In *Venus and Adonis*, then, we see in little most of the major themes that will occupy us in the rest of this book: the rejection of a transcendent perspective, the possibly redemptive role of nature, the tension between the mortal and the immortal, the idea of the landscape and of animals as vehicles that mediate human motive, and the curative possibilities of art and belief.

133 See my discussion of *Venus and Adonis* in Tom MacFaul, *Poetry and Paternity in Renaissance England: Sidney, Spenser, Shakespeare, Donne and Jonson* (Cambridge: Cambridge University Press 2010), especially p. 154.

The following chapters address a series of necessarily overlapping concerns. As we have seen, one of the principal fascinations of Renaissance understandings of the natural world is the difficulty people had in making crisp distinctions between modes of natural existence even as they tried to order their understanding of the world. We are the inheritors of the Enlightenment's relatively successful efforts to divide up the natural world into manageable and relatively separate spheres,[134] so that we are able to think of physics, chemistry, biology and psychology in rather different paradigms. Renaissance thinkers clearly wanted, at least at times, to make something like these distinctions, but were still so tied up in the older habit of analogical thinking that they could not hold onto divisions of experience for long. Still, some ordering of the natural world does obtain reasonably robustly, and that offers a structure for the following chapters. The first deals with the countryside, the earth itself and its vegetable products, showing how this zone, however contested and often marginal, is nonetheless the most productive arena for human experiences of translation and transformation. The second chapter considers animal life, frequently used as a way of making sense of human relations and human motivation, but just as often complicating them. The third chapter deals with the human arts of diet and health, often overlapping with natural magic, showing how these are embedded in wider structures, and how human attempts at mastery are often compromised by the very materials humans need to use. A number of plays reappear in more than one chapter – *Macbeth*, *The Winter's Tale*, *As You Like It*, *Love's Labour's Lost* and *Cymbeline*, for example – in order to show how different natural perspectives bring to light different aspects of each play's use of the natural world to effect its resolution. Shakespeare's art of nature is crucially perspectival, and this structure of revisiting is designed to bring out the complex and often contradictory image of the world that each play constructs; it also enables one to see that the most striking – and, for that matter, critically enabling – context for an individual Shakespeare play can be another play by the same author. The final short chapter, however, deals with one play which brings all of the book's themes together: *The Tempest*, Shakespeare's crowning contemplation of the natural world as a whole. That chapter also brings together all the main issues handled in the rest of this book.

In one of the most acute comments on Shakespeare's art in general, William Warburton describes *The Tempest* and *A Midsummer Night's*

134 See Michel Foucault, *The Order of Things: An Archaeology of the Human Sciences* (London: Tavistock Publications, 1970), and Latour, *We Have Never Been Modern*.

Dream as 'the noblest Efforts of that sublime and amazing Imagination, peculiar to *Shakespeare*, which soars above the Bounds of Nature without forsaking Sense: or, more properly, carries Nature along with him beyond her established Limits.'[135] This book is above all an effort to explore how he manages to carry the natural world so far without losing sight of humanity's place in it. Shakespeare wants to preserve a sense of human specialness, but uses the natural world, which is always compromised and compromising, to challenge claims to specialness of the more masterful or individualistic sort.

[135] In *Johnson on Shakespeare*, ed. Walter Raleigh (London: Oxford University Press, 1908), p. 64. Cf. Palfrey's suggestion, in *Late Shakespeare*, p. 21, that Shakespeare's characteristic art is to 'surprise the world into new forms'.

CHAPTER 1

Country matters

In Shakespeare's time, the radical distinction between urban and rural life which became so important around the time of the Industrial Revolution had not yet emerged,[1] but the London of his theatres was increasingly distant from the natural world. The theatres themselves were on the margins of the city, in places where the city authorities' writs wouldn't run, but their audience was mostly urban. In representing the rural world to an urban audience, they were engaged in an uneasy process of translation. As with Plato's concern that art is a mere representation of a representation, there is an anxiety about art's ability to translate the natural with a double artifice. The theatre is a place of translations, a liminal space, and it is never more so than when it is representing the country. The rural world itself, in these circumstances, is invoked as an *other* place, something yearned for, but also a place that, in its liminality, enables translations and transformations more radical and potentially redemptive than those of the city, which are founded on mere commercial exchange (even though the theatre itself was a firmly commercial enterprise). The result is that the rural world is invoked as a possible place of natural transformations, but those transformations are always a matter of compromise, being enabled by people taking a flexible and responsive attitude to their environment, rather than trying to master it.

Such transformations were occurring in a changing environment: the Reformation involved an attempt to desacralize the landscape, but was not necessarily all that successful in doing so; indeed, that effort often resulted in new kinds of piety, and it did not do away with the sense that the landscape

[1] See W. G. Hoskins, *The Making of the English Landscape* (1955; Toller Fratrum: Little Toller Books, 2013), pp. 129–51. Hoskins argues that the people of Tudor England took their wild places so much for granted that there are no descriptions of such environment as 'scenery' (p. 131). That is true up to a point, but much of the material in this chapter suggests they did have a sense of its beauty, and even its precariousness. See also Andrew McRae, *God Speed the Plough: The Representation of Agrarian England, 1500–1660* (Cambridge: Cambridge University Press, 1996).

was a divinely written book.[2] The specialness of places and people becomes contested as a result: particularity may be preserved (with some difficulty), but the idea of somewhere or someone being transcendentally superior is challenged. The environment was also changing as a result of the Great Rebuilding of England,[3] enclosure, and of changing climatic conditions.[4] All of these factors led to a renewed search for a stable, ideal rural space. The space of the countryside, treated increasingly as the truly natural place, in opposition to an artificial urban (and theatrical) environment, is the only place where real overlap between people may happen, and therefore where real, meaningful dramatic transformations may take place. It is the supposedly lower aspects of humanity rather than the privileged and special that enable change; the result is that the mediation of the natural environment is usually a matter of uncomfortable compromise rather than grand transformation. One of the deepest human fantasies about an Other place is that it might enable one to reach some Archimedean point from which one might radically change the world, but Shakespeare shows that things are not like that: one never gets to a transcendent 'world elsewhere'.[5] But one can get to a different kind of more natural world where there is at least the possibility of translation and the emergence of a kind of grace. Such translation, at its most perilous, may radically challenge particular identity, but at its best it purges the worst aspects of human claims of specialness, including the problems associated with sovereignty and gender difference.

In *Paradise Lost*, when Satan comes to tempt Eve, we encounter within a long epic simile one of the most powerful evocations of the rural world in the period:

> Much he the place admired, the person more.
> As one who long in populous city pent,
> Where houses thick and sewers annoy the air,
> Forth issuing on a summer's morn to breathe
> Among the pleasant villages and farms
> Adjoined, from each thing met conceives delight,
> The smell of grain, or tedded grass, or kine,
> Or dairy, each rural sight, each rural sound;
> If chance with nymphlike step fair virgin pass,

[2] See Alexandra Walsham, *The Reformation of the Landscape: Religion, Identity, and Memory in Early Modern Britain and Ireland* (Oxford: Oxford University Press, 2011).

[3] See W. G. Hoskins, 'The Rebuilding of Rural England, 1570–1640', *Past and Present* 4 (1953), 44–59.

[4] See Geoffrey Parker, *Global Crisis: War, Climate Change and Catastrophe in the Seventeenth Century* (New Haven: Yale University Press, 2013).

[5] *Coriolanus*, III. iii. 135.

What pleasing seemed, for her now pleases more,
She most, and in her look sums all delight.
(IX. 444–54)[6]

The countryside here is a place of leisure and pleasure for the visitor, but it's also clear that it is the working rural world. The smells here are refreshing but not emptily pure: they have the pungency of cowshit and drying grass, evoking the processes of digestion. Though all the business of the rural world is focalized into fascination with the country lass, the world is also valued on its own terms, the girl being merely a summing up of her environment rather than an incongruous addition to it. The terms of the epic simile make it clear that the city is the equivalent of the Hell from which Satan has come, and there seems for a moment to be a sense in which the rural world can redeem the infernal qualities of the city. By drawing an analogy between the countryside and the unfallen world of Eden, Milton implies that there are aspects of at least relative unfallenness in the rural world: the simile's process of translation (hell = city, paradise = country) brings up the theologically unorthodox possibility that there may be relative unfallenness, even though the fact that this is only a simile makes that idea deniable.

For a moment, indeed, Satan's evil intentions are suspended by this beauty: 'That space the evil one abstracted stood / From his own evil, and for the time remained / Stupidly good, of enmity disarmed' (lines 463–5). The fact that he *stood* for this moment points to his fallen state and suggests that it might be redeemed.[7] The word 'space' here refers to a spot of time, but it also implies that the suspension of evil has to do with being embedded in a good space; the time taken over the simile enacts that suspension into stupor and in doing so it makes the rural space and the time of the delay equivalent. In the rural world, as in the Garden of Eden more specifically, space and time cooperate, taking us away from the conflict of those dimensions that is so essential to the development of narrative. The attainment of such redemptive harmony, for however brief a space, is one of the central drives of Renaissance literature. Helen Cooper argues that 'The essence of the pastoral mode is the search for an ideal; but not an escapist one. The shepherd must turn from his pipes to his flock; the golden Arcadian world is always broken, the perfection of art brought

6 References to John Milton, *Paradise Lost*, ed. Alastair Fowler, 2nd edition (London: Longman, 1997).

7 The word 'stood' is crucial in Milton's epics as a contrast to the Fall: God created man 'Sufficient to have stood' (*Paradise Lost*, III. 99), and, when Christ defeats Satan in *Paradise Regained*, the key moment comes when he 'stood' on the Temple (IV. 561) – references to John Milton, *The Complete Shorter Poems*, ed. John Carey, 2nd edition (London: Longman, 1997).

into conflict with natural mutability, through war or corruption, by winter and age and death. But the breaking only makes the value and appeal of the pastoral more intense. Life does not conform to the patterns of art, but there must be a *point of contact*. The shepherd's voice is the voice of the poet in the brazen world trying to reach the golden, the voice of Man in the fallen world trying to regain paradise'.[8] The pastoral mode, then, offers some potential for redemption, a model for heaven on earth, a sense of contact between them, even if that is treated as a fiction or an anticipation of a transcendent heaven.[9]

Whereas Milton contrasts the rural world with the stench and overcrowding of the urban environment, in *As You Like It* the forest is put into competitive contrast with the world of the royal court:

> DUKE SENIOR. Now, my co-mates and brothers in exile,
> Hath not old custom made this life more sweet
> Than that of painted pomp? Are not these woods
> More free from peril than the envious court?
> Here feel we not the penalty of Adam,
> The seasons' difference, as the icy fang
> And churlish chiding of the winter's wind,
> Which when it bites and blows upon my body
> Even till I shrink with cold, I smile and say,
> 'This is no flattery: these are counsellors
> That feelingly persuade me what I am.'
> Sweet are the uses of adversity,
> Which like the toad, ugly and venemous,
> Wears yet a precious jewel in his head;
> And this our life, exempt from public haunt,
> Finds tongues in trees, books in the running brooks,
> Sermons in stones, and good in everything.
> (II. i. 1–17)

The speech is a self-conscious set-piece of self-consolation, but it is cut across with tension and irony. The ducal court, after all, is not a specific place, but a moveable institution, dependent on the ruler's presence; this is the court, nor are we out of it. At first, the Duke seems to be saying that he has recovered an Edenic world, with none of the seasonal change thought to be the consequence of Adam's fall: we don't feel such things *as* the cold of winter, he seems to say. However, the word 'as' turns out to mean that we don't feel that cold as a punishment, but rather as good

8 Helen Cooper, *Pastoral: Mediaeval into Renaissance* (Ipswich: D. S. Brewer, 1977), p. 7, emphasis added.

9 See also Cooper, *Pastoral*, p. 95.

counsel that reminds us of our human condition, giving us good lessons. How we receive things matters, changing their meaning. There is a sense of an escape to a deeper reality in the rural world, away from the artificial life of the court. But in another sense it is an escape from reality, from 'public haunt'; the people are replaced by trees, stones and streams. Even the naturalness of the country is mildly called into question: the artifice of the court is emphasized by the alliterative quality of the phrase 'painted pomp', but the rural world is also presented in alliterative terms ('tongues in trees', 'books in . . . brooks', 'sermons in stones') which highlight a degree of similarity. Amiens' response to this is ambiguous; he says, with some irony,

> I would not change it. Happy is your Grace
> That can translate the stubbornness of fortune
> Into so quiet and so sweet a style. (lines 18–20)

On the surface, he seems to assent to his master, to be saying he has no wish to leave the forest, but it's clear that there's an undertow of resentment, hinting that 'it's all very well for *you*; I wouldn't be able to make the best of it as you do'. Ironically, this is the kind of courtly equivocation and flattery that the Duke thinks he's escaped (underscored by Amiens' own alliteration). The magical power – the 'Grace' – of the monarch is acknowledged, but that power is double-edged: it can translate suffering into happiness, but it also translates the countryside into the court by carrying the court into the country. His courtly, rhetorical *style* is a kind of transformative grace, but of a limited and limiting kind.[10] As with the Midas of myth, everything the Duke touches turns to courtliness. He can never really see the rural world on its own terms, can never escape his destiny as Satan for a moment seems to. Translations are possible, but not complete changes. Satan brings along the 'hot hell' that is always with him, just as Donne brings 'the spider love' into 'Twickenham Garden'; fallen things, such as language and human consciousness, cannot be left behind – indeed they are often needed to effect translations.

Those translations often take place in a 'second world', away from the normal business of life, and one of the primary functions of the rural world in Shakespeare's plays is to afford such a change of agenda. The next section of this chapter will show that these second worlds are very much liminal, compromising spaces, rather than being radically different or escapist. Human histories are compromised but not forgotten or

[10] For Calvin's association of rhetoric with a limited kind of grace, see Bouwsma, *John Calvin*, p. 117.

abandoned. The ensuing section demonstrates that those histories can be thoroughly absorbed into the rural world, as it becomes a space where people die; in those cases, a gendered relationship to the natural world enables humans' absorption into the earth, demonstrating that the (mostly male) claim to stand outside nature is vain. Such claims are often made with particular force by kings, and the following section shows how even they are compromised by the land they believe they rule. The final section of the chapter shows how local attachments and hospitality enable a happier kind of compromise with nature, allowing for earthly happiness. Humans' claims to mastery, or to insist on 'a world elsewhere' are shown to be vain.

Second worlds

One of the more valuable commonplaces of Shakespeare criticism is that an escape to a second world – usually a non-urban environment – is needed to resolve social and emotional tensions built up in the more socially realistic first world of a play, particularly a comedy.[11] As Anne Barton puts it, the comedies use this device to achieve a 'clarification and renewal attained, paradoxically, through a submission to some kind of disorder, whether festive or not'.[12] This is well put, because it is all too easy to make this version of Shakespeare's comic method into too neat a formulation: the disorder is natural, but also deeply and persistently paradoxical, not as easily put away or contained as a festivity might be; the boundaries between the first and second world are not secure. Probably the earliest instance of this movement, in *The Two Gentlemen of Verona*, is decidedly peculiar. Banished from Milan because of his plans to elope with the Duke's daughter Silvia, Valentine finds himself in the lawless world of the wilderness. The outlaws he encounters there quickly decide that he will make an excellent 'king for our wild faction' (IV. i. 37). The wild rural world seems to be suffering from a power vacuum: it needs a king to make it whole.[13] As often in Shakespeare, the rural world is not precisely located; here, the outlaws seem as English as they are Italian, swearing 'By the bare scalp of Robin

11 The classic statement of the idea is Northrop Frye, *Anatomy of Criticism: Four Essays* (1957; Princeton: Princeton University Press, 2000), pp. 181–2; for further refinements, see Harry Berger, Jr., *Second World and Green World: Studies in Renaissance Fiction-Making* (Berkeley: University of California Press, 1988), pp. 13–17, and Elliot Krieger, *A Marxist Study of Shakespeare's Comedies* (London: Macmillan, 1979).

12 Anne Barton, *Essays, Mainly Shakespearean* (Cambridge: Cambridge University Press, 1994), p. 92, drawing on C. L. Barber, *Shakespeare's Festive Comedy: A Study of Dramatic Form and its Relation to Social Custom* (1959; Princeton: Princeton University Press, 2012).

13 The trope of outlaws in need of a leader is quite a common one: it occurs, for instance, in *Common Conditions* (1576), where pirates are in similar need of a captain, and there is something similar in Beaumont and Fletcher's *Beggars' Bush* (1618).

Hood's fat friar' (line 36). Absurdly, but significantly, Valentine seems an appropriate choice as king because of his skill in languages; such a skill, like the poetic *style* of *As You Like It*'s Duke, may be necessary to translate the rural world into other terms.

Valentine's use of his new regal role, indeed, enables the redemption of the outlaws' world. Rather than the rural second world saving the courtly first world, then, it is the translation of civility and wildness into each other's terms that brings about the play's resolution.[14] When the Duke is brought into Valentine's company, he instantly forgives Valentine, and accedes to all of his other requests. Is this the transformative effect of the natural environment, or does it rely on the rather lazy contempt for people's motives that generally dominates this play? Possibly, it is a matter of coercion in this case, the Duke having to ransom himself (though it's not clear whether he is a captive). Possibly, though, the forgiveness relies on the Duke recognizing Valentine's new regal status, however iffy it may be.

The Duke's disparagement of Valentine early in Act Five goes so far as to refer to him as a 'peasant' (V. ii. 35), but by the end of the play he is 'a gentleman and well derived' (V. iv. 146), a man of 'unrivalled merit', 'worthy of an empress' love' (lines 144, 141). Rather arbitrarily, it might seem, he has a 'new state' (line 144); the Folio text here reads 'new statute', which may indicate that such status can be imposed by the Duke making his will into law, that he can be given a new style (in the sense of title) by the simple act of human choice. Yet there is some doubt as to whose choice enables all this. When Valentine is offered his new status as king of outlaws, his potential new subjects frame the choice in revealing terms:

> 2 OUTLAW. Are you content to be our general?
> To make a virtue of necessity
> And live as we do in this wilderness?
> 3 OUTLAW. What say'st thou? wilt thou be of our consort?
> Say 'Ay' and be the captain of us all:
> We'll do thee homage and be ruled by thee,
> Love thee as our commander and our king.
> 1 OUTLAW. But if thou scorn our courtesy, thou diest.
> (IV. i. 59–66)

This doesn't seem to be much of a choice. Valentine can no more escape regality than the Duke in *As You Like It* can. They declare their wild justice to be courtesy, and their consorted will makes everything happen. There is

[14] Roberts, *The Shakespearean Wild*, p. 41, argues that 'though the men seem to have infiltrated the Wild, they are too thoroughly imprisoned in their own preconceptions to experience its liberating effects. For them the forest is a male Wild, differentiated from the city by its outlaw population'. This forest world is, she rightly suggests 'strangely flat and perfunctory' as a result.

an implicit punning connection between the wilderness and the power of the human *will*, which can transform necessity into virtue.

This is pointed up further when Valentine soliloquizes:

> How use doth breed a habit in a man!
> This shadowy desert, unfrequented woods,
> I better brook than flourishing peopled towns:
> Here can I sit alone, unseen of any,
> And to the nightingale's complaining notes
> Tune my distresses and record my woes.
> O thou that dost inhabit in my breast,
> Leave not the mansion so long tenantless,
> Lest, growing ruinous, the building fall
> And leave no memory of what it was.
> Repair me with thy presence, Silvia;
> Thou gentle nymph, cherish thy forlorn swain.
> [*Shouts within.*]
>
> What hallowing and what stir is this today?
> These are my mates, that make their wills their law,
> Have some unhappy passenger in chase.
> They love me well; yet I have much to do
> To keep them from uncivil outrages. (V. iv. 1–17)

There are some connections here with the Duke's love of solitude in *As You Like It*, but the sentiment is more ambiguous in itself. Valentine is on a civilizing mission, but he fears that, like the desacralized buildings of the Reformation landscape, he might lose his own identity. Valentine's subjects are fundamentally lawless, and this is a play in which law is often subverted.[15] Yet, in the end, he is able to redeem them, telling the Duke that they have 'worthy qualities' (V. iv. 153) despite them being confessed criminals, one even having killed a man. This is not so much a healing natural world as one of chaos in which anything goes. Yet that world allows some kind of mediation between people, giving Valentine the grace to forgive his false friend Proteus, even for the attempted rape of Silvia. Valentine accepts Proteus's 'sorrow' as a 'sufficient ransom' for his sins (lines 74–5), because, as he says, 'Who by repentance is not satisfied / Is nor of heaven *nor earth*' (lines 79–80; emphasis added). If 'By penitence th' Eternal's wrath's appeased' (line 81), then earthly man should accept it too; but this is very glibly put, and it's clear that Proteus has not yet reached his full repentance. He has to admit his inconstancy to Julia before

[15] For instance, Proteus's violation of the 'law of friendship' in the very moment that he mentions it (III. i. 5).

he can be truly reclaimed: he recognizes the ease with which men change their minds, but this is not so much a matter of *metanoia* (the change of mind that is requisite to repentance) as a fresh sight of Julia, which makes him wonder 'What is in Silvia's face, but I may spy / More fresh in Julia's with a constant eye?' (lines 114–5). The wilderness has enabled this fresh vision (but whether it can truly be called constancy is another matter). The idea of wildness implies a notion of the human will that is not under conscious or rational control, partly because the will is considered to be fallen, 'infected', as Sidney put it (see Introduction); that lack of conscious control, though, enables the access of grace – the salvific force that humans cannot will into being on their own terms. The wilderness suspends human plans, and disposes people into their correct pattern, without their own stir.[16] It is the source of a grace otherwise unavailable in civil society, but it is, paradoxically, a rather rough magic, a grudging grace.

The contempt for human motive that informs *The Two Gentlemen of Verona*, driving us into a wilderness of arbitrary will, is more fully articulated in *A Midsummer Night's Dream*. Most famously, of course, Puck declares 'Lord, what fools these mortals be!' (III. ii. 115), thinking their lives a 'fond pageant' to entertain himself and Oberon (line 114). Titania, even though she is in love with the ass-headed Bottom, wants to purge his 'mortal grossness' (III. i. 160), implying that there is something deeply wrong about human solidity. Puck, in turn, calls Bottom 'the shallowest thick-skin of that barren sort' (III. ii. 13), and though he may refer merely to the mechanicals, there is a sense in which the phrase resonates to take in all humans. 'Barren' here means stupid, but it has clear connotations of being unproductive, and we may balk at the term: humans, like the Indian child's mother, reproduce, whereas fairies do not. In the forest, to be human is to be contemptible, but we may consider that mortal grossness is more genuinely connected to the natural world than the airy thinness of the fairies.

Humans' gross solidity means that they are more capable of real change – up to and including mortality – than the fairies, and it is humans rather than spirits who are really transformed in the forest. Bottom is 'translated' (III. i. 119), something that Helena also wants to happen, desiring early in the play that she be 'translated' into the apparently more loveable Hermia (I. i. 191). She also claims that 'Things base and vile, holding no quantity, / Love can transpose to form and dignity' (lines 232–3). Unlike Titania,

[16] Anne Barton, *Essays, Mainly Shakespearean*, p. 174, argues very convincingly that 'The involuntary plays a significantly new part in the late plays'; yet there are traces of its importance from the very beginning of Shakespeare's work.

who believes that the lower parts of mortal humanity need purging, Helena thinks that the low parts of the human – presumably involving one's vegetal and animal souls – can be translated into something more valuable, and indeed that they may be necessary for human dignity. The base aspects of nature are important: though the transformations of the play are effected mainly by Oberon's potions, it is significant that those transformations all take place while the lovers are sleeping on what Puck calls 'the dank and dirty ground' (II. ii. 75); Oberon, in bringing about the final translations of love, has to 'rock the ground whereon these sleepers be' (IV. i. 86). Whereas the fairies fly through the air, humans are deeply *grounded* in nature, for good or ill; they are bottomed out, as it were; Robert Pogue Harrison argues that, throughout history, 'The *humus* [earth] grounds the human,' largely through burial rites;[17] but other forms of grounding may work just as well. This grounding enables translation, acting as a mediating condition. The humans end up, to use Theseus's resonant phrase, 'earthlier happy' (I. i. 76) than any airy fairy can be.

A Midsummer Night's Dream contains some of Shakespeare's most resonant poetry of the natural world. This poetry leaves criticism rather at a loss, as it seems like a pure evocation of a natural atmosphere, a poetry of pure being rather than articulated meaning. Yet there are some crucial differentiations in this poetry which, by distinguishing human and immortal attitudes to nature, subtly enable us to see how complicated human interaction with the rural world is:

PUCK. How now, spirit! whither wander you?
FAIRY. Over hill, over dale,
Thorough bush, thorough brier,
Over park, over pale,
Thorough, flood, thorough fire,
I do wander every where,
Swifter than the moon's sphere;
And I serve the Fairy Queen,
To dew her orbs upon the green.
The cowslips tall her pensioners be,
In their gold coats spots you see:
Those be rubies, fairy favours,
In those freckles live their savours.
I must go seek some dewdrops here,
And hang a pearl in every cowslip's ear.
(II. i. 1–15)

17 Robert Pogue Harrison, *Forests*, p. 7.

The fairy goes frictionlessly *through* and *over* the natural world, rather than getting embroiled in it. There is something superficial about the way it clothes nature, and the courtly imagery here accordingly touches on standard critiques of the superficiality of courtliness. The relationship of the fairy monarch to her country is insubstantial and arbitrary. Humans, by contrast, can live more solidly and weightily in the world: Hermia remembers that she and Helena 'Upon faint primrose beds were wont to lie, / Emptying our bosoms of their counsel sweet' (I. i. 215–6). Where the fairy gives out its favours without any sense of loss, the girls empty themselves out, and are concomitantly aware of the fragility of the flowers they lie on. The 'spots' and 'freckles' of the flowers here may be a sign of nature's fallenness, but they are translated into favourable beauty spots by the fairies' perspective. Shakespeare's tendency, unusual for his time, to 'number the streaks of the tulip', involves making blemishes signs of life's savour,[18] and life is to be savoured because it is transient. Unlike the fairies, the humans have a sense of time passing and of the rhythms of seasons: Lysander, Hermia and Helena, for instance, once met in the wood 'To do observance to a morn of May' (line 167). Love is embedded within such natural cycles: Helena thinks Hermia's voice is, to Demetrius, 'More tuneable than lark to shepherd's ear, / When wheat is green, when hawthorn buds appear' (lines 184–5). This sense of temporally linked sympathies is in sharp contrast to the lofty jarring of the fairies. Titania's quarrel with Oberon has made 'the green corn' rot 'ere his youth attained a beard' (II. i. 94–5); fairies not mortals are the cause of barrenness.[19]

Oberon and his crew are, then, a kind of airy nothing; the imaginative sympathies of humans are required to give things a local habitation and a name. Humans are more connected to the wood than the fairies are. Demetrius's pun that he is 'wood within this wood' (line 192) emphasizes that connection: though folly and madness ('wood'-ness) are humans' lot, the pun also connects to their wooing (Helena says, shortly after, that women 'should be woo'd' – line 242). The wood may be a 'desert place' (line 218), but it is turned into a place of plenitude by human emotion. As Helena says, 'Nor doth this wood lack worlds of company, / For you, in my respect, are all the world' (lines 223–4). Respect, here, means perception,[20] the human imaginative ability to translate things and imbue them with meaning.

[18] See Samuel Johnson, *Rasselas*, chapter 10.

[19] Borlik, *Ecocriticism*, p. 120 helpfully situates the play in the context of the climate and food crisis of the mid-1590s.

[20] cf. *Cymbeline*, II. iii. 135.

How far the translations work is very much a moot point. In the play's epilogue, Oberon says of the new married couples that 'the blots of Nature's hand / Shall not in their issue stand' (V. i. 409–10); he seems for a moment to claim the power to wash away Original Sin, though in fact he goes on to qualify this by saying that their children won't have moles, harelips or scars. Puck, meanwhile, is the spirit that is sent 'To sweep the dust behind the door' (line 390). This seems like another mode of cleaning mortality's sinfulness,[21] but it's possible that his action is the equivalent of sweeping the dust under the carpet rather than getting it out of the house. The hints of natural redemption are raised only to be partially withdrawn; they are provisional and tentative, a matter of perspective.

The wood is a neutral zone which allows for adjustments of perspective. The rude mechanicals leave the city for their play rehearsal because they do not want to be 'dogged with company, and our devices known' (I. ii. 104). As with the Duke in *As You Like It*, the desire to escape 'public haunt' is the major motive for going to the countryside, which is negatively conceived as a place free of people. Yet the wood is in fact highly populated, full of life. This is partly because, as Theseus says, humans tend to project and imagine animate things, supposing a bush a bear (V. i. 2–22). Yet this is not as anthropocentric a form of projection as we might assume. It involves an assumption of an animate universe, certainly, but the connections are two-way: if Nature is given a kind of consciousness, humans are made natural, their connections to one another mediated through the natural world while the autonomy of that world is given proper respect. The alienation and isolation of human consciousness are suspended through nature's mediation. The lovers express this blurring beautifully when they wake from their sleep on the ground:

> DEMETRIUS. These things seem small and undistinguishable,
> Like far-off mountains turnèd into clouds.
> HERMIA. Methinks I see these things with parted eye,
> When everything seems double. (IV. i. 186–9)

This doubleness, in which the boundaries of the world are seemingly dissolved, resembles the unfathomable bottomlessness of Bottom's dream. As C. L. Barber puts it, 'the perceived structure of the outer world breaks down [and] the body and its environment interpenetrate in unaccustomed ways, so that the seeming separateness and stability of identity is lost'.[22] Lost, or re-found as a result of shifting and blurring one's perspective.

21 Barber, *Shakespeare's Festive Comedy*, p. 158 argues that 'with the dust, out go evil spirits'.
22 Barber, *Shakespeare's Festive Comedy*, p. 153.

The rural world, in this play, represents that which is not available to consciousness but which nonetheless influences us. At the same time, it has more autonomy than the countryside in Shakespeare's other plays because no human lives there.

A place where no one lives is a troubling concept: we think of the old canard about trees falling silently in woods. The idea of such a place fascinated the Romantics: following on from Gray's idea that 'fully many a flower is born to blush unseen, / And waste its sweetness on the desert air',[23] Wordsworth in 'Nutting' is troubled and enticed in equal measure by violets which 're-appear / And fade, unseen by any human eye' (lines 30–1), making his heart luxuriate 'with indifferent things, / Wasting its kindliness on stocks and stones, / And on the vacant air' (lines 39–41). Like Spenser's Guyon in the Bower of Bliss, though informed by a different code of morality, he resists this luxurious temptation, and ravages the place; the bower and its plants 'Deformed and sullied, patiently gave up / Their quiet being' (lines 45–6).[24] These last lines are resonant with meaning: the phrasing could simply be a circumlocutory way of saying that the bower stopped being silent, but there is also a sense of Christlike suffering as the plants lose their life, and a contradictory sense that their true *being* only emerges at this moment of destruction and death, that meaningful life only comes out when man violates nature. The 'Spirit in the woods' of which Wordsworth warns in the poem's final line may emerge only when man comes to destroy it. Similiarly, in *A Midsummer Night's Dream,* nature seems fallen and limited only when there are humans around to experience it. Left to its own absence of device, it seems unfallen and infinite, going on 'in maiden meditation, fancy-free', but without 'a local habitation and a name' (II. i. 164; V. i. 17). Shakespeare, like Wordsworth, presents the natural world as *indifferent* to human concerns.[25]

But even the wood in *A Midsummer Night's Dream* is 'near Athens', the cradle of Western civilization; Shakespeare's other representations of the rural world are more populated and therefore even more problematically marginal. We are (almost) always on the fringes of the civilized and the natural. *Love's Labour's Lost* is one of Shakespeare's more obviously outdoor plays, yet its outdoorsiness is in fact basically artificial. Though the

[23] 'Elegy Written in a Country Churchyard', lines 55–6. References to *The Poetical Works of Gray and Collins*, ed. Austin Lane Poole (London: Oxford University Press, 1919).

[24] References to William Wordsworth, *The Major Works*, ed. Stephen Gill, revised edition (Oxford: Oxford University Press, 2000).

[25] Wordsworth's 'indifferent things', points to the Stoic idea of *adiaphora*, things that are neither good nor bad, picked up and emphasized by Hooker in the Reformation as a way to avoid disagreements on minor doctrinal matters.

countryman Costard is one of the major characters, he is a bumpkin imported for entertainment purposes, a 'swain' to be 'our sport' alongside the equally exotic and absurd Don Armado (I. i. 179). Costard has his own sport with Jaquenetta in the 'curious-knotted garden' of the King (line 246), and has some further fun misdirecting his betters' letters, but his translation to the courtly world does not make it more natural. It is a failure of hospitality rather than a love of nature that makes the King keep the ladies out of his home (and, seemingly, out of his park as well): the Princess comments that 'The roof of this court is too high to be yours, and welcome to the wide fields too base to be mine' (II. i. 92–4), perhaps implying that any claim on the skies is a mark of royal hubris, but mainly highlighting an absurdly artificial and uncomfortable meeting in which the court is transported to the countryside for diplomatic purposes.[26] Though the King tries to get the Princess to dance 'on this grass' (V. ii. 185), her refusal to do so accords with a refusal to accept the compromised terms of their meeting; the natural world here is not a place of happy mediation but a compromise based on the men's attempt to break their oath as little as possible.[27]

A deliberate and stylized withdrawal into the natural world, then, doesn't always enable and mediate love as it does in such plays as *A Midsummer Night's Dream*, for the natural world needs to be taken on its own terms. By contrast to *Love's Labour's Lost*, where the world of the country is included in a fundamentally courtly structure and world view, *The Merry Wives of Windsor* is apparently a citizen comedy, but one where an atmosphere of rusticity prevails, despite the proximity of the royal court. The fact that the actual presence of the court and king at the time of the play's action is doubtful may be the enabling condition of this particular mixture of world views.[28] Windsor is a royal town, but only on occasion; as such, it is a remarkably changeable place, shading between city, country and court with unusual ease. Characters can easily walk in the royal park before dinner, can quite casually set up duels in fields on either side of town, and can merrily send Falstaff out to the meadows to be dunked in the Thames.[29] That atmosphere of partial rusticity enables a sense of sanity to prevail in Windsor.

Anne Page, the play's principal love-object, is a relatively minor character, speaking little; yet her sanity rings out in what little she has to say, giving

[26] Given the Princess's reference to pavilions later, we might see this meeting as analogous to such diplomatic meetings as the Field of the Cloth of Gold.

[27] See Chapter 3 for further discussion of *Love's Labour's Lost*'s process of purgation and the effort to do away with artificiality.

[28] Caius claims to be heading off to court several times, but others mention the absence of the king.

[29] Fowler, *Renaissance Realism*, p. 7, points out that the play's 'geography is unusually consistent' for drama of the time.

us confidence as to the validity of her marital choice. Rejecting both Caius and Slender as her suitors, she says

> Alas, I had rather be set quick i' th' earth,
> And bowled to death with turnips.
> (III. iv. 86–7)

No one who hears this little lament could possibly fail to side with her; alongside the Blackadderish wit, we also get an impression of groundedness: she is not a girl to build castles in the air like the vain misses of London comedy.[30] Anticipating such an exaggerated version of rustic punishment may help avoid it: it is Falstaff in the end who is such a butt, a 'Jack a Lent' (V. v. 127).[31] Falstaff, indeed, almost invites such a punishment, parodically anticipating Lear when he goes out into the park saying 'Let the sky rain potatoes, let it thunder to the tune of "Greensleeves", hail kissing-comfits and snow eringoes' (lines 19–20). He expects alien, sophisticated grocery to come his way (potatoes being a recent import, kissing-comfits being breath-sweets, and eringoes an exotic aphrodisiac candy; Greensleeves was the new pop-tune of the 1580s),[32] in contrast to Anne's earthier and more familiar turnips.

Nonetheless, Windsor is a town, not the deep rural world (if there really is such a thing). Its climax comes in a royal park, not out in the fields, and that climax is a translation into courtly terms. Mistress Quickly, playing the Queen of the Fairies, sends the fairies to clean the Castle and the chairs of the Order of the Garter 'With juice of balm and every precious flower' (line 62). The natural and the courtly are held in a precise and precious but consciously fictive and precarious balance:

> And nightly, meadow-fairies, look you sing,
> Like to the Garter's compass, in a ring.
> Th' expressure that it bears, green let it be,
> More fertile-fresh than all the field to see;
> And '*Honi soit qui mal y pense*' write
> In em'rald tufts, flowers purple, blue and white,
> Like sapphire, pearl, and rich embroidery,
> Buckled below fair knighthood's bending knee:
> Fairies use flowers for their charactery.
> (lines 65–73)

30 E.g. Gertrude Touchstone in *Eastward Ho!*

31 To be buried alive is also Aaron's punishment in *Titus Andronicus*.

32 Despite the abiding myth, it was *not* written by Henry VIII; it is an Italianate tune, whose modes place it very much as a new thing in the late Elizabethan period. See Giorgio Melchiori's Arden3 notes to these lines – Melchiori also points out the allegedly aphrodisiac qualities of both potatoes and eringoes.

As so often, the natural and the supernatural shade into one another. It is not at all clear here whether the language of flowers and fairies, or the language of courtly *impresas* and jewels is primary; we cannot see which world view *represents* the other. We might therefore even wonder whether Mistress Quickly represents Queen Elizabeth or vice versa. The translation, for a moment, is perfectly mutual. Yet Falstaff, like Ovid's Actaeon, and like Calidore in *The Faerie Queene*, intrudes on and interrupts this perfect circuit of natural and political expression. His difference from his literary precursors, though, is significant: he is intended to intrude – indeed, the whole masque was set up for his intrusion. As Herne the Hunter, Falstaff is a figure of 'winter time' (IV. iv. 30) intruding on a spring fertility ritual, but we should be wary of taking the ritual aspect of the scene too seriously.[33] Shakespeare seems keen to suggest that such rituals always involve circular translations and compromised mediations, that there is no essential truth to be got at in them, no radically other world to be accessed through them. If there is a second world, it is also *this* world.

Gender and mortality

It is only in the processes of living and dying in the real world, rather than the theatrical otherworld of ritual, that people really engage with nature, and to do so involves real risks. A natural space is most fully focalized by someone dying in it, and the relationship of the mortal person to the place of their death is often construed in highly gendered terms. Shakespeare's most famous moment of a character being absorbed into nature is the death of Ophelia in *Hamlet*, as described by Gertrude:

> There is a willow grows askaunt the brook,
> That shows his hoary leaves in the glassy stream,
> Therewith fantastic garlands did she make
> Of crow-flowers, nettles, daisies, and long purples
> The liberal shepherds give a grosser name,
> But our cull-cold maids do dead-men's fingers call them.
> There on the pendant boughs her crownet weeds
> Clamb'ring to hang, an envious sliver broke,
> When down her weedy trophies and herself
> Fell in the weeping brook. Her clothes spread wide,
> And mermaid-like awhile they bore her up,
> Which time she chaunted snatches of old lauds,

33 Keith Sagar, *Literature and the Crime against Nature: From Homer to Hughes* (London: Chaucer Press, 2005), pp. 80–1 argues that Falstaff is a kind of fertility god, 'however degraded'.

As one incapable of her own distress,
Or like a creature native and indued
Unto that element. But long it could not be
Till that her garments, heavy with their drink,
Pulled the poor wretch from her melodious lay
To muddy death. (IV. vii. 166–83)

The account is so obviously mediated that it hardly needs the Gravediggers' discussion of Ophelia as a possible suicide in the next scene to emphasize how much Gertrude is making the best of things, telling a story that will enable her to be buried in Christian ground. Gertrude's 'There is' opening points to similar scene-setting formulae in Latin poetry (Virgil and Ovid's *est locus* trope). The effect is to make the scene the primary agent, Ophelia herself almost incidental. The great property of nature seems to be to cross boundaries (hence all those hyphenated names). There are many crossings here (even the word 'brook' implies a stream that can be crossed). A woman who is associated with 'country matters' (III. ii. 116), she is the play's great escapee from the prison that is Elsinore. That escape may be ultimately a muddy death, but she finds her way more readily into her own element than anyone else; her dissolution is much easier than Hamlet's, despite his wish that his flesh would melt and purify into dew. Hamlet believes that his father's 'form and cause conjoined, preaching to stones, / Would make them *capable*' (III. iv. 126–7, emphasis added), but the play fails to bear out this longing for the natural world and man to become so capable of common, immanent action;[34] by contrast, Ophelia's *incapability* of her own distress is a kind of negative capability, more properly on terms with the natural world than anyone around her.

If Denmark is 'an unweeded garden', as Hamlet says, perhaps we should blame the groundskeepers for Ophelia's accident: they should surely have coppiced the badly angled willow. Joking aside, Ophelia is rather a weed, though not something 'rank and gross in nature' as it turns out.[35] She is unnecessary to the play's sense of order, bringing inconvenient and embarrassing flowers into the court. One mystery that no critic seems overly keen to pluck is the question of whether Hamlet has actually slept with Ophelia: her bawdy songs clearly imply that he has, but almost all commentators seem eager to protect the prince from the charge of abandonment. Gertrude, perhaps, knows better: her apotropaic mention of those liberally named 'long purples' suggests something along those

[34] Richard C. McCoy, *Faith in Shakespeare* (Oxford: Oxford University Press, 2013), p. x, shows how Hamlet's words bespeak a longing for 'a kind of Eucharistic miracle' that might cure the kingdom.

[35] Desdemona is also called a 'weed' (IV. ii. 67) when suspected of sexual looseness.

lines. On the other hand, she may identify her lost potential daughter-in-law with the 'cull-cold maids' who won't even mention cocks. The point, of course, is that Ophelia's virginity is as doubtful as her suicide, and as the Queen's complicity in Old Hamlet's murder. Women are a mystery much deeper than the mystery Hamlet so fondly supposes is his own: they share in the mystery of mortal nature, which cannot – in principle – be analysed or turned into a neatly Baconian weedless garden.

The association of the natural environment with wild and dangerous sexuality is still more acute in *Titus Andronicus*, where it exists almost solely as a locale for rape. Yet the boundaries between the urban civilization of Rome and the wildness of nature are all too easily crossed in this play. As with the suicide of Ophelia, there is a use of descriptive language in relation to the rape of Lavinia that beggars modern belief: we feel that anyone who could describe the incident would be better to offer help than to offer such choric comment. While this may be a Renaissance convention,[36] we can't help feeling that the sheer lengthiness of the description serves to naturalize both rape and suicide, suggesting that these are baffling female activities that resist rationalization just as much as they obviate assistance. In the case of Lavinia, whose name associates her with the country,[37] it's possible that the description of the natural scene even hints at her responsibility for her violation.

Inciting her sons to kill Bassianus and to rape Lavinia, Tamora describes the place she claims that her victims have led her to:

A barren detested vale you see it is;
The trees, though summer, yet forlorn and lean,
Overcome with moss and baleful mistletoe;
Here never shines the sun, here nothing breeds,
Unless the nightly owl or fatal raven;
And when they showed me this abhorrèd pit,
They told me, here, at dead time of the night,
A thousand fiends, a thousand hissing snakes,
Ten thousand swelling toads, as many urchins,
Would make such fearful and confusèd cries,
As any mortal body hearing it
Should straight fall mad, or else die suddenly.
No sooner had they told this hellish tale,
But straight they told me they would bind me here

36 See Frank Kermode, *Shakespeare's Language* (London: Allen Lane, 2000), pp. 7–14.

37 Lavinia, in Virgil's *Aeneid*, was the name of the founding hero's new wife, and the landing place in Italy to which he was destined was Lavinium.

Unto the body of a dismal yew,
And leave me to this miserable death.
(II. iii. 93–108)

The description is even more peculiarly mediated than Gertrude's description of Ophelia's suicide, this time by clear dishonesty: Bassianus and Lavinia have *not* described the place thus; it is a misrepresentation of a supposed representation. Tamora seems to conjure a place of mischief out of nothing – or at most out of her own lasciviousness, for the victims have just caught her dallying with Aaron. In a much more negative way than in *A Midsummer Night's Dream*, human intentions are transformed and subverted in this forest: victims are made criminal here, criminals portray themselves as victims. The inversions that are essential to her plot derive from the creation of this place, which Aaron calls a 'loathsome pit' (line 193), and which we might associate with Tamora's vagina. Its barrenness is partly ironic given her pregnancy by Aaron, but accurate in that she will not give the emperor true offspring. Her plots will also kill off any more fruitful sexuality in her enemies' family.

The darkness and confusion of this place result in the cutting off of true speech, for once Quintus and Martius have fallen into the pit, they become silent, unable to answer the accusations against them, which come in the form of oral, epistolary and physical evidence (i.e. the gold Aaron has buried as well as the body of Bassianus). The cutting off is particularly acute in the case of Lavinia, who loses the tongue and hands that might tell of her rape. In a sense, she becomes part of the natural environment, Marcus describing her lost hands as 'her two branches' and 'aspen leaves' (II. iv. 18, 45) and her empty mouth as 'a crimson river of warm blood' (line 22). The chaotic power of nature has overcome the Andronici: as Marcus says, 'One hour's storm will drown the fragrant meads' (line 54). The hunting sequence had begun with Titus saying 'the morn is bright and grey, / The fields are fragrant and the woods are green' (II. ii. 1–2), but now that sensuous distinctiveness has been thrown into darkness and confusion. Lavinia has supposedly *shown* this terrible place to Tamora; and, in a sense, she has, in that she has accused Tamora, whose sexual deviancy might otherwise have gone unrevealed. Like an Actaeon, Lavinia has stumbled on a secret place of nature and released forces that destroy her. Lavinia has revealed Tamora to herself: as with Gertrude and Ophelia, the ekphrastic description of a natural place has enabled a transference of guilt and punishment to occur between women. Gertrude, who *may* be nearly as guilty a woman as Tamora, is in a sense preserved by Ophelia's sacrifice. At its worst, the natural world becomes a place where proper distinctions between people can be lost, based on the tendency to tar all women with the same brush that we see in Hamlet, who may not taint his mind against his mother, but whose sense of feminine frailty muddies his attitude to Ophelia. As we will see, the wilderness is also a place where the more improper, excessive valuation of human specialness is abandoned; but in *Titus* it is a viciously feminine place where human dignity is unfairly sacrificed.

The loss of selfhood in the natural world is not wholly a feminine province, however. In Shakespeare's most masculine play, *Timon of Athens*, the wild rural world is an arena for angry contemplation of the failings of homosocial bonding and society in general. Timon does not dissolve into the elements like Ophelia, though, nor does he lose verbal capacities like Lavinia: he sets up an enduring and textual monument in the countryside which preserves his curse on mankind. The play is vague about exactly how Timon kills himself, but his grave is on 'the very hem o' th' sea' (V. iv. 66). The play is particularly interested in such boundaries between natural realms, and that between the natural and the civilized. When Timon leaves Athens, he turns back to address the 'wall / That girdles in those wolves' (IV. i. 1–2), but he also wishes that it would collapse into the earth; clearly Timon believes that artificial boundaries do not really separate human nature from other forms of nature. In the woods, he expects to 'find / Th' unkindest beast more kinder than mankind' (lines 35–6), but instead he finds the resources of the earth itself.

One key resource he discovers is stones. Lone prophets sometimes speak to stones,[38] but Timon instead throws them at his various visitors. The earth, it seems, provides him with the means to preserve his privacy. Yet its gifts are of many kinds: it also gives him food – which he needs – and gold – which he doesn't. Having decided that there is no balance or order in the world, saying 'All's obliquy; / There's nothing level in our cursèd natures / But direct villainy' (IV. iii. 18–20), Timon tries nonetheless to find some level base, some common denominator of humanity, by digging in the earth, asking it to 'yield me roots' (line 23); yet what he finds is not the basic staff of life, but the very thing that has caused all his troubles, gold. Only when he curses nature, in significantly gendered terms, calling it 'damnèd earth, / Thou common whore of mankind that puts odds/ Among the rout of nations' (lines 42–4) does he find the basic thing he needs. When he emphasizes commonality, he gets the root of difference;

[38] e.g. Milton at the end of *The Ready and Easy Way to Establish a Free Commonwealth*.

when he emphasizes nature's differentiations, he gets – eventually – a turnip (compare Anne Page, above). Later, he calls Nature 'Common mother' (line 177), but the echo of the phrasing used when he called it a common whore identifies the principles of nurturing with more meretricious properties. Later it is 'bounteous huswife Nature', which produces a 'full mess' for men (lines 420–1); its very generosity is sloppy. Nature's 'infinite breast' (line 178) though bounteous is also undiscriminating. There is something intolerable about the idea of the infinite, once solely the property of God, being attributed to a feminized Nature. It is also intolerable because that infinite nature is a property of Timon himself – his hunger, which causes him to lament that 'nature being sick of man's unkindness / Should yet be hungry' (lines 176–7). Timon can speak about nature but cannot stand apart from it and tame it to his will.

Apemantus emphasizes Timon's lack of transformative grace; he is not like *As You Like It*'s Duke in being able to translate the woods with and into a sweet and instructive style:

What, think'st
That the bleak air, thy boisterous chamberlain,
Will put thy shirt on warm? Will these moist trees
That have outlived the eagle page thy heels
And skip when thou point'st out? Will the cold brook,
Candied with ice, caudle thy morning taste
To cure thy o'ernight's surfeit? Call the creatures
Whose naked natures live in all the spite
Of wreakful heaven, whose bare unhousèd trunks,
To the conflicting elements exposed
Answer mere nature; bid them flatter thee.
(lines 221–31)

Even as he insists on Nature's indifference, Apemantus fills the environment with intentions, history, energetic and purposive conflicts. Those conflicts, furthermore, are with an angry heaven; that heaven may be introduced in order to emphasize the relative feebleness of Timon's rage, but it certainly makes this place move and live. Neither Timon nor Apemantus may find sympathy in Nature, but they do find something more vivacious than the empty formalities of social life as represented in the play's first three acts. Their discourteous quarrel nonetheless has a kind of perverse fondness in it.[39] The idea of their being a general 'thievery' in the natural world, where

[39] On this, see Tom MacFaul, *Male Friendship in Shakespeare and his Contemporaries* (Cambridge: Cambridge University Press, 2007), pp. 141–9.

'Each thing', from sun and moon down, steals energy from something else (lines 435–42) could be just a negative way of looking at patterns of natural sympathy rather as Timon's friendship with Apemantus is based on Blakean opposition.

The doubleness of nature is emphasized in all of this, and Timon's attitude to it is double, passionately ambivalent. He calls out

> O blessèd breeding sun, draw from the earth
> Rotten humidity; below thy sister's orb
> Infect the air! Twinned brothers of one womb,
> Whose procreation, residence, and birth
> Scarce is dividant, touch them with several fortunes,
> The greater scorns the lesser. Not nature
> (To whom all sores lay siege) can bear great fortune
> But by contempt of nature. (IV. iii. 1–8)

The human burden of this peculiar and difficult speech is clear enough: however close people are, differences in their fortune make them inimical; there are no bonds of sympathy in human nature. Yet this unnatural antipathy seems, paradoxically, to be founded in nature. The final sentence seems to mean that even someone who is in a (natural) condition of great fortune (which has resisted the sores that the world provides) can only carry off his fortune by acting contemptuously towards his natural kin, but the way of putting it abstracts a self-involuted, even cancerous enmity of nature to nature. The reason for attacking nature is that it is unnatural, highlighting the way in which nature self-deconstructs. Yet there is something blessed here, some higher source of value that transcends the fallen world, even if its good influence is somehow turned awry in its results. Later, he tries to separate out the ideal and transcendent source of life from the natural world, referring to the sun as 'Hyperion' (line 184); one might compare Hamlet's insistence that his father was a Hyperion figure to Claudius's satyr (*Hamlet*, I. ii. 140): in both cases there is the desire to make the masculine source of life transcendent, even if the speaker himself is embedded in feminine Nature. This seems like a stalled critique of a creating deity: god (equivalent to the sun) is necessarily good, and is necessarily good precisely because he is the origin of everything (the alliterative connection of 'blessed' and 'breeding' effects this); yet what is created is diseased; the only thing that redeems the deity is that Timon wills the disease, albeit after the fact – this god at least answers prayers, though retrospectively. A willed contempt redeems the world, or at least sets man's relationship to the divine on some kind of comprehensible footing, allowing him to die. Timon's opinions about the natural world are in the end less important than his involvement in it; he cannot find any transcendent perspective on nature.

King and country

A ruler is supposed to have power over his *country*, but the nature of his authority over the land itself is highly precarious.[40] Like Timon ordering the sun about, but with more sanction, King Lear commands the storm that is already taking place. He calls the elements 'servile ministers' (III. ii. 21), expressing anger and contempt at these elements for apparently joining with his daughters against him (service may be a crucially valuable part of human nature, but servility is to be avoided); yet he also seems to think that the elements can be pressed into his own peculiar form of service. He famously demands

> Blow, winds, and crack your cheeks! rage, blow!
> You cataracts and hurricanoes, spout
> Till you have drenched our steeples, drowned the cocks!
> (lines 1–3)

Partly calling down vengeance on himself, partly calling it onto his daughters, he is in some ways pleased at the storm's indifference, its lack of respect of persons.[41] Yet he also seems to affirm his own powers over his kingdom, and its weather ('our steeples' seems to use the possessive royal we).[42] He refuses to criticize the elements for 'unkindness' (line 16), saying that they owe him no 'subscription' (line 18); the elements are of course kind, in the sense that they are natural, but the odd idea that they might owe a *written* contractual deference expressed by the idea of subscription bespeaks the really weird alienation of this scene.

The idea that the weather might act as a vengeful force on behalf of but not in the control of a king is picked up in *Macbeth*, where the protagonist anticipates that Duncan's murder will provoke an elemental crisis:

40 There is some doubt as to whether authority over the country is a metonym for authority over the people or vice versa. It may be that the two come as a package, but how that package is tied together is very uncertain.

41 Egan, *Green Shakespeare*, p. 145 draws a telling parallel between Lear's challenge to the storm and Cnut's challenge to the waves.

42 In this moment, for once, he reveals himself to be a post-Reformation monarch.

pity, like a naked new-born babe,
Striding the blast, or heaven's cherubin, horsed
Upon the sightless couriers of the air,
Shall blow the horrid deed in every eye,
That tears shall drown the wind. (I. vii. 21–5)

The very excessive language of this still taps into the language of royal power (the couriers are the king's messengers), suggesting that the king has agents whose powers he knows nothing of and whom he would do well not to trust. There are powers in the natural world which human action unleashes, but which humans don't control.

In *Lear*, even those loyal to the king are fearful of the storm that has been invoked, because it is not clear whether its force operates on his behalf or against him. The loyal Gentleman says that the King is 'minded like the weather, most unquietly' (III. i. 2); he communicates his own disquiet, perhaps because he's unsure whether the weather is affecting the King or vice versa. Gloucester is similarly uneasy, saying that 'Man's nature cannot carry / Th' affliction nor the fear' (III. ii. 48–9): the generalization is rather typical of the play (and particularly of Gloucester), but we may question how far it can really apply to the king, a being who in some senses stands outside simple human nature, having two bodies, one of which may be as transcendently eerie as the newborn, angelic figure of pity invoked by Macbeth.[43] Kent, shortly after, says 'The tyranny of the open night's too rough / For nature to endure' (III. iv. 2–3), perhaps continuing his role as a critic of Lear in suggesting a connection between the king's tyrannous actions and the storm; in which case, it might constitute either a nemesis for that tyranny or its natural continuation. In response, Lear says 'Let me alone', a line of weird and contradictory resonance: on the one hand, he may be asking to be allowed to stay out in the storm and die; on the other, he may be insisting on his own uniqueness and exceptionality,[44] believing that only *his* nature can endure this.

It seems that Lear seeks the heath in order to be solitary, but he's barely left alone there for a moment. This is as blank a form of nature as one can imagine:[45] as Gloucester says, 'for many miles about / There's scarce a bush' (II. iv. 301–2). Yet not only is the hovel discovered, but Lear

43 See E. H. Kantorowicz, *The King's Two Bodies: A Study in Mediaeval Political Theology* (Princeton: Princeton University Press, 1957).

44 The phrase has connotations of 'leave it to me' – with a sense that one is specially capable: e.g. *Shrew* IV. ii. 71, *12N* II. iii. 134.

45 See Maus, *Being and Having in Shakespeare*, p. 128, on the fact that most of *King Lear* takes place in marginal areas, not being part of the property-system; see also Egan, *Green Shakespeare*, p. 132. It is not explicitly a heath, but given the absence of even a bush, it's either a heath or moorland.

is constantly accompanied by his motley court. He would like to think himself alone with nature, but loyal attendants (Edgar as Tom, Kent as Caius, and Gloucester *in propria persona*) minister to his needs; even the hovel is described as providing 'some friendship' (III. ii. 62). The failure of real abandonment in this play is as ironic as the company Timon is forced to keep in his self-imposed exile. A similar irony can be found in Lear's sense that he has found (in Tom) 'the thing itself' (III. iv. 106), man in his most basic state, one of the 'naked wretches' he apostrophizes in the one moment when he is left alone on the heath (line 28). In fact, the play doesn't really present common folk, despite giving the illusion of touching ground-bass of man as thing itself: the Old Man (Gloucester's tenant – IV. i. 13) who brings Gloucester to Edgar plays a small role; but most country folk are represented by Edgar in his various disguises. The servant who kills Cornwall is – ironically enough – his master's 'villain' (III. vii. 77), and a 'peasant' (line 79), but his significant role lasts less than ten lines before he's summarily done away with. The country as a whole has a rather illusory and elusive presence in the play.

Edgar, in many respects, embodies and represents the country, both as a natural environment and as its inhabitants.[46] When he flees from his father's house he says

> I will preserve myself, and am bethought
> To take the basest and most poorest shape
> That ever penury, in contempt of man,
> Brought near to beast. My face I'll grime with filth,
> Blanket my loins, elf all my hairs in knots,
> And with presented nakedness outface
> The winds and persecutions of the sky.
>
> (II. iii. 6–12)

The peculiar passive construction ('am bethought') of his plan indicates a giving up of characteristically human rationality; the contempt of man expressed here may be attributed to the abstract force of penury, but the impression given is a general contempt for the idol of human identity, a contempt that will lead Edgar to consider himself 'nothing' (line 21). The filth he wears radically grounds him while at the same time turning him into an elf-like spirit, able to move through the play with fairy flexibility a little like Puck's, and to translate himself like Bottom. He chooses his role as a madman because 'The country gives me proof and president [i.e. precedent]' for it (line 13), yet in taking on the role he seems to be testing

[46] See Simon Palfrey, *Poor Tom: Living "King Lear"* (Chicago: University of Chicago Press, 2014).

and proving himself, playing the prodigal as well as taking on a role like heirs to kingdoms going about in disguise among their subjects (such as Prince Hal, and the title character in Middleton's *The Phoenix*), touching the earthy bass/base string of *hum*ility.

In doing so, he acquires a degree of knowledge and power. Coming to the illusory Dover Cliff, he seems to be beating the bounds of his future kingdom. In evoking the cliff in the first place, he shows his ability to manipulate the environment more effectively than Lear, who could only tell the weather to do what it was already doing. When he takes Gloucester to the hospitable shadow of a tree, he seems in full command of the natural world: Gloucester says that 'a man may rot even here' (V. ii. 8), but Edgar denies this gloomily unfruitful notion, insisting that 'ripeness is all' (line 11). Lear, in perhaps his greatest moment of insight, laments that 'they told me I was every thing' (IV. vi. 104–5), but Edgar, who is more prepared to become nothing, can more readily ride out the storms of nature. If the fact that he is given the play's final line in the Folio indicates that he is the successor to the kingdom, it is because he has earthed himself most effectively. Edgar's humility succeeds Lear's claims of mastery, but both men lose their special identity in the process.

The idea of successors to the kingdom proving themselves in the marginal natural environment is also central to *Cymbeline*, where there is a quieter but almost equally unsettling compromising of human individuality. The play takes us off to the Welsh mountains for its translations; the princes Guiderius and Arviragus have been brought up there, perhaps in compliment to Prince Henry being installed as Prince of Wales in 1610: if so, the play's proving of the princes substitutes in literary-dramatic terms for the earlier custom of Princes of Wales getting actual military-administrative experience on the Welsh borders (as was the case with Henry VIII's elder brother Arthur). The boys' status as 'mountaineers' refreshes the royal family (as well as connecting Guiderius/Prince Henry to one of his future kingdoms). The fact that their daily hunting prepares them so well for war with the Romans may also act as a justification for James I's oft-criticized lengthy hunting trips. That the princes are therefore able to rescue their father in battle may point at hopes of resolving tensions between James and his elder son.[47]

The play's use of its natural environment is more intriguing than such slavish political allegory might suggest, however. Denied her choice of

47 See Fred B. Tromly, *Fathers and Sons in Shakespeare: The Debt Never Promised* (Toronto: University of Toronto Press, 2010) for the trope of sons rescuing their fathers.

husband, Imogen wishes that she were 'A neat-herd's daughter, and my Leonatus / Our neighbour shepherd's son' (I. i. 149–50); this anticipates the way the pastoral countryside will partly enable resolution in *The Winter's Tale*, but in this play a more rugged and painful country experience will be necessary. Posthumus makes no plans to improve his fortunes once he is banished, saying that he will simply 'abide the change of time, / Quake in the present winter's state, and wish / That warmer days would come' (II. iv. 4–6); this more passive attitude to the weather allows a happier ending than the futile commands to the storm we saw in *King Lear*.[48] Yet a passive attitude to nature goes alongside a deeper reverence for it: where Lear saw servility in the elements, the mountaineers have a more sacred sense of service in nature, one which involves wise passivity and receptiveness. Belarius says, 'This service is not service, so being done, / But being so allowed' (III. iii. 16–17); he may mean that his own service has been taken amiss by the king, but he also connects the sentiment to the 'morning's holy office' they are undertaking (line 4): he is going to 'tread these flats' while the young men climb the hill (line 11), so that each should do the office appropriate to their age. Such a sense of decorum, tied to landscape, enables mediation of difference: Guiderius may disagree with Belarius's belief that there is 'no life [compared] to ours' (line 26), and Arviragus may think it 'bondage' (line 44), but they can also accept that this is based on their different experiences of the world.[49] The 'goodly day' (line 1) can accommodate a rich range of experience and perspective like a Bruegel landscape.

When Imogen comes into this environment, she is first of all forced to encounter 'wildness' (III. iv. 9); she is referring to Pisanio's troubled expression, but the word also ties her to the transformative effects of the wilderness where she will meet her brothers. As she travels through the wilderness, Imogen has had to make 'the ground my bed' (III. vi. 3), but this grounding has not been redemptive as it was in *A Midsummer Night's Dream*; she is in some senses alienated from it, and indeed Belarius nearly believes that she is 'a fairy' (line 41 – the fact that she eats means that she

48 See Palfrey, *Late Shakespeare*, pp. 88–96, for a more negative reading of Posthumus's passivity.

49 Bradin Cormack, *A Power to Do Justice: Jurisdiction, English Literature, and the Rise of the Common Law, 1509–1625* (Chicago: The University of Chicago Press, 2007), pp. 238–9 argues that these experiences on a 'threshold line' test the efficacy of political sovereignty in a particularly acute way and more generally that 'in the late tragicomedies Shakespeare conceives of dramatic action both in terms of the distances between distinct jurisdictions and in terms of the threshold reality separating them. In so doing, he stages the legal equation by which imperial identities emerge as themselves a threshold reality'. Though I conceive of these thresholds more naturalistically than legally, Cormack's argument about the creative/ constitutive potential of such spaces has much in common with my own.

isn't one). In fact, her travelling and sleeping on the ground has made her ill, in such a way that she rejects the company of her brothers (IV. ii. 5–14), with whom she has (or ought to have) natural familial sympathy. They are notably more affectionate to her than she to them, perhaps because she has not found her true nature: when she says 'clay and clay differs in dignity, / Whose dust is both alike' (lines 4–5), she seems to press a notion of difference that is more appropriate to the court than the country. She will need to die and be reborn again to purge this element of her courtly, alienated self.[50]

The princes, it is clear, are much more associated with the natural world than Imogen is: Belarius repeatedly praises 'divine Nature' as represented in them (line 169; see also III. iii. 79). When they find Imogen/Fidele apparently dead, their funereal tributes to 'him' embed Imogen in nature, while denying her mortality:

> GUIDERIUS. Why, he but sleeps.
> If he be gone, he'll make his grave a bed.
> With female fairies will his tomb be haunted,
> And worms will not come to thee.
> (lines 215–8)

Arviragus offers her grave 'fairest flowers', such as harebells and eglatines, which will, he says, be brought by a 'ruddock', 'with charitable bill' (lines 219–28), but rather brilliantly Guiderius (even though he started it) pulls his brother back from the indulgence in such flowery sentimentality, telling him not to 'play in wench-like words with that / Which is so serious' (lines 230–1). Conjuring up images of a dutiful and naturally caring Nature, in which the robin redbreast tends to graves, is seen as a sentimental distraction from real grief. Nonetheless, the lines enable and embody a connection between the siblings that is involuntarily redemptive, binding them to the land and its products.

In accepting mortality, acknowledging that 'Golden lads and girls all must, / As chimney-sweepers, come to dust' (lines 262–3), the princes connect themselves to their people and their environment. The golden lads may be dandelions, golden at first, becoming like chimney brushes as they fade; yet that fading enables their fertility.[51] It is odd that this beautiful

[50] On her near- or apparent starvation, see Chapter 3.

[51] The idea that 'golden lads' refers to dandelions, and 'chimney-sweepers' to dandelion clocks in Warwickshire dialect is very enticing; it is often stated, e.g. Bill Bryson, *Shakespeare: The World as a Stage* (London: Harper Perennial, 2008), p. 192. It would be lovely if it were true; but it may be a canard. Another, more convincing, possibility is that 'chimney-sweepers' refers to ribwort, 'whose seeds come to dust and travel on the wind', as Jonathan Bate observes in *Shakespeare and the English Romantic Imagination*, 2nd edition (Oxford: Clarendon Press, 1989), p. 141.

dirge is sung (or spoken) over Cloten as well as over Imogen/Fidele: Belarius even says of both of them 'Upon th' earth's face / You were as flowers, now withered' (lines 285–6),[52] despite the fact that he knew and despised Cloten. But this may accord with the fact that the natural environment has enabled principles of undifferentiation to operate. That undifferentiation goes so far, in fact, that Imogen will mistake Cloten's body for that of Posthumus. If Imogen was once too courtly and too apt therefore to dwell on distinctions, the other extreme has now won out, which is just as undesirable: the levelling principle of death does away with all particularity.

The natural environment, then, does not bring us to clear and distinct recognitions of truth in this play. Indeed, there is more blurring when Imogen tells the Roman soldiers who find them that Cloten's body (which she thinks Posthumus) is that of 'Richard du Champ' (line 377), associating him with the fields before strewing his body 'With wild wood-leaves and weeds' (line 390); the irony that Cloten gets 'the prettiest daisied plot' the Romans can find (line 398) is one of Shakespeare's more peculiar redemptive movements. Where the sentimental poetry over the dead Fidele was a relief from seriousness, here the poetic language is undercut by the comic irony of its application to a headless clot.

Yet there is a semi-tragic irony in all this too, for Cloten is really dead. Though Imogen and Posthumus are almost insistently differentiated from him in the play's early scenes (e.g. I. i. 16–24), they too will die. The beauty of the play's conclusion relies as much on the recognition of mortality as it does on the absurdly drawn-out plot recognitions that make up most of the final scene. Posthumus's greeting to his wife is justly famous, poignantly bringing death into play: 'Hang there like fruit, my soul,/ Till the tree die' (V. v. 263–4). There is something unnatural and precarious in this, however. What has happened to Edgar's idea that ripeness is all? Won't a fruit rot if it stays on a tree? The fact is, there is something above nature in this play's resolution: the operation of the gods has been necessary to redeem Posthumus, whose actions have shown him not so superior to Cloten. Indeed, it's just about possible to double the roles,[53] which would give a deeper irony to Imogen's mistake about the body. If Imogen has been reborn through nature, it is because she hadn't really sinned. Posthumus is different; his misapprehensions of Imogen, and all women, require outside agents for a recovery. Yet he himself, it seems, does *not* see, or at least does not hear Jupiter, who speaks to Posthumus's family in his dream and whose words Posthumus does not register. When he wakes from his sleep

[52] There is a crux here: the Folio reads 'Upon their faces'; I adopt Butler's Cambridge ed. reading.

[53] See Simon Palfrey and Tiffany Stern, *Shakespeare in Parts* (Oxford: Oxford University Press, 2007), p. 53.

he wonders 'What fairies haunt this ground?' (V. ii. 197). The ground itself may be as important in this transformative moment as the gods that flit across it. His wise passivity comes out when he says, of the gnomic written prophecy, 'Be what it is, / The action of my life is like it, which / I'll keep, if but for sympathy' (lines 211–3). His own phrasing is as gnomic as the prophecy's (in sympathy with it), and his meaning is nicely double: he is pleased that there is sympathy in the world – *sunt lacrimae rerum* – and he is consequently able to engage sympathetically with himself and therefore with the world and with his own wife. Underneath this too, there may be a sense that he is accepting an intuition of divine grace, seeing a match between his outward state (the action of his life) and the mystery of inner salvation, for which he cannot claim responsibility: his own actions, ungraceful as they have been, cannot cause salvation (and couldn't, even if they were better, according to Protestant doctrine), but the sense that the overall action of his life *fits* with the prophecy and with a larger process of the growth of grace in the play. From this moment grows that imaginative if peculiar tree: a tree of knowledge from which the fruit will not be taken becomes a new covenant between them, and the image as a whole involves a refusal to insist on knowledge of absolutes.

If Imogen has not sinned, she nonetheless gets purged through the play's environmental processes: purged, that is, of her special status as a princess. Imogen's resigned but reasonably cheerful belief that she can escape from her fate is one of her most endearing features, but its upshot is rather complicated. Pisanio tells her that if she will not stay at court to be besieged by Cloten's love-suit 'Then not in Britain must you bide' (III. iv. 134). It's hard to see exactly why this should be: perhaps, like the banished Duke of *As You Like It* she necessarily trails around a court-atmosphere that she cannot escape (at least when she is in Britain); perhaps her position as a married-but-not-married princess makes her so anomalous that the country (as opposed to the bubble-world of the court) rejects her.[54] Her response is bracing:

> Hath Britain all the sun that shines? day? night?
> Are they not but in Britain? I' th' world's volume
> Our Britain seems as of it, but not in 't;
> In a great pool a swan's nest. Prithee think
> There's livers out of Britain. (lines 136–40)

[54] There may also be a parallel with Cordelia, whose return to England seems so anomalous that Lear asks her 'where did you die?' (IV. vii. 48, F and Q1 reading)

The sentiment is far from straightforwardly nationalistic: even if there's a certain pride in Britain's uniqueness, there's also a sense of its awkwardness. In fact, of course, she does not go out of the country, for only in her own country can she shuffle off her strangeness and become, in Cleopatra's terms, 'no more but e'en a woman'. Like Cleopatra, and like Elizabeth I in real life, she had wanted to be a milkmaid (a 'neatherd's daughter' would be such),[55] and the processes of the play have enabled that desire, returning her to a natural state in removing her peculiarity, but not her particularity. The play presents us with the dangerous blurring of human identity that the natural world can sometimes bring about (Posthumus/Cloten) but pulls back from its tragic consequences; it also more positively removes the transcendent, superhuman quality of royalty from Imogen.

The nation's peculiarity is harder to remove: Cymbeline goes some way to this by agreeing to give tribute to the Roman emperor, but Britain remains a swan's nest, a supplementary appendix to the volume of the world. Elsewhere, we see a similar tension in the idea of national specialness, even in the most notable articulation of the idea – John of Gaunt's great speech in *Richard II*. York there highlights an idea of secondariness and artificiality, in calling England 'our tardy, apish nation' too apt to copy Italian fashions with 'base imitation' (II. i. 22–3). Gaunt's set-piece speech almost consumes itself in doubleness: England *was* special but has now been abased: having been 'This royal throne of kings, this sceptred isle, / This earth of majesty, this seat of Mars, / This other Eden, demi-paradise (lines 40–2), it has been 'leased out' and 'bound in with shame' (lines 59, 63). It was a 'little world' (line 45), able to defend itself, but a breeder of martial men; it was as famous as the tomb of Christ, a 'dear dear land' (line 51) but has now 'made a shameful conquest of itself' (line 66).

To say the least, this is overdetermined: England is a place of peace and war, a land and a people, isolated but able to domineer over the world far from home; it is defended but also bound in by the sea; it is like Christ's tomb, which implies that it is redemptive, but it is also fallen; it is *dear* – many times – in that it is beloved, but also expensive (and therefore can be rented out); it is valuable for mothering and nursing kings, and yet its current king has sold it. Gaunt's encomium-cum-lament therefore traces not only the ironies of nostalgic nationalism, but some of the key tensions in attitudes to the natural environment. Like Imogen's 'swan's nest', the country is both an aspect of the natural world and a

[55] For Elizabeth's expression of a wish to be a mere milkmaid, see Elizabeth I, *Collected Works*, p. 170; Cleopatra probably echoes her in saying that she is 'No more but e'en a woman, and commanded / By such poor passion as the maid that milks' (*Antony and Cleopatra*, I. xv. 73–4).

rather separate pendant to it. Speaking his dying words, Gaunt separates himself from such a contradictory formation of the environment he is *of* but not *in*.

But perhaps the King of such a nation can contain its contradictions, having an essential, special relation to his country. When Richard himself returns from Ireland, he declares

> I weep for joy
> To stand upon my kingdom once again.
> Dear earth, I do salute thee with my hand,
> Though rebels wound thee with their horses' hoofs.
> As a long-parted mother with her child
> Plays fondly with her tears and smiles in meeting,
> So weeping, smiling, greet I thee, my earth,
> And do thee favours with my royal hands.
> (III. ii. 4–11)

Richard demands that his land not feed the rebels, and that it bring forth spiders, toads and adders to resist them (lines 12–20). This extraordinary speech takes us a long distance, seeming almost to invoke the rebellion it seeks to forestall.[56] Richard moves from maternal imagery – which in any case seems inverted as he rather than the land is the mother – to its radical opposite, the poisonous antagonism of spiders, toads and snakes, which are nonetheless as natural as a maternal relation. Yet, typically, he qualifies his invocation, calling it a 'senseless conjuration', which he fears that his lords will 'mock' (line 23).[57]

His conjuration becomes that of a witch, and its senselessness is as double as the adder's tongue: it is *instinctive*, but it is also foolish; his senselessness is needed to evoke sensitive feeling in his land. The earth has feeling only when it is violated: in a peculiarly backwards way, by insisting that the earth has feeling, Richard seems to guarantee the success of the rebellion that will create that feeling.[58] As in Wordsworth's 'Nutting', it is only through violation that earth is able to become sentient. Human action is needed to make the natural world meaningfully respond.

[56] See Maus, *Being and Having in Shakespeare*, p. 27.

[57] Perhaps the point is that they are *mocking* it, in the sense that they are imitating it, by kneeling like the King himself; turning against them, he insists on his own unique right to a relation with the land, but in doing so, he abjures a *common* relationship with the land and thereby alienates his supporters.

[58] Egan, *Green Shakespeare*, p. 83, argues that 'In *Richard 2*, belief in Tillyardian correspondence between the human and cosmic planes is right even though wrong: believing makes it so'.

Localism and hospitality

If the grandeur of a King's ownership is shown to be ineffective or self-thwarting, though, the idea of more local attachments has more resonant force, and this is frequently conveyed through hospitality in the countryside. *Richard II* illustrates and even half-articulates the imaginative problem of national ownership, whose full emotional force only seems to emerge at moments of separation (death, rebellion). A different but possibly more redemptive kind of nostalgic alienation within the natural environment can be found in Shakespeare's strangest and least necessary rural idyll, the Gloucestershire scenes of *Henry IV Part 2*. To some, these have seemed the deepest countryside scenes, on a par with the Dingley Dell sequences of *The Pickwick Papers*: Hazlitt, for instance, argues that 'The meanest circumstances are shewn through an atmosphere of abstraction that dignifies them: their very insignificance makes them more affecting';[59] yet the characters' minds here are all pointed elsewhere. Shallow's servant Davy's mind is on the litigation of his friend William Visor (against Clement Perks of the Hill), as well as on the sack William Cook lost at Hinckley Fair (V. i. 20–33); these trivial matters give an expansive sense of rural life which is accentuated by the general preoccupation with food. The other characters, most notably Shallow himself (significantly, a Justice of the Peace, the Crown's local representative), are nostalgic for their youth in London: in a strange sense, we only feel the significance of rural life through thoughts of the city; yet the 'chimes at midnight' perhaps resonate more deeply in Gloucestershire than they ever did in the London days Shallow and company recall. Danby argues that at this point in the play, the world has broken down into 'mutually exclusive spheres',[60] and in a sense this is true, but there is also a sense of these spheres speaking quietly to one another; the local and the national are connected, legally and emotionally. The scenes' only real effect is decisively to demonstrate Falstaff's cynical shallowness to us, but they have no larger effect on the characters of the play. Shallow hopes that 'our old acquaintance be renewed' (III. ii. 294), but such renewal is not really the function of the rural world. What we encounter instead is something more radically self-sufficient; as Silence says, 'now comes in the sweet o' th' night' (V. iii. 49–50). It has no relation to history, or even to the men's lives. If anything, it involves an acceptance

[59] In *The Romantics on* Shakespeare, ed. Jonathan Bate (London: Penguin, 1992), p. 193. See also Orson Welles's film, *The Chimes of Midnight* (1966).

[60] *Shakespeare's Doctrine of Nature*, p. 83.

of mortality. Night is this play's time of handovers, after all, from father to son, from youth to age.

The lords who witness Richard II's greeting to his country may seem to mock the King's possessive conjuration, but Falstaff's cynicism cannot invalidate this version of pastoral. The scenes embody a sense of localism set in quiet opposition to the nationalism (even internationalism) of the history plays' main sequences – the kind of localism, indeed, to which some environmentalists now argue we need desperately to return.[61] The delicate invocation of Silence's home deep in the country could not be more different from the grand but strangely artificial declaration of space that we find in *Henry V*, where the Chorus's forced and meta-theatrical creation of a France to invade is troublingly uncertain and alien. This France is finally embodied in Princess 'Kate', whose awkward wooing by Henry reflects the fruitless trouble of taking someone else's country for one's own temporary glory. Despite the comic misunderstandings of the Gloucestershire scenes, that world is undoubtedly more real than the phantom glory of the invasion of France.

Yet Gloucestershire of course is a fantasy, though of a peculiar kind: it is an all-male geriatric ward, its homosocial fellowship dependent on the absence of women. Shakespeare's most powerful rural idylls of liberal hospitality, by contrast, are centred on ideal femininity. Bohemia in *The Winter's Tale* is a very strange place: it is a landlocked country with a coast, a highly sociable desert, a place of seasonal confusion and confusion between indoors and outdoors – to say nothing of its hungry bears. This fluid locale, in which identities are more easily swapped than elsewhere, is presided over by Perdita, queen of the feast, a figure of great integrity even as her identity remains in abeyance.

Unlike the Gloucester scenes, the pastoral scenes in Bohemia clearly play a crucial role in their play, filling up a gap in nature. Whereas Silence speaks of 'the sweet of the night', Autolycus brings us into the countryside by singing of 'the sweet o' the year' (IV. iii. 3). Yet this refers to spring, and the season here, quite clearly, is summer, the time of sheep shearing. Perdita laments that she has no 'flowers o' th' spring' for Florizel's 'time of day' (IV. iv. 113–4); the invocations of spring at high summer (both Autolycus and Perdita mention daffodils) constitute a delicate approach to the issue of time's trans-shifting.[62] Yet they also play a key role in the play's sense of

61 E.g. Bill McKibben, *Eaarth: Making a Life on a Tough New Planet* (New York: St Martin's Press, 2010).

62 Palfrey, *Shakespeare's Possible Worlds*, p. 247, has a different, but complementary take on this: 'As Perdita always intuits, any feeling of ease is a dangerous dream: too weightless, somehow factitious,

life's completeness: it is precisely the high summer of life that Leontes has lost for himself and Hermione.

That season, though, is a troublesome one. Perdita associates it with the 'streaked gillyvors, / Which some call Nature's bastards' (lines 82–3), flowers that she refuses to keep in her garden, despite Polixenes' eloquent insistence that the art that makes them 'is an art / That Nature makes' (lines 91–2).[63] She perhaps has an intuitive sense of the damage done by accusations of bastardy, making her primly defiant of anything that whiffs of sexual impropriety (including Autolycus's songs – line 219). The high summer of life has seen great pain inflicted in the play's earlier scenes, but the pastoral goes some way to healing this.

Hermione has been calumniated precisely for being too good a hostess in her ability to make Polixenes stay in Sicily.[64] Perdita comes under similar peril partly as a result of her hostess-ship at the summer festival. Her Shepherd foster-father gives her counsel on hospitality:

> Fie, daughter, when my old wife lived, upon
> This day she was both pantler, butler, cook,
> Both dame and servant; welcomed all, served all;
> Would sing her song, and dance her turn; now here,
> At upper end o' th' table, now i' th' middle;
> On his shoulder, and his; her face o' fire
> With labour, and the thing she took to quench it
> She would to each one sip. (lines 55–62)

The social promiscuity and heated passion of the country housewife mingles with energetic multi-tasking role-changes, but in that social atmosphere there seems to be no risk involved – *honi soit qui mal y pense*, one might suggest, is more appropriate as a watchword of pastoral than courtly manners. Perdita cannot quite live up to this role model, but it does underpin the simple dignity of her household management.

And it is worth stating that this is a household, not an outdoor festival: we are told several times that there are people at the *door*. Yet this, the second-longest scene in Shakespeare, is an outdoorsy indoor scene, just as the longest scene – the final scene of *Love's Labour's Lost* – is an indoorsy outdoor scene. The rural world, as place of translations, is always a liminal

liable to be sucked down a hole any second. The pastoral scene's long spring-and-summer extension, for instance, is the merest suspended moment'.

63 For the orthodoxy of both Polixenes' and Perdita's positions here, see Tayler, *Nature and Art*, pp. 135–7.

64 See Wilbur Sanders, *The Winter's Tale* (Boston: Twayne, 1987), p. 8.

place, a place of overlap.[65] The disguised Polixenes and Camillo have intruded on the Shepherd's home. They find better hosts than they are guests: unlike in Classical/ Biblical stories of gods or angels testing out human hospitality, it is the guests who are tested and found wanting. Whereas a monarch might normatively make any house s/he visited his/her Court, translating it into his own sphere, Polixenes' disguise here prevents that from being the case: Perdita remains Queen of the Feast. The result is that, despite the King's stinging rebukes to her and her family, Perdita can say

> I was not much afeard; for once or twice
> I was about to speak, and tell him plainly
> The self-same sun that shines upon his court
> Hides not his visage from our cottage, but
> Looks on alike. (lines 442–6)

This is a boldly levelling sentiment, given further life by the pun on 'son' which quietly asserts that Florizel is as at least as keen on her cottage as he is on his father's court. Of course the political implications of the sentiment are defanged by the fact of her status being as good as that of Polixenes; yet, however tiresomely elastic the secret princess trope of romance narrative is, Shakespeare gets something out of it here. The sun is a model of regality and the integrity that ought to go with it (selfsameness); it does not hide its face, and we might think that any king who does so devalues the coin of kingship.

Compared to this false representation, Perdita herself has a natural authority, enabling her to say to the Prince, in her last gesture of assumed authority, 'Will't please you, sir, be gone?' (line 446). She then says 'I'll queen it no inch farther' (line 454); turning the word *queen* into a verb is extraordinarily powerful here: doing replaces being when being has become a matter of misrepresentation. Perdita, whom Florizel wishes were 'A wave o' th' sea' (line 141), is a doer, an embodied action:[66] as he says to her 'What you do / Still betters what is done' (lines 135–6); 'all your acts are queens' (line 146). In the light of this, the question of her mere royal identity doesn't much matter (and perhaps that's a reason why the play skips over the proof of her identity). The *inch* she refers to reminds us,

65 Hence I'm inclined to disagree with Estok's point – valuable though it is in itself – that the pastoral scenes of the play are bracketed away from its consequential plot. – *Ecocriticism and Shakespeare*, p. 96.

66 See Hazlitt's use of this line in his discussion of Hamlet's 'yielding flexibility' of character – in *Hamlet: Bloom's Shakespeare through the Ages*, ed. Harold Bloom (New York: Infobase Publishing, 2008), p. 155.

too, of the firmest claim of regality in Shakespeare – Lear's 'every inch a king' (*King Lear*, IV. vi. 107) – but here the spatial language is in service of a denial that paradoxically affirms and fixes. Such arrested motion and embodied action may remind us of the greatest Renaissance depictions of Nature: Botticelli's Primavera for instance. The paradoxicality and double doubleness of Nature is here firmly captured and given human life, just as the statue is brought to life at the play's end (on this, see Chapter 3).

Florizel, despite the evident power of his love, has a problematic relationship to this image of nature. He wants Perdita to 'Apprehend / Nothing but jollity' (lines 24–5), but rather troublingly compares himself to an Ovidian god descending for the purposes of seduction or rape (lines 27–31). His glorious invocation of her mode of action notwithstanding, his declaration of faith suggests a degree of alienation from nature even stronger than that of the Olympian gods: he asserts

> It cannot fail, but by
> The violation of my faith, and then
> Let nature crush the sides o' th' earth together,
> And mar the seeds within! Lift up thy looks.
> From my succession wipe me, father, I
> Am heir to my affection. (lines 476–81)

The word 'affection' has been a curse in this play: Leontes is infected by 'Affection' at the moment his jealousy strikes (I. ii. 138). Florizel is subject to a father's curse, perhaps the worst thing that could happen in the thinking of the time.[67] There is a rebellion against nature here, and his apocalyptic oaths anticipate Marvell's 'The Definition of Love', in which love is an impossibility that might destroy the whole world. As John Pitcher points out, the lines are 'uncomfortably close' to apocalyptic sentiments in *King Lear* and *Macbeth*.[68]

What, then, is the redemptive force in *The Winter's Tale*, and is it sufficient to correct for the play's destructive impulses? At its simplest, it is women redeeming men. In part, as we will see in Chapter 3, Paulina's (and others') medicinal *art* is needed. But there are other complex forces at work. One of the play's keywords is 'grace', and it is certainly possible for a Christian reading of the play to insist that the order of grace redeems the order of nature. Things, however, are not that orthodox, for grace is not here as separate from nature as orthodoxy would insist. Whether

67 See Tom MacFaul, *Problem Fathers in Shakespeare and Renaissance Drama* (Cambridge: Cambridge University Press, 2012), pp. 6, 154.

68 Arden 3 edition, note to these lines.

or not there's a Catholic sentiment at work, or whether Shakespeare is attempting a pretty piece of paganism, this play does seem frequently to suggest that children are not born into Original Sin. Most powerfully, of course, Polixenes claims that he and Leontes were in childhood

> as twinned lambs that did frisk i' th' sun
> And bleat the one at th' other: what we changed
> Was innocence for innocence; we knew not
> The doctrine of ill-doing, nor dreamed
> That any did. (I. ii. 67–71)

The doctrine of Original Sin seems something that people have to be *taught* – and teaching the doctrine, the language seems to suggest, leads to its consequences in 'ill-doing'. Believing something makes it true. The use of pastoral imagery here suggests that innocence rather than sin is the basic common denominator of human experience. As we'll see in Chapter 2, the idea of animal innocence has some power at the time, partly as a way of escaping from the harshness of predestination; here, the imagery of lambs ties childhood to the idea of Christ's redemption as well as insisting on innocence. Polixenes says that if they had stayed in 'that life', 'we should have answered heaven / Boldly, "Not guilty;" the imposition cleared / Hereditary ours' (lines 71, 73–5). His awkward phrasing here seems to imply not only that they were innocent, but that their innocence was *redemptive*, clearing away hereditary sin. Despite the partly joking sense that women cause men to fall (or at least trip – line 76), Polixenes' lines associate the pastoral world of childhood with the order of grace, conflating the classical golden age with the garden of Eden, and thus enabling the Bohemian pastoral scenes to be redemptive.[69]

A further push to the idea of nature as unfallen comes when Paulina frees Perdita from gaol; she argues that

> This child was prisoner to the womb, and is
> By law and process of great Nature thence
> Freed and enfranchised, not a party to
> The anger of the King, nor guilty of
> (If any be) the trespass of the queen.
> (II. ii. 57–61)

This is on the face of it a claim from natural law, that the child is not guilty of the crimes of the parents, but the framing of the argument, with its enjambments and pauses, almost seems to go further, even hinting at

[69] See the fine and challenging reading of the play in Egan, *Green Shakespeare*, pp. 124–31.

freeing the child from the sins of the parents (right back to Adam and Eve) and underpinning that freedom with the invocation of great Nature, the Magna Mater, whom Perdita later invokes as 'great creating Nature' (IV. iv. 88). This resonantly assonant phrase is beautifully self-involuting: Nature is great because it creates, it makes great things, it even creates itself; for Paulina, it is a little more orderly, having laws and processes to back itself up.[70] As such it makes the petty tyrannies of Leontes (and even those of Polixenes) rather otiose.

If grace – or at least providence – is connected to Apollo too (III. i. 22), his distant perspective is less effective, his oracle only causing death and destruction. Apollo, whose Homeric epithet was 'he who strikes from afar', is something of a flyover deity, detached from the natural world, and rather wantonly killing Mamillius as punishment for Leontes not believing in his oracle. Transcendent knowledge, however unfallen, is insufficient to bring about happy endings, it seems. Rural space, rather, does the work of grace. Leontes commands Antigonus to 'bear' the infant Perdita

> To some remote and desert place quite out
> Of our dominions, and that there thou leave it
> (Without more mercy) to it own protection,
> And favour of the climate. As by strange fortune
> It came to us, I do in justice charge thee,
> On thy soul's peril, and thy body's torture,
> That thou commend it strangely to some place
> Where chance may nurse or end it.
>
> (II. iii. 176–83)

The order to 'bear' the child may oddly call forth the bear that kills Antigonus. Like Lear banishing Cordelia, this king has a sense that anything that happens outside his own realm cannot be his responsibility or even quite real to him; the child is *strange* in the sense that Leontes thinks her the Bohemian Polixenes' offspring, and that strange desert place and climate will be its guardian. As with Autolycus, whose attempted misdemeanours come to good, Leontes' attempted curse becomes a blessing. Climatic forces do indeed operate thus: a storm may kill the sailors who take Antigonus to Bohemia, but for the Shepherd and Clown who pick up Perdita, ''Tis a lucky day . . . and we'll do good deeds on 't' (III. iii. 138–9). The contraction here has a certain subtle power that is part of this play's atmosphere: in many cases we have seen phrases like 'i' th'' and 'o' th' permeate *The Winter's*

[70] Roberts, *The Shakespearean Wild*, p. 165 associates Paulina with the Magna Mater. See also Helen Cooper's discussion, in *Pastoral*, p. 175.

Tale's language,[71] and I think they quietly capture the way in which people are softly but firmly embedded in their environment in this play. More declaratively, Antigonus lays Perdita '*upon* the earth / Of its right father' (lines 45–6, emphasis added); he is wrong to do so, and is killed by a bear for it: despite his dream of Hermione, he has accepted Leontes' crazed notion of Perdita's paternity.[72] Believing this place to belong to Polixenes, he gives the child up, but such royal possession is not in fact as strong a force as he believes. Perdita, through the agency of the shepherds, will integrate herself into this environment, not just laying upon it because of her supposed paternity. Her attitude, insisting on the common grace of the sun, like that of the shepherds choosing to do good deeds, changes the world by taking the right perspective on it rather than by trying to master it.

An integrated but non-possessive attitude to the rural world is embodied in Autolycus's song, the immediate preface to the sheep-shearing scene:

> Jog on, jog on, the foot-path way,
> And merrily hent the stile-a;
> A merry heart goes all the day,
> Your sad tires in a mile-a.
> (IV. iii. 123–6)

Autolycus, whose name means 'lone wolf',[73] is able to take a disinterested but not transcendent perspective. His song is not quite his own speech, being part of a tradition, but accepting its precepts enables him to engage with the world. A mercurial figure, who almost against his own will catalyses the play's happy ending, he represents the flexibly reactive approach to the natural world that most often brings about happiness in Shakespeare's works. Walking through the countryside merrily affirms one's place in the world, making light of obstacles such as stiles – but also making light of transformative obstacles such as literary/ regal *style*.

This brings us back to *As You Like It*, a play whose easy hospitality makes obstacles lighter than any other Shakespeare play; the play's whole attitude is like that embodied in Autolycus. The perfunctory plot is so easily resolved because of the play's rural atmosphere, in which people easily transform their world. Touchstone's notion that 'Your "If" is the

71 See the fine discussion of such contractions in Russ McDonald, *Shakespeare's Late Style* (Cambridge: Cambridge University Press, 2006), pp. 86–7.

72 See Shell, *Shakespeare and Religion*, pp. 206–15 for a long and valuable discussion of the nature of divine punishment on Antigonus.

73 See Pitcher's Arden 3 note to the List of Roles.

only peacemaker; much virtue in "If"' (V. iv. 102–3) is the play's key sentiment:[74] conditionality and provisionality abound in Arden, enabling smooth mediation of human difficulties, but without the total suspension of motive that characterizes earlier rural plays such as *The Two Gentlemen of Verona* and *A Midsummer Night's Dream*. Though it may initially seem that the Duke's regal style is the agent of translations, a richer and stranger effect of the environment itself is crucial.

We are told at the play's beginning that the banished Duke 'is already in the forest of Arden, and a many merry men with him, and there they live like the old Robin Hood of England' (I. i. 114–6); the merry world here created doesn't seem like the result of any active agency or movement – the Duke simply already *is* there, without apparent movement, like Keats being already with the Nightingale. Young gentlemen 'flock' to him with a simple pastoral ease, and they 'fleet the time carelessly, as they did in the golden world' (lines 117–8). Life becomes an easy stream of being, without plotting or cares; they never seem to be attempting to get the dukedom back and they're only like Robin Hood's men in lifestyle – there's no suggestion that they are bandits. Orlando insists that he will not be an outlaw (II. iii. 31–5), and though he does become one for a moment in demanding food (II. vii. 87ff.), he only does so in order to provide for Adam's necessities – and even this turns out not to be necessary, thanks to the Duke's hospitality (see Chapter 3, below). Even the usurping Duke Frederick describes his brother as having 'ranged' (I. iii. 68), with scant recognition of causality and with a suggestion of animal, purposeless wandering such as the word has in Wyatt's 'They flee from me', though without Wyatt's sense of 'busily seeking with continual change'.[75] Despite others' hopes that there will one day be 'a better world' (I. ii. 284), presumably on the Duke's restoration, there is a passive sense that the world will not go the faster for our driving.[76] In joining her father in exile, Rosalind is convinced that she goes 'To liberty and not to banishment' (I. iii. 138). The play is Shakespeare's most radical exploration of human freedom.

As the play's title probably implies, that freedom is partly Epicurean, involving a liberation from unnecessary fears:[77] there is no concern with time and causality. When Orlando insists that 'There's no clock in the

[74] For a useful commentary on this, see McCoy, *Faith in Shakespeare*, pp. 78–9.

[75] References to Sir Thomas Wyatt, *The Complete Poems*, ed. Ronald A. Rebholz (Harmondsworth: Penguin, 1978).

[76] The phrase is Marvell's.

[77] On Shakespeare's Epicureanism, see Jonathan Bate, '"Hide thy life": The Key to Shakespeare', *Times Higher Education Supplement*, 6 August 2009.

forest' (III. ii. 300–1) he sounds a keynote of refusal to be tied to time's dominion (though he does admit still that there is 'time o' day,' at least for lovers' meetings).[78] Yet this invocation of a golden world is highly artificial. In addition to the invocations of Robin Hood, there are further highly conscious and conspicuous invocations of the Classical Golden Age and of ancient pastoral literature, suggesting that the play's characters have *willed* themselves into a set of literary tropes and styles. Yet their willing seems strangely passive and easy-going, a matter of acceptance rather than the affectation we saw in *Love's Labour's Lost.*

The cottage that Rosalind and Celia buy is a strange mixture of the real and the conspicuously literary. They buy it from the absentee landlord Carlot,[79] who has neglected Corin, his tenant, and whose failings in hospitality contrast so strongly with the welcome given at the court in exile. In doing so, they gazump the prospective purchaser Silvius, and we might feel some unease at the idea of the townies buying up country property thus on a whim. Yet Corin is clear that Silvius 'little cares for buying anything', owing to his love for Phoebe (II. iv. 90). Silvius, in fact, is rather an ersatz 'swain', more a literary figure than any other in the play. Celia expresses the girls' more genuine appreciation of the rural world with lovely simplicity: 'I like this place / And willingly could waste my time in it' (lines 94–5). The word 'waste' here is curiously loaded as it is in Wordsworth's 'Nutting' (see above): it is clear that this forest is *not* a waste, not what would be called a desert or wilderness, yet time spent here is strangely unfruitful.[80] Her simple liking of the place is a refreshing change from her father's excessive claims of pastoral translation, and her translations are correspondingly breezier. When Rosalind describes her house to Silvius, she breezily says ''Tis at the tuft of olives here hard by' (III. v. 75); olive trees are of course an unlikely feature of a northern European forest, and Rosalind's phrasing nicely captures the awkward fusion of flora, the earthily Anglo-Saxon word 'tuft' tugging against the obviously classical olive trees rather as her own good sense undermines the swooningly literary lover/shepherd Silvius affects to be. The rural world needs to be treated with a little scepticism in order that it have its beneficial effects.

[78] See the discussion of the play's emphasis on time in Fowler, *Renaissance Realism*, pp. 42–3; Jaques does say that Touchstone has a 'dial' in his pocket (II. vii. 20), but it would hardly be much use there.

[79] For a discussion of possible contemporary allusions in the name see Juliet Dusinberre's note to III. v. 109 in the Arden 3 edition.

[80] On the problem of 'waste' land, see Scott, *Shakespeare's Nature*, p. 66.

A degree of contestation over the meaning of the rural world is what gives *As You Like It* its energy, though that does not require that one perspective trumps another. Jaques, hardly the play's most admirable character, is at least right to condemn Orlando for vandalizing trees by sticking his wretched poems to them, politely saying 'I pray you mar no more trees with writing love-songs in their barks' (III. ii. 259–60), and Rosalind later supports the argument (line 360). Touchstone's sense that 'the tree yields bad fruit' (line 116) reminds us that what Orlando calls his own '*civil sayings*' (line 128) are out of place here; as Corin says, 'Those that are good manners at the court are as ridiculous in the country as the behaviour of the country is most mockable at the court' (lines 45–8); yet without the poems' presence we would barely notice the trees in the forest. In the end, decisions over such issues don't matter much: Touchstone is surely right when he says 'let the forest judge' (line 122). As with his suspending judgement in the idea of *If* as the only arbiter, Touchstone insists on a wisely passive stance as the way to a simplifying resolution.

Simplicity, though it is a literary convention of pastoral as much as the language of pastoral lovers, is a convention of a different kind, one that tries to develop the basic properties of human life, and few literary characters articulate it as well as Corin: 'I am a true labourer: I earn that I eat, get that I wear, owe no man hate, envy no man's happiness, glad of other men's good, content with my harm, and the greatest of my pride is to see my ewes graze and my lambs suck' (lines 73–7). We may dispute Touchstone's response that this is a 'simple sin' (line 78), but it is important that he says it, and that there is argument over the notion of simplicity (Touchstone thinks it simple-mindedness) – and, for that matter, over what constitutes a sin. No idea, however sane, is allowed final authority here. The forest may be there to judge, but it keeps its judgements to itself. Where Perdita has authority in her simple desire to 'milk my ewes, and weep' (*The Winter's Tale*, IV. iv. 450), there is an epicurean refusal of excess emotion in *As You Like It*, and that is effected by its cheerfully agonistic dialogic style, which is associated with the freedoms of a hospitable world.

That even applies to the play's songs, which are framed in ways that give ironic distance to their simple or even simplistic rural sentiments. Amiens's 'Under the greenwood tree' is undermined by the fact that Jaques demands its continuance in order to further his melancholy ('I can suck melancholy out of a song as a weasel sucks eggs' – II. v. 12–13). In this song the only enemy is 'winter and rough weather' (line 8), and it seems to be a celebration of a rural idyll in which there is no serious competition or ambition, but the final verse, written by Jaques, suggests that the idyll is an asinine loss of 'wealth and ease' motivated by 'stubborn will' (lines 52–3). This seems a fairly simple conflict over the value of the escape to the woods, but we must also recognize that it was Amiens (as we saw at the beginning of this chapter) who initially hinted at scepticism, and it is Jaques at the play's end who stubbornly stays in the forest. 'It was a lover and his lass', sung by the Pages, is undermined by Touchstone, who says that 'there was no great matter in the ditty' and that 'I count it but time lost to hear such a foolish song' (V. iii. 34–5, 39–40), but we may wonder if 'time lost', like the time Celia wants to waste, is ever really lost in such matters. The song itself insists that we 'take the present time' (line 30), and that 'life was but a flower' (line 28); perhaps the nobleness of life is merely to 'pass' 'o'er the green corn-field' (line 18), measuring life in rural space and not in clocktime.

Certainly the play's political plot is easily resolved: Duke Frederick is converted by a hermit the moment he comes to 'the skirts of this wild wood' (V. iv. 159); those *skirts* are important: all wildness is relative, marginal, liminal, edgy, neither one thing nor another. Duke Senior takes the conversion (translation) very much in his stride, only commenting that it's done Orlando and Oliver good, as it dowers their marriages with Oliver's confiscated lands and with the Dukedom for Orlando (lines 168–9). Once he's commented on this he loses interest, though, insisting that they all 'forget this new-fall'n dignity / And fall into our rustic revelry (lines 174–5). The repetition of *fall* here has a delicate and complex irony: it hints that the return to courtly dignity will be a fall; yet it also implies that to stay for the moment in rusticity is a fall in status; if it is a fall, it might be a fall for the better, then, a *felix culpa*; finally, as the play has been so preoccupied with spring (and the Pages' song has highlighted this), there may be a hint of a turn to autumnal matters.

The competing roles of nature and providence/grace in bringing about this resolution are much less insistent in *As You Like It* than in *The Winter's Tale* or *Cymbeline*. Yet the play does start off with a discussion of nature as compelling in its way as that between Perdita and Polixenes. Here, Nature is set against 'the good huswife Fortune', whom Celia wants to mock (I. ii. 31–2); Rosalind acidly comments that 'the bountiful blind woman doth most mistake in her gifts to women' (lines 35–6), but insists that Nature is as responsible for the problems of the world (and women) as much as Fortune is, for Fortune 'reigns in gifts of the world, not in the lineaments of Nature' (lines 41–2). Fortune, it seems, can destroy the things Nature makes:

> When Nature hath made a fair creature, may she not by Fortune fall into the fire? Though Nature hath given us wit to flout at Fortune, hath not Fortune sent in this fool [Touchstone, who has just entered] to cut off the argument?
>
> ROSALIND. Indeed there is Fortune too hard for Nature, when Fortune makes Nature's natural the cutter-off of Nature's wit. (lines 43–50)

This banter between the cousins is absolutely typical of Shakespeare's use of the idea of Nature: the wit the girls claim is demonstrated in the very moment of its assertion, and that wit is *natural* and dynamic, spontaneously responsive to a dramatic entrance; the idea that wit is a property of Nature rather than of unfallen reason is a little unconventional; the unorthodoxy is also a little self-undermining, for if wit is *natural*, it is surprising that the word is more typically used of a fool. It is acceptable to be one of the 'fools of nature' that Hamlet evokes: to be so may be in fact to be a 'pure wit' like Costard in *Love's Labour's Lost*. Nature's doubleness is cheerfully accepted, as it enables one to bear the stubbornness of fortune – perhaps better than the mere style of the Duke. Rosalind's sanguine flexibility makes her an even more powerful – and rather subtler – embodiment of the natural world than Perdita. Roberts argues that the wild world is 'de-Natured' in the play,[81] but I think that the play makes clear that there was never a simple wild or a simple nature.

Place is fundamentally human, and cannot really be apprehended in any meaningful way by a transcendent deity: as Robert Pogue Harrison argues, 'gods are not the original founders of place – mortals are. An immortal god may bless a place that has already been founded, but such a god cannot introduce the mark of finite time necessary to ground it'.[82] This chapter has shown that while the rural world is a place of translations, it is never simply so, because people bring the weight of their own histories and identities to it. The translation is never an entirely neutral matter: it is dangerous, in that it may in the worst cases remove all human particularity; yet it can be a blessing, as it can remove the vanity of human specialness – the claims to transcendence that are associated particularly with regality – and can make them 'earthlier happy' as a result. Taking the right stance on

[81] *The Shakespearean Wild*, p. 48.
[82] Robert Pogue Harrison, *The Dominion of the Dead* (Chicago: The University of Chicago Press, 2003), p. 23.

the ground, participating humbly in natural process, leads to happiness, and that may be a foreshadowing of grace. In the next chapter, we will see other kinds of transformation at work, when people attempt to simplify their characters and motives through thinking about their relations with non-human animals.

CHAPTER 2

Man and other animals

In the post-Cartesian world, the distinction between humans and animals became crucial and absolute, but many more recent thinkers have suggested that our continuity with animals is in some way defining of our humanity. Alasdair MacIntyre has argued that our relationship to animals is a crucial way of accepting our human dependence on others and therefore of the limits of our rational autonomy: 'Human identity is primarily, even if not only, bodily and therefore animal identity and it is by reference to that identity that the continuities of our relationships to others are partly defined'.[1] As we saw in the Introduction, Shakespeare's contemporaries saw considerable continuities between our animal and our human identities, and Shakespeare, this chapter will show, persistently uses animal imagery to define human relationships. Jacques Derrida and, in a rather different way, Donna Haraway have argued that our self-recognitions depend on seeing ourselves through the eyes of animals.[2] In Shakespeare's time too, the use of animals to help ponder one's own nature was a powerful heuristic tool.[3] Kate Soper has argued, following Bakhtin, that 'Where medieval scholasticism had repelled the body in order to sustain the "humanity" of man, in other words, his propinquity to God relative to the beasts, Rabelais and other thinkers of the Renaissance (notably Pico della Mirandola, Giambattisto Porta, Giordano Bruno, Tommaso Campanella and Marsile Ficino) employed it as a principle of a new Promethean humanism';[4] that is, they insisted on man's *willed* differentiation from other animals: it was not a

[1] Alasdair MacIntyre, *Dependent Rational Animals: Why Human Beings Need the Virtues* (London: Duckworth, 1999), p. 8.

[2] Jacques Derrida, *The Animal that I Therefore Am*, ed. Marie-Louise Mallet, trans. David Wills (New York: Fordham University Press, 2008), Donna Haraway, *When Species Meet* (Minneapolis: University of Minnesota Press, 2007); see also Pat Shipman, *The Animal Connection: A New Perspective on What Makes Us Human* (London: Norton, 2011).

[3] See Erica Fudge, *Brutal Reasoning: Animals, Rationality, and Humanity in Early Modern England* (Ithaca: Cornell University Press, 2006).

[4] *What Is Nature?*, p. 96.

given, but something one had to strive towards. At the same time, animals could teach one something about oneself, some deeper truth. To take a particularly striking example, Ben Jonson had a pet fox, which he tried to tame 'as well for the abating of my disease as the delight I took in the speculation of his nature'.[5] The idea that a fox's presence could in some way act as a corrective therapy to a man's illness is striking – if rather archly expressed in context – but even more striking is the idea that one can engage in 'speculation' through an animal: the word's roots are tied to the idea of a looking-glass, suggesting that one can find some element of the self – however refracted – in non-human animals. There is an impulse of self-taming and mastery at work here, but also a fascinated delight in otherness and connection.

Individual animals may help focus our thinking about humanity, at least momentarily. The apparent simplicity and unity of their motives can also be used as a way to simplify human motive and to explain otherwise unaccountable changes in human relationships; Gail Kern Paster argues that 'identification across the species barrier was compelling for the early moderns because it seemed both to reinforce affective self-experience and to offer an escape from it into the imagined self-sameness of animal passion';[6] but what starts off as an apparent simplification of humanity often results in a complication of it, as the sheer proliferation and variousness of animality makes its presence felt.[7] The result is a blurring of human motive and relationship, a blurring that is typical of Shakespeare.[8]

In his Colloquy, *Amicitia*, Erasmus gives a bewildering range of examples of pairs of animals that have sympathy or antipathy to one another; each case seems unique, but no overall pattern firmly emerges. In this dialogue Ephorinus describes, for example, a monkey being tied to a tortoise, which made the monkey void its bowels and have fits 'so that we had to release him from his chain and revive him with a mixture of water and wine'. Ephorinus's friend John responds 'But there's no reason for a monkey to dread a tortoise'; to which Ephorinus sagely comments 'Perhaps some reason concealed from us but known to nature'.[9] The whole dialogue is

5 Cit. Donaldson, *Ben Jonson*, p. 407.

6 Gail Kern Paster, *Humoring the Body: Emotions and the Shakespearean Stage* (Chicago: University of Chicago Press, 2004), p. 50.

7 Philip Davis, *Shakespeare Thinking*, p. 12, argues that 'Sometimes thought in Shakespeare is so powerful in its language that the object of the thought, at a level prior to personality, becomes more present than the person thinking it.'

8 For Shakespeare's tendency to blur motives that are clearer in his sources, see Stephen Greenblatt, *Will in the World: How Shakespeare Became Shakespeare* (London: Jonathan Cape, 2004).

9 *The Colloquies of Erasmus*, trans. Craig R. Thompson (Chicago: University of Chicago Press, 1965), p. 1041.

full of such anecdotes of mysterious attractions and repulsions between animals. The sheer number of examples is perhaps set up as a resource for rhetorical *copia*, offering a variety of ways of analogizing human likes and dislikes, but when such examples are deployed, the animals themselves seem to come, momentarily, to life, offering a real challenge to the idea of human integrity and uniqueness. Shylock, asked to account for his hatred of Antonio in *The Merchant of Venice*, takes a very Erasmian line, saying that 'Some men there are love not a gaping pig; / Some that are mad if they behold a cat',[10] and claims that just a there is 'no firm reason' for disliking the pig or 'a harmless necessary cat', so he (Shylock) can offer 'no reason' 'More than a lodged hate and a certain loathing' for Antonio (IV. i. 47–60). The imagery of animal nature here takes us away from *reason*, even as it focuses us on the particularity of human passion. Antonio, who thinks himself special in a negative way, 'a tainted wether of the flock, / Meetest for death' (lines 114–5) cannot be saved from this animalistic hatred by the normal processes of the law of contract. He presents himself as an almost Christlike scapegoat for others' sins, but Portia is able to save him, removing his claims of exceptionality, by reminding us of some more basic laws: 'thou shalt not kill' trumps Shylock's bond. The particularity of contract is trumped by the generality of the Decalogue.

Two major impulses can be identified behind the use of animals and animal imagery in Shakespeare's plays: on the one hand the desire to simplify motive and pick out individuals; this goes together with characters' desires to be unique. On the other hand, there is the desire to connect with others, and this leads to a blurring of the sense of human motive and specialness. As with his use of other aspects of the natural world, Shakespeare deploys animals and animal imagery in order to acknowledge human specialness, while purging it of its pretensions to mastery and separateness. The first section of this chapter deals with the early history plays, which exhibit perhaps the most persistent preoccupation with bestial nature; animal imagery in these plays is used to pick people out, give them motifs of individuality, but those motifs come to have their own life, blurring motive and making men monstrous. The next section deals with monstrous visions of human nature, in which the idea of the human as the sum of animal creation is shown to be grotesque and debasing rather than triumphant; animals in those cases are used as ways of thinking about unmotivated but natural antipathies. The third section shows how

[10] As if to support Shylock's example, Bertram in *All's Well* says that before he discovered Parolles's baseness, he could 'endure anything . . . but a cat' (IV. iii. 237).

those antipathies paradoxically offer a source of human sympathy and connectedness, and perhaps even of redemption. The final short section considers the two most notable dogs on the Elizabethan and Jacobean stage, showing how dogs, as a kind of lowest-common-denominator animal, may both embody ideas of familial connectedness and reflect the demonic tendencies of individualism.

The animal world of the early histories

The *Henry VI* plays contain an extraordinarily rich stream of animal imagery, so that the world of late medieval England comes to seem more like a bestiary than a history of human doings. Animal language is used here partly in order to create a sense of vivid identity for the great personages of the past, but also partly as a vector for human connections of sympathy and antipathy. Henry VI, meeting his new Queen, longs for 'sympathy of love' (*2 Henry VI*, I. i. 23); yet what emerges is a fundamental and powerful enmity: when Henry pities his uncle Gloucester's doom, she responds:

> Be woe for me, more wretched than he is.
> What, dost thou turn away and hide thy face?
> I am no loathsome leper, look on me.
> What? art thou like the adder waxen deaf?
> Be poisonous too, and kill thy forlorn queen.
> Is all thy comfort shut in Gloucester's tomb?
> Why then Dame Margaret was ne'er thy joy.
> Erect his statue and worship it,
> And make my image but an alehouse sign.
> Was I for this nigh wracked upon the sea,
> And twice by awkward wind from England's bank
> Drove back again unto my native clime?
> What boded this, but well forewarning wind
> Did seem to say, 'Seek not a scorpion's nest,
> Nor set no footing on this unkind shore'?
>
> (III. ii. 73–87)

This passage is revealing in a number of ways: the antipathy between Henry and Margaret is mapped onto an antipathy between England and her native France; the imagery of poisonous animals, hurled at Henry, rebounds onto the Queen herself and the nest she has invaded and infested. In opposition to this, Gloucester's fundamental *kindness* (in the full sense) was earlier signalled by the Queen's mocking reference to his 'nest' (II. i. 184), which she believed that his wife had tainted. The infection or *influenza* of animal imagery, once released, goes beyond its local rhetorical purposes and leads us to a deeper truth. One effect of this is that Margaret's offspring, however natural and legitimate, will not succeed to the English throne, as they are made alien, antipathetic and inimical to England.

Henry's pity for Gloucester's tragedy is perhaps the most extravagant expression of pity for another's fall in Shakespeare:

> Thou never didst them wrong, nor no man wrong;
> And as the butcher takes away the calf,
> And binds the wretch, and beats it when it strays,
> Bearing it to the bloody slaughter-house,
> Even so remorseless have they borne him hence;
> And as the dam runs lowing up and down,
> Looking the way her harmless young one went,
> And can do nought but wail her darling's loss,
> Even so myself bewails good Gloucester's case
> With sad unhelpful tears, and with dimm'd eyes
> Look after him, and cannot do him good,
> So might are his vowèd enemies. (III. i. 209–20)

This articulation of innocence and impotence is as self-pitying as it is sympathetic. In making himself into a cow (too full of the milk of human kindness?), Henry unmans himself, but also limits his emotional range, arriving at the useless simplicity of a farm animal; this arguably cuts off any possibility of true or practical feeling for the son he will disinherit in Part 3. Animalizing the Lancastrian royal line, then, destroys their regal pretensions. And all the other characters are also affected by the plays' animal world.

Gloucester's enemies try to simplify him, York sophistically calling him 'an empty eagle . . . set / To guard the chicken from a hungry kite' (lines 248–9). This simultaneously slanders the Protector and disempowers the King he was to protect. Warming to this theme, Suffolk presents him as a fox set to guard 'the flock' – an implicit plural which disindividuates Henry. This rhetoric is fairly transparent and unpersuasive; it is the crowing spin of those who are winning. The conspirators against Gloucester even seem to know this, but it does not prevent their version from having its imaginative, infecting effect. York, in turn, constructs himself in soliloquy by using animal terms:

> My brain, more busy than the labouring spider,
> Weaves tedious snares to trap mine enemies.
> Well, nobles, well; 'tis politicly done,
> To send me packing with an host of men:

> I fear me you but warm the starvèd snake,
> Who, cherished in your breasts, will sting your hearts.
> (lines 339–44)

These terms pick up from his more public language, suggesting that his own plans – even his whole nature – emerge from the rhetorical construction of Gloucester earlier in the scene. Animalistic treachery, once started, doesn't remain in the control of those who deploy it: rather the reverse.

A little later, Suffolk becomes, in Henry's terms, a bird of ill omen (III. ii. 40), and the serpentine image set up by Margaret (see above) and remotivated by York then gets tied to Suffolk in Salisbury's account of the people's rage against Gloucester's murderers (lines 259–69). Once this has become a public motif, it is beyond any individual's control. The Commons, who are 'like an angry hive of bees' (line 125) take on the force of the serpentine infection, which can now go anywhere. Suffolk tries to redirect this effect by cursing his enemies:

> Poison be their drink!
> Gall, worse than gall, the daintiest that they taste!
> Their sweetest shade a grove of cypress trees!
> Their chiefest prospect murdering basilisks!
> Their softest touch as smart as lizards' stings!
> Their music frightful as the serpent's hiss,
> And boding screech-owls make the consort full!
> All the foul terrors in dark-seated hell –
> (lines 321–8)

This is directed at Henry, Warwick, Salisbury, the people, all indiscriminately. Yet, though it was Margaret who urged him to these words, calling him a 'coward woman' and demanding 'Hast thou not spirit to curse thine enemy?' (lines 307–8), she goes on to stop him, saying

> Enough, sweet Suffolk, thou torment'st thyself,
> And these dread curses, like the sun 'gainst glass,
> Or like an overchargèd gun, recoil,
> And turns the force of them upon thyself.
> (lines 329–32)

Suffolk's language has hardly been sweet, and it's possible that Margaret breaks him off due to the demonic turn that he's taking – she may only want *natural* curses – but the Queen's inconsistency here doesn't much matter; indeed, one major effect of the ricocheting of animal imagery is the compromising of individual character consistency. In this play and its sequel, as elsewhere in Shakespeare (and as in D. H. Lawrence's writings), it's as if a whole shadowy otherworld were taking place behind the primary human drama, another animalistic dimension, with its own attractions and repulsions sometimes working with, sometimes against the conscious alliances and enmities of the historical characters, sometimes simplifying them, sometimes making them more complex. The overcharged nature of the language has its own power, turning upon itself and upon all things. Suffolk may insist that he has 'eagles' blood', not fit to be sucked by 'drones' (IV. i. 109), but this fantasy of identity is fundamentally compromised and self-defeating – after all, the image of the eagle was first introduced in order to pick out Gloucester for destruction.

York later describes his supporters Warwick and Salisbury as his 'two brave bears' (V. i. 144), an image that almost inevitably results in the contest becoming a bear-baiting. The animal imagery here, which anticipates the more famous imagery of Macbeth (and Gloucester – *King Lear*, III. vii. 54) tied to a stake, reminds us of the connection between the cruel contests of theatre and those of the bear ring.[11] In so doing it trivializes history. A certain dampening of the animal imagery does seem to ensue, particularly once Warwick ties the image of the bear to his heraldic badge of a baited bear (lines 202–3). In a sense, then, animal imagery can become simply iconic, representative, and can lose its force.

Yet the relationship between animality and human inscription is not always one of humans attempting to stamp their identity on the world. Jack Cade's statement about animals gives a different kind of keynote to the play:

> Is this not a lamentable thing, that of the skin of an innocent lamb should be made parchment? that parchment, being scribbled o'er, should undo a man? Some say the bee stings, but I say, 'tis the bee's wax; for I did but seal once to a thing, and I was never mine own man since. (IV. ii. 78–83)

The bondage of the lower classes depends on the use (or abuse) of animal nature. It *undoes* a man, unmakes his superiority to the animals, removes his self-possession. Yet this doesn't only apply to the lower orders. The textualizing and rewriting of animal life presented here also offers an ironic comment on what we have seen going on among the aristocrats: once verbal play is made of animals, they take on their own power, removing any sense of self-ownership.

The play ends with York talking about Salisbury as 'That winter lion, who in rage forgets / Agèd contusions and all brush of time' (V. iii. 2–3).

11 See Andreas Höfele, *Stage, Stake and Scaffold: Humans and Animals in Shakespeare's Theatre* (Oxford: Oxford University Press, 2011).

The animal re-emerges as a timeless symbol, 'like a gallant in the brow of youth' (line 4), able to repair himself. In this simile within a metaphor, a man is an old lion who is like a young man: through such a process of revitalization something new enters the world of the play. The fixed self may be compromised by the process, but the power of time is brushed off. Only through animals time is conquered, one might say. What might be a mere motif, crucially, has come to life and become a source of meaningful, autonomous motive.

The chain of animal imagery becomes even more intense and tangled in *Henry VI Part 3*, as the nation gets more fully embroiled in the complexities and tergiversations of civil war. Supposedly noble animals are presented as objects of fear: Warwick is presented as a falcon to terrify the King and his supporters (I. i. 47), Clifford as a 'pent-up lion o'er the wretch / That trembles under his devouring paws' (I. iii. 12–13) in his vengeance on the innocent Rutland. More conventionally, York sees his followers as 'lambs pursued by hunger-starvèd wolves' (I. iv. 5), though he himself is more startlingly like a swan swimmingly helplessly against a tide (lines 19–20). As he is defeated, he can still insist on his regal claims by claiming to be a 'phoenix' (line 35), but Northumberland calls him a 'cur', not worthy of further combat (lines 56–7). Queen Margaret, in turn, is sketched through a bewildering range of animalistic language: she is 'She-wolf of France, but worse than wolves of France, / Whose tongue more poisons than the adder's tooth!' (line 111–2), has a 'tiger's heart wrapped in a woman's hide' (line 137) and is 'more inhuman, more inexorable, / O, ten times more, than tigers of Hyrcania' (lines 154–5). Perhaps no other character in Shakespeare is presented as being so naturally unnatural; the animal imagery is incoherent, excessive but insufficient: she's a tiger, but worse than a tiger; a wolf but worse than a wolf, and therefore like an adder; and what conceals all this is a woman's skin, yet the woman's skin is admitted to be animalistic in the word 'hide'. The animals here seem to take on their own life, to become self-descriptions rather than ways of understanding Margaret. All this fecundity of animal imagery derives from her maternal rage, which is both natural and unnatural, and which subverts the heraldic nobility of more masculine claims to power and status.

Richard of Gloucester tries to clarify and focus the play's animal imagery in the next scene, describing his father's valour thus:

> I saw him in the battle range about,
> And watched him how he singled Clifford forth.
> Methought he bore him in the thickest troop

As doth a lion in a herd of neat,
Or as a bear, encompassed round with dogs,
Who having pinched a few and made them cry,
The rest stand all aloof and bark at him.
So fared our father with his enemies,
So fled his enemies my warlike father;
Methinks 'tis prize enough to be his son.
(II. i. 11–20)

As we have just seen York taunted and killed, this can only be ironic – indeed, it seems so ironic that it looks either like political spin or wishful thinking. Singling his father forth, Richard imagines a nobler version of war, and a more fixed, crystallized notion of human identity than is really available amongst the savage herds of civil war. Part of Richard's appeal is his ability to stand forth as an individual, 'like no brother' (V. vi. 80), in the midst of undifferentiated, animalistic humanity, but this speech, undercut a moment later by the appearance of three suns in the sky and by the news of York's death, only serves to emphasize that his version of individuality is a precarious fantasy.

When Henry wants to be merciful to his defeated enemies, Clifford speaks against him in a manner that starts calmly, but gathers force from its use of animal imagery:

My gracious liege, this too much lenity
And harmful pity must be laid aside.
To whom do lions cast their gentle looks?
Not to the beast that would usurp their den.
Whose hand is that the forest bear doth lick?
Not his that spoils her young before her face.
Who scapes the lurking serpent's mortal sting?
Not he that sets his foot upon her back.
The smallest worm will turn, being trodden on,
And doves will peck in safeguard of their brood.
(II. ii. 9–18)

The king is initially gentle as a lion, but even that comes to seem a paradox; descending the animal hierarchy prompts more sense of passion: Henry becomes a bear, but one in its maternal aspect (bears were thought to lick their offspring into shape) before becoming a serpent, symbol of evil. The protean nature of this imagery is more bewildering than clarifying, humiliating the king into the form of a worm before momentarily reasserting some form of gentleness in the peaceful, forgiving motif of a dove, which in turn is made to peck rather than coo. Clifford's main point is that 'Unreasonable creatures feed their young' (line 26) and that Henry's disinheriting of his son has caused all of the reversals of nature we have seen so far in the play. The point is simple, but the animalistic presentation of it confuses rather than simplifies. Henry admits that 'Full well hath Clifford played the orator, / Inferring arguments of mighty force' (lines 43–4), and though he is persuaded, there is a sense in which these arguments overbear him rather than appeal to his intellect or conscience. Nature, here, in a proto-Hobbesian manner, is more might than right.

On his own, Henry is less convinced of the urgency of such arguments. Sent away from the Battle of Towton, he sits on a molehill and ponders the course of things, seeing himself as a shepherd watching the dawn, which in turn is 'like a mighty sea/ Forced by the tide to combat with the wind; / Now sways it that way, like the self-same sea / Forced to retire by fury of the wind' (II. v. 5–8). He sits on the molehill and dreams of a 'happy life' as a 'homely swain' (lines 21–2), merely counting the hours, and allotting himself his shepherd tasks. The 54-line speech is perhaps the fullest expression of a pastoral ideal of stasis in Shakespeare,[12] and it frames a longing for godlike detachment and omniscience along with a dutiful (perhaps Stoical) submission to determinism. The sheer length and undramatic tedium of the speech means that it is pretty much bound to be cut in modern productions, but this is a mistake; it is worth its length precisely because of its tedium, which hypnotically pulls us away from the battle. To become the shepherd, the highest ideal of the king, most fully in charge of time and life, is to detach oneself from history and animal nature. Yet, like the mole on whose hill Henry sits, he becomes blind to the goings-on of the world as he imagines a wholly sufficient omniscience. Henry's quasi-divine perspective abstracts all forces into the 'self-same'-ness of the sea. Such abstraction has its attraction but is radically undermined by the ensuing appearance of two of Shakespeare's most abstract characters, 'a son that hath killed his father' and 'a father that hath killed his son' (line 54 SD, line 78 SD):[13] the removal of identity entailed by Henry's attitude may lead to such horrifying mistakes. The ideal of a perfect king as identified with a sundial here anticipates Richard II's sense of himself as 'numbering clock' (*Richard II*, V. v. 50); once the idea of royalty has been abstracted into such a mechanism, it loses all life. We may prefer even a Richard III.

[12] See the discussion in Helen Cooper, *Shakespeare and the Medieval World* (London: Bloomsbury, 2010), p. 135.

[13] See the discussion of this sequence in John Wilders, *The Lost Garden: Shakespeare's History Plays* (London: Macmillan, 1978), pp. 16–17.

Henry accordingly becomes 'a deer whose skin's a keeper's fee' on his capture (III. i. 22), linking him, ironically, to Jack Cade, but otherwise the animal imagery after this pastoral moment becomes more abstract and incidental (e.g. IV. vii. 25, IV. viii. 49–50, V. ii. 11–15, V. iv. 80, V. vii. 10–12). When Somerset says 'he that will not fight for such a hope / Go home to bed, and like the owl by day, / If he arise, be mocked and wondered at' (V. iv. 55–7),[14] he indicates that animality has become something incongruous as the civil wars draw to a close. Henry ties the chain of animal imagery up by remarking on the portentous nature of Richard of Gloucester:

> The owl shrieked at thy birth, an evil sign;
> The night-crow cried, aboding luckless time;
> Dogs howled, and hideous tempest shook down trees;
> The raven rooked her on the chimney's top,
> And chattering pies in dismal discords sung.
> (V. vi. 44–8)

Henry presents Richard as 'an indigested and deformèd lump' (line 51), and this figure is lumped together with all the animality that has forced its way through the play. Yet if he absorbs all the savagery here, he also absorbs all the associated life and motive.

In Richard's own play, he seems the only adequately living creature; everyone else seems strangely listless, easily swept along in his plans, and this is partly because he seems to summarize or epitomize all animals. *Richard III* is full of supernatural imagery, particularly when Richard is accused of being a devil, and in the various curses which are bandied about,[15] but natural, animalistic imagery is nearly as dominant, at least in the first few acts of the play.[16] Richard himself is a naturally unnatural figure: however vicious he is as a result, he also has much more life than any other character. In his wooing of Anne, he sophistically invokes 'rules of charity' (line 68), and she replies:

14 Brome picks up on this image in *The City Wit*, where Josina says 'I would not be wonder'd at like an Owle among my neighbors'. References to *The Dramatic Works of Richard Brome*, 3 vols. (London: John Pearson, 1873), I: 340 (the edition has no line numbers).

15 The origin of much of this is Queen Margaret. See Deborah Willis, *Malevolent Nurture: Witch-Hunting and Maternal Power in Early Modern England* (Ithaca: Cornell University Press, 1995).

16 Jeanne Addison Roberts comments that the animal imagery used of Richard moves him 'into the realm of the Wild', becoming 'a contaminated outsider greatly to be feared by guardians of Culture. His is not simply a double step down on the Chain of Being, from male below female to animal, but an invasion of a Wild which blurs the margins of culture. His Wild, however, overlaps animal and male Wilds and is energized by lust not for women but for power. Animals seem to occupy a more honorable place than women.' – *The Shakespearean Wild*, p. 57.

> Villain, thou knowst nor law of God nor man:
> No beast so fierce but knows some touch of pity.
> RICHARD. But I know none, and therefore am no beast.
> ANNE. O wonderful, when devils tell the truth!
> (I. ii. 70–3)

Here we see a neat encapsulation of the paradoxical nature of animality: animals are invoked as a reference point for human pity, but Richard *transcends* (or claims to transcend) animality, and therefore must be supernatural, a figure of wonder if also a demonic figure. As a result, the play's invocations of animal imagery, while they give life to Richard, fail to reduce him to mere bestiality. He is animal, but only insofar as to be animal is to be an object of wonder.

Anne goes on to call Richard 'diffused infection of a man' (line 78); not only is he poisonous, but there is something decentered, destabilizing about him. The boundaries of his selfhood are porous, and he is marvellously capable of infecting others – including his surprisingly successful wooing of Anne herself. She is won over by him, despite the fact that she thinks 'Never hung poison on a fouler toad' (line 147).[17] Margaret later tries to curse him, referring to him as 'this poisonous bunch-backed toad' (I. iii. 245),[18] but if he is *already* a cursed toad, it's hardly possible for her to curse him more. Indeed, in Margaret's language he is one cursed since birth:

> Thou elvish-marked, abortive, rooting hog!
> Thou that wast sealed in thy nativity
> The slave of nature and the son of hell!
> Thou slander of thy heavy mother's womb!
> Thou loathèd issue of thy father's loins!
> (lines 227–31)

Richard cheerfully turns this insult back on Margaret, but is hardly hurt by it. He is not, after all, abortive, and if he was born as the slave of nature that does give him a certain irreducible resilience. Anne calls him 'hedgehog' (I. ii. 102), and that seems to confirm his imperviousness, even as it attempts (like the word 'hog' above) to ridicule his heraldic emblem of the boar. In *Henry VI Part 3*, Richard claims that he can 'Change shapes with Proteus' (III. ii. 192), and like Proteus's, his animalistic transformations make him harder rather than easier to pin down.

When Richard recalls his killing of the Lancastrian Prince Edward, he contemplates his victim in terms of near-wonder:

17 Is there a hint of the princess and frog myth here?
18 *Sic*: 'bunch-backed' is much better than 'hunchbacked', I think.

A sweeter and a lovelier gentleman,
Framed in the prodigality of nature–
Young, valiant, wise, and (no doubt) right royal–
The spacious world cannot again afford.
(*Richard III*, I. ii. 242–5)

Yet this wonder redounds on Richard himself, for Anne has now accepted him as a replacement for the dead prince. Nature's prodigality in creating one as lovely as Edward implies that there is something aberrant in natural goodness, and that Richard himself is a more appropriate production. That is not to say that Richard is normal: he is, in his way, as exceptional as Edward. Being 'like no brother' and 'myself alone' (*Henry VI Part 3*, V. vi. 80–3), he is the uniquely special product of Nature at its most naturally unnatural, reformed from its prodigal tendency to create men who are too good. He is the boar to Edward's Adonis.

However, if Nature's weirdest work is to produce such creatures as hedgehogs and toads, objects of wonder, it also produces more standard animals, and Richard is allied to them too. Perhaps the most common animal imagery in *Richard III* is of dogs, about whom Shakespeare is famously ambivalent (with the ambivalence tending ultimately to the negative).[19] The issue may be that dogs were the lead species in a changing of attitudes about animals: the first animal to be fully absorbed into the family, and therefore becoming the first to whom human categories could be applied.[20] Richard calls Anne's attendant 'Unmannered dog' (I. ii. 39), with a possible pun on a lack of manliness, while also suggesting that the human value of manners can be applied to such a creature. Most dog imagery, though, is aimed at Richard himself, such as Margaret's (I. iii. 215) and her warning that 'when he fawns he bites' (line 289). Such language is intended to declass Richard, in spite of his claim that he 'was born so high', like an eagle (line 262).[21] Yet Richard himself defangs such insults by accepting his own *sub*-doglike nature from the start. He admits that 'dogs bark at me as I halt by them' (I. i. 23); this suggests not only that dogs feel superior to him, however, but that they recognize and perhaps fear something in him. His description of his own form is half-lament, half-celebration:

I, that am rudely stamped, and want love's majesty
To strut before a wanton ambling nymph;
I, that am curtailed of this fair proportion,

19 See Caroline Spurgeon, *Shakespeare's Imagery and What It Tells Us* (Cambridge: Cambridge University Press, 1935), pp. 195–9.
20 See Thomas, *Man and the Natural World*, pp. 100–8.
21 Cf. I. i. 132–3.

Cheated of feature by dissembling nature,
Deformed, unfinished, sent before my time
Into this breathing world, scarce half made up.
(lines 16–21)

Nature here is conceived as a bad, fake artist. But if this is so, then Richard may represent some deeper truth. He is 'sent before [his] time' in the sense that he was born prematurely, but the phrase is imaginatively resonant, even implying that he is a man of the future, an anachronism. If he cannot strut before a nymph, so much the better, as he will not be easily seduced by such non-human, sirenical femininity. He is half a man, certainly, but there is also perhaps a pun in the word 'curtailed', whose stress here *cur*tailed may imply something doglike; if so, he is a half-human, half-animal chimera, and as such a figure who can stand outside humanity but who can still comment authoritatively on it.

The play's animal imagery, however important it may be in setting up Richard's nature, thins out after its first act. We might expect Richard's henchmen Ratcliffe and Catesby, who were traditionally associated with a Rat and a Cat, to develop some animalistic qualities, but there's a resolute refusal to develop this. In the middle of the play there is a good deal of talk of stoniness as opposed to natural kindness (e.g. III. vii. 223–4; IV. i. 98), but other modalities of natural imagery are absent. Richard himself becomes 'a base foul stone, made precious by the foil / Of England's chair, where he is falsely set' (V. iii. 250-1), but other than standard references to his heraldic image, and to his victims as lambs to his wolvish nature (e.g. IV. iv. 22–3), little animality emerges as Richard comes to the throne. As he becomes King, he conceals his animality, which makes it all the more troubling when it returns.

Only when he is decisively thought of as a tyrant can animal imagery return in any sustained way. This re-emergence is startlingly invoked by Margaret, who seems to conjure the beast forth from his mother's womb:

From forth the kennel of thy womb hath crept
A hell-hound that doth hunt us all to death:
That dog, that had his teeth before his eyes
To worry lambs and lap their gentle blood,
That foul defacer of God's handiwork,
That excellent grand tyrant of the earth,
That reigns in gallèd eyes of weeping souls,
Thy womb let loose to chase us to our graves.
O upright, just, and true-disposing God,

How do I thank thee that this carnal cur
Preys on the issue of his mother's body.
(IV. iv. 47–57)

However ironically Margaret intends the word, there is a sense in which Richard really is 'excellent', in that he is prodigiously unusual. He is opposed here, not to natural creation but to God's, an idea that seems to turn him into an apocalyptic figure, almost the Antichrist (is that the sense in which he is sent before his time?). Yet the dog imagery anchors him here, preventing him from assuming such grandeur of evil: he seems more trivial, like Spenser's Blatant Beast, which represents mere slander rather than bringing apocalypse.[22] When Richmond re-enlivens the imagery of Richard as a boar, he seems to be making him into some apocalyptic force (one might think again of the Venus and Adonis legend), but there's a similarly naturalizing anchor:

The wretched, bloody, and usurping boar,
That spoiled your summer fields and fruitful vines,
Swills your warm blood like wash and makes his trough
In your embowelled bosoms – this foul swine
Is now even in the centr[e] of this isle. (V. ii. 7–11)

This is grotesque, viscerally natural language which takes its echo of Psalm 80 and presses it close inside the human body. Boars and pigs were notorious eaters of humans, and this imagery invokes a real horror at a violence in the centre of the realm, but it then turns a bit more realistic when Richmond adds, matter-of-factly, 'Near to the town of Leicester, as we learn' (line 12). Evil is among us, precisely located, in the East Midlands, rather than operating as any kind of transcendent force. Richard may want to be inspired by 'fiery dragons' (V. iii. 350), but he is not really a supernatural being. He may be a vice figure, but the animal imagery of the play prevents his evil from being truly demonic; whatever he is – not quite human, certainly – he is natural rather than supernatural. Derrida argues that the strangely persistent connection between beasts and kings in Western thinking shows an attempt to naturalize (and perhaps thereby to contain) the monstrous qualities of sovereignty (both animals and monarchs being above the law),[23] and nowhere is this more acute than in the figure of

[22] Also presented as a dog of hell: *The Faerie Queene*, VI. xii. 35. References to Edmund Spenser, *The Faerie Queene*, ed. A. C. Hamilton, text ed. Hiroshi Yamashita and Toshiyuki Suzuki (Harlow: Longman, 2001).

[23] Jacques Derrida, *The Beast & the Sovereign*, 2 vols., ed. Michel Lisse, Marie-Louise Mallet and Ginette Michaud, trans. Geoffrey Bennington (Chicago: University of Chicago Press, 2009–11).

Richard III, a figure of excess who is both above and below normal human motivation. He is a monster, a figure of wonder, but he is also *natural.*

Monstrous humanity

The fact that animals share something with us, while being fundamentally different, means that they are extremely useful for conveying the ripples of sympathy between people that fall short of anything as absolute as empathy. We have seen that the traditional model of the soul gave man a soul in common with animals and, in Shakespeare's own time, Giordano Bruno argues that 'the human species displays, in the particularities of its individuals, the variety of all other species together'.[24] As with Bacon's conception of man's compoundedness, man is distinguished from the other animals, but only in being *more* animal than they are, a summing up or epitome of animality. Bruce Boehrer argues that the failure to manage a clear distinction between human and beast 'opens up a new realm of conceptual possibilities by generating a second field of binary discrimination parallel to the first: the things that conform to the man/beast opposition and things that do not'; those things that do not conform are monstrous, and so 'the man/beast opposition ceases to stand for the world as it absolutely is but stands instead for the world as it absolutely *should be*'.[25] The variousness of animal creation therefore seems to offer a model for human variousness, but it also presents a problem for the definition of humanity, often making it monstrous.

That definition is complicated by the idea of metempsychosis, one of the ideas we saw in the Introduction as enabling man's connection to nature. The idea is generally treated lightly in Shakespeare's time, but with a sense that it might just be true. In *Twelfth Night*, when Malvolio is imprisoned for his supposed madness, the ensuing scene would be anything but comic to its original audience,[26] obliquely reflecting a fear of what might happen when new philosophies and ideas are imposed. English people had suffered many changes of religion in the sixteenth century, being forced to change their deepest beliefs according to the changes of monarchical regime, and a similar process of belief-change was at least imaginably possible on scientific as well as religious matters. The doctrine that Malvolio is capriciously asked

24 Giordano Bruno, *Cause, Principle and Unity*, p. 16.

25 Boehrer, *Shakespeare among the Animals*, pp. 3–4.

26 Colin Burrow, *Shakespeare and Classical Antiquity* (Oxford: Oxford University Press, 2013), p. 98, argues that Shakespeare's references to metempsychosis are 'almost always jokes', but, though the other examples he adduces are jokey, this one has more threat to it.

to accept is the idea of metempsychosis, the belief in transmigration of souls commonly attributed to Pythagoras. Not only does this reflect a fear of the need to swallow new ideas, but the ideas themselves are ones which destabilize man's privileged position in the universe. Significantly dressed as a priest, the clown Feste catechizes the imprisoned madman, in a parody of all-too-familiar religious inquisitions and persecutions:

CLOWN. What is the opinion of Pythagoras concerning wild-fowl?
MALVOLIO. That the soul of our grandam might happily inhabit a bird.
CLOWN. What think'st thou of his opinion?
MALVOLIO. I think nobly of the soul, and no way approve his opinion.
CLOWN. Fare thee well. Remain thou still in darkness. Thou shalt hold the opinion of Pythagoras ere I will allow of thy wits, and fear to kill a woodcock lest thou dispossess the soul of thy grandam. Fare thee well. (IV. ii. 50–60)

What might be mere opinion can be imposed by authority here. 'Happily' mainly means 'perhaps', but it also implies some happiness in the possibility: when our dead ancestors can no longer go to Purgatory and be prayed for, it might be comforting to imagine we still have some connections with them in animal form. Even if we don't assent to this opinion, though, we may entertain it as a possibility and this can lead to caution (or even fear) in our treatment of animals. Trying on new ideas like this destabilizes all our attempts to hold unitary, clear beliefs. Marlowe's Faustus in his last moments, wishes

Ah, Pythagoras's *metempsychosis*, were that true,
This soul should fly from me and I be changed
Unto some brutish beast.
All beasts are happy, for, when they die,
Their souls are soon dissolved in elements.
(A Text, V. ii. 107–11)

Faustus here characteristically wants to have his cake and eat it, moving from one metaphysical idea to another, wishing that his soul could transmigrate, in Pythagoras's scheme, and then wishing that the transmigrated soul could dissolve without further translation, returning to the orthodox scheme in which animal souls are mortal. He is under the pressure of imminently heading to Hell, but his position might be taken as an acute instance of anyone contemplating the possibility of predestined damnation – a condition in which it may be highly consoling to grasp for other metaphysical schemes. Thinking something may make it so.

Donne's *Metempsychosis* (1601 – around the same time as *Twelfth Night*) uses the doctrine of the transmigration of souls for rather mysteriously satirical purposes,[27] but the poem gets distracted from its satirical intent as Donne finds the idea of transmigration imaginatively interesting for its own sake; trying on an ironic intellectual position such as this involves taking it seriously to some degree, admitting that it is at least a possible truth. In his preface to the poem Donne reminds his readers that

> the Pythagorean doctrine doth not only carry one soul from man to man, nor man to beast, but indifferently to plants also: and therefore you must not grudge to find the same soul in an emperor, in a post-horse, and in a mushroom, since no unreadiness in the soul but an indisposition in the organs works this. And therefore, though this soul could not move when it was a melon, yet it may remember and now tell me at what lascivious banquet it was served. And though it could not speak when it was a spider, yet it can remember and now tell me who used it for poison to attain dignity.[28]

There is a clear sense of the doctrine's absurdity here, but also a relish for its consequences. The reference to a mushroom, for instance, is silly, but its proximity to the mention of an emperor also makes it point to the idea of courtly arrivistes, who were called mushrooms because they sprung up overnight. The idea of melons at lascivious banquets and spider-poisons used by the ambitious adds a pleasing sense of paranoia to such vicious courtly activities by suggesting that the non-human substances involved are somehow witnesses to vice. The overall effect is to endue the world with more conscious life than a complacent philosophy would normally expect.

The soul focussed on in the poem goes through a bewildering variety of bodies: it is, in turn, the apple in Eden, a mandrake, a sparrow, two fishes, a whale, a mouse, a wolf, a dog-wolf, an ape and Themech, fifth daughter of Eve. There is no real sense of orderly progress here, and the idea of transmigration is mostly used to show a sense of chaotic entanglement in nature rather than to show a sense of order. The soul may encapsulate variety, but that variety is not hierarchically comforting; it is likened to Noah's Ark,

> That swimming college and free hospital
> Of all mankind, that cage and vivary
> Of fowls, and beasts, in whose womb, Destiny

[27] M. van Wyck Smith, 'John Donne's *Metempsychosis*', *RES* 24 (1973), 17–25, 141–52, plausibly argues that the poem is an attack on Robert Cecil, chief minister at the end of Elizabeth's reign; it's possible that the satire is more general, showing the progress of the idea of vain religious thinking and schism.

[28] 'Epistle', lines 24–34.

Us, and our latest nephews did install
(For thence are all derived, that fills this All)
Didst thou in that great stewardship embark
So diverse shapes into that floating park,
As have been moved, and informed by this heavenly spark.
(lines 23–30)

This is not an order like the great chain of being, but a miscellaneous grab-bag, an unstable, floating thing, with the disorder of a hospital or college rather than the order of a church. Even God's steward-*ship* involves an adventitious pun. This menagerie is untidy, and God seems barely in control of it.

The poem ends with the soul's first transformation into a woman:

Keeping some quality
Of every past shape, she knew treachery,
Rapine, deceit, and lust, and ills enow
To be a woman. (lines 506–9)

From the mouse that killed an elephant we get treachery, from the wolf rapine, from the wolf-dog deceit, and from the ape lust, and this is summed up in woman. The cherished notion of man as microcosm is inverted in woman. This seems sufficiently final, but Donne then goes on to reflect that Cain (who marries this woman, his sister), despite being the source of murder, is the Promethean inventor of useful things; this leads to the conclusion that we can't disentangle the useful from the vicious, and that we can only be guided by 'opinion' (line 520). All that we have learned from exploring the doctrine of transmigration is a radical relativism, and a destabilization of human dignity, as varied opinions of the world alter its very nature. In Donne's poem, man takes on all of the riddling doubleness of the natural world, which is complex, entangled, paradoxically sometimes *un*natural, a subject for opinion and speculation. Man may be the epitome of creation, but that creation is complex and uncertain, impossible for individuals to control. It is subject to opinion, and to sudden changes of perspective.

The consequence is that people are less in control of their own motives than they might think. Animal imagery has a tendency not only to blur, but also to *pre-empt* human motive, on the basis of others' conceptions and beliefs. Shylock, in *The Merchant of Venice*, complains that Antonio 'call'dst me dog before thou hadst a cause' (III. iii. 6), and this insult becomes its own motive and cause, driving Shylock to subhuman action. He sees poetic justice of a kind in his actions, warning 'Since I am a dog, beware my fangs' (line 7); Antonio has caricatured and reduced him, and this reduced self will be the violent force impelling the plot. With his mixture of ingenuous decency and casual condescension, Antonio had earlier suggested that 'The Hebrew will turn Christian, he grows kind' (I. iii. 178); Shylock will indeed become more *natural*, but in the wrong direction, turning animalistic in the bad sense rather than the redemptive. When Shylock later insists on cutting out his pound of flesh, Gratiano that his savageness 'almost mak'st me waver in my faith / To hold opinion with Pythagoras, / That souls of animals infuse themselves / Into the trunks of men' (IV. i. 130–3). There is a sense of wonder here, but also of paradox: Gratiano wishes that Shylock be 'damned', but at the same time calls him a 'dog'; but if he were a dog, he couldn't be damned.

Don John in *Much Ado about Nothing* is a rather diminished version of Richard III and Shylock, whose animalistic nature is more perfunctorily elaborated. Resenting his reconcilement to his legitimate brother, he says

> I had rather be a canker in a hedge than a rose in his grace, and it better fits my blood to be disdained of all than to fashion a carriage to rob love from any. In this (though I cannot be said to be a flattering honest man) it must not be denied but I am a plain-dealing villain. I am trusted with a muzzle and enfranchised with a clog, therefore I have decreed not to sing in my cage. If I had my mouth, I would bite; if I had my liberty, I would do my liking. In the mean time, let me be that I am, and seek not to alter me. (I. iii. 27–37)

He is attached to his own nature, for which he has a degree of contempt, in opposition to Richard's delight. He knows that he is a dog, unwillingly tamed, but he cannot rise above that nature and get any perspective on it as Richard does; rather, he just takes a grim satisfaction in the fixity of self that being a dog gives him. As a result, he fails to be a satisfying villain: in fact, another imaginary villain has to be conjured up in his place, the thief 'Deformed' whom the Watch create from their mishearing of Borachio (III. iii. 125–6). 'Deformed' is like the ghost of Richard III, flitting through the play, a formless being that emerges from 'fashion' rather than nature.

A sense of the peculiar, pre-emptive, undermotivated fashioning of people pervades *Troilus and Cressida*, which has probably the most extensive range of animal imagery in any of Shakespeare's plays, largely due to the range of insults flung out by Thersites. The effect of the animal imagery here is systematically to diminish the heroic/romantic characters of the play; where ancient epic and medieval romance emphasize the significance of human difference, based on the particularizing distinction of persons entailed by combat and by love, Shakespeare's play denies any attempts to give people such distinction, in spite of its characters' notorious preoccupations with reputation, order, and opinion.[29]

Pandarus, at the beginning of the play, tries to assert the superiority of aristocratic heroes to common soldiers. He refers to the latter group as 'Asses, fools, dolts! chaff and bran, chaff and bran! porridge after meat. I could live and die in the eyes of Troilus. Ne'er look, ne'er look, the eagles are gone; crows and daws, crows and daws' (I. ii. 241–4). Yet if the distinction is so evident, why so repetitiously insist on it? He also overdoes the point as he tries to focus Cressida's attention on Troilus, with the result that he calls even Achilles 'a very camel' (line 249). The *Iliad* has a deep seriousness in its recognition that its distinguished heroes will become food for dogs and all manner of birds (I. 4–5), but the use of animals in *Troilus* almost immediately becomes absurd and incoherent.

Ajax (largely through Thersites' choric mouth) is the central focus for this absurdity and incoherence. Before Pandarus and Thersites can get their oars in, Cressida's Alexander introduces Ajax:

> This man, lady, hath robbed many beasts of their particular additions: he is as valiant as the lion, churlish as the bear, slow as the elephant; a man into whom nature hath so crowded humours that his valour is crushed into folly, his folly sauced with discretion. There is no man hath a virtue that he hath not a glimpse of, nor any man an attaint but he carries some stain of it. He is melancholy without cause, and merry against the hair; he hath the joints of everything, but everything so out of joint that he is a gouty Briareus, many hands and no use, or purblind Argus, all eyes and no sight. (lines 19–30)

Some think that this may be Shakespeare's portrait of Ben Jonson;[30] I am sceptical, not least because the young Jonson was not the large, slow, bearish man he later became, but was a scrag.[31] It is more instructive to see Ajax as a failed version of a key humanist trope: Man as microcosm or epitome of nature. This is the flipside of the ideal Renaissance man, self-contradictory rather than self-sufficient, at odds with the world and its purposes rather than objectively aware of them. If the existence of the ideal man – Ophelia's version of Hamlet, who is the 'glass of fashion and the mould of form' (III. i. 153) – may clarify and distinguish those around him, the existence of such a figure as Ajax infects all around him with his incoherence.

[29] See Bradshaw, *Shakespeare's Scepticism*, pp. 151–2.

[30] See Arden 3 Introduction, pp. 9–10.

[31] Dekker, *Satiromastix*, V. ii. 294–5: 'Horace was a goodly corpulent gentleman, and not so lean-cheeked a scrag as thou art'. References to *The Dramatic Works of Thomas Dekker*, ed. Fredson Bowers, 4 vols. (Cambridge: Cambridge University Press, 1953–61).

When he makes his own proper appearance, he insults Thersites as a dog (and a toadstool, a porcupine, etc. – II. i. 1–52), but he has himself been set up as a dog, in Ulysses' and Nestor's plan to make the 'Two curs' 'tame each other' (I. iii. 389). The point of all this may be that the moment one sets someone up as a dog in conflict, anyone whom that dog fights becomes reduced to the level of a dog themselves. So incoherent is Ajax that he is at odds with *everyone*, which makes everyone else – being in conflict with him – a dog too. Likewise, when Ajax is called an elephant (II. iii. 2), this seems to have the effect of making Achilles also an elephant (line 105); though Ajax is an elephant because he is stupid and slow, and Achilles because he is unbending, the animal imagery tends to blur rather than enable rhetorical distinction.

One of the play's key concepts is Ulysses' idea that 'One touch of nature makes the whole world kin' (III. iii. 175). Complex and resonant as this notion is (and we will make more of it later), the main thrust seems to be that any trace of human weakness links us to everyone else, but not in a positive way: any weakness Achilles shows removes any distinction he may once have had; his slightest vanity makes him like Ajax and therefore a candidate for oblivion rather than renown. In general, the sense of human kinship in this play is not positively presented: kinship between Hector and Ajax means that the former decides not to fight the latter to the death, but this leaves us unsatisfied, with a sense that their combat was ill-motivated in the first place. The summary of Hector's attitude, rather than seeming truly noble, just creates a sense of half-heartedness:

> This Ajax is half made of Hector's blood,
> In love whereof, half Hector stays at home;
> Half heart, half hand, half Hector comes to seek
> This blended knight, half Trojan and half Greek.
> (IV. v. 83–6)

Ajax's incoherence is emphasized for another reason, and Hector is also hereby associated with it. Human identity, distinction, and meaningful motive are diluted.

This dilution is of a piece with other aspects of the play's sense of nature. Natural impulses seem half-hearted and insufficient, mere rhetorical ploys with no real motive behind them. Hector argues eloquently for the naturalness of marriage:

> Nature craves
> All dues be rendered to their owners: now,
> What nearer debt in all humanity

Than wife is to the husband? If this law
Of nature be corrupted through affection,
And that great minds, of partial indulgence
To their benumbèd wills, resist the same,
There is a law in each well-ordered nation
To curb those raging appetites that are
Most disobedient and refractory.
(II. ii. 173–82)

Nature and the law of nations are allied here, and shown to be cognate forces against mere refractory *will*, but this is not enough: ten lines later, casually and without real motive, Hector proposes that they keep the adulterous Helen anyway.[32] The sense of a will that runs counter to nature is also the subject of Troilus's lament on 'the monstruosity in love', 'that the will is infinite and the execution confined' (III. ii. 81–2). Cressida agrees, saying 'They that have the voice of lions and the act of hares, are they not monsters?' (lines 88–9). The invocation of the category of the monstrous is the only way to account for the natural unnaturalness of human will;[33] even though Troilus's position dissents from Hector's in insisting on the infinitude of the will and the inadequacy of performance, that very infinitude may be numbing, teasing us out of thought. Man may be the epitome of the animal world, but that just makes the infinite will beastly and arbitrary. Hector's claim that keeping Helen is 'a cause that hath no mean dependence / Upon our joint and several dignities' (II. ii. 192–3) attempts to shore up mere will with the idea of human dignity, but it is as blindly incoherent and undermotivated as anything Ajax does.

Cressida, who will later be a 'Bifold' figure, who 'is and is not Cressid' (V. ii. 144, 146), has a sense even at the peak of her love for Troilus that she has 'an unkind self' (III. ii. 149). She has therefore something of the fundamental, paradoxical doubleness of nature itself. She naturalizes her infidelity in advance when she hopes that she will not be called

As false
As air, as water, wind, or sandy earth,
As fox to lamb, or wolf to heifer's calf,
Pard to the hind, or step-dame to her son.
(lines 191–4)

32 See the important discussion of Hector's apparent caprice in Bradshaw, *Shakespeare's Scepticism*, pp. 132–9.

33 See Boehrer, *Shakespeare among the Animals*, p. 4. See also Wes Williams, *Monsters and their Meaning in Early Modern Culture: Mighty Magic* (Oxford: Oxford University Press, 2011).

Though the list of animals (and stepmothers) is proverbial, the invocation of the four elements as exemplars of falsity is surprising: we may infer that she means that these elements are false *to* one another, but she doesn't say this; falsehood and incoherence seem essentially embedded in nature at its most basic.

Troilus develops this idea when he says

> Within my soul there doth conduce a fight
> Of this strange nature, that a thing inseparate
> Divides more wider than the sky and earth,
> And yet the spacious breadth of this division
> Admits no orifex for a point as subtle
> As Ariachne's broken woof to enter.
> Instance, O instance, strong as Pluto's gates,
> Cressid is mine, tied with the bonds of heaven;
> Instance, O instance, strong as heaven itself,
> The bonds of heaven are slipped, dissolved and loosed,
> And with another knot, five-finger-tied,
> The fractions of her faith, orts of her love,
> The fragments, scraps, the bits and greasy relics
> Of her o'er-eaten faith, are bound to Diomed.
> (V. ii. 147–60)

This is as stirring a lament for the incoherence of nature as anything we find in Donne's *Anniversaries*. The sheer strangeness of nature is brought home here: that which ought to instantiate harmony – a spider's web – comes to represent subtlety and competitiveness (Arachne's struggle with Minerva) as well as brokenness; the things which ought to harmonize – the natural world and the God who made it – are at odds but without clear distinction between them; that which ought to guarantee bonding is loose, and is in any case paradoxical – the classical custom of swearing by aspects of the underworld; yet that which is broken is also bonded to something new. Even fragmentariness is not quite coherently fragmentary or satisfyingly broken. Human caprice and insistence on specialness or distinction has brought us to this pass, but distinctions here are slipped and loosed, creating strange linkages.

The chief oddity of the play, then, is that there are still bonds at work, even if they seem very strange and unnatural. Aeneas and Diomedes feel *sympathy* with one another, but only insofar as both want to kill the other (IV. i. 25–7). Thersites, meanwhile, perhaps the play's most *typical* character, can refuse battle, and thus resemble Hector, but only on the basis of his potential opponent being a bastard like himself. Battle is presented as a hunt (e.g. V. vi. 29–31) or as a bull-baiting (V. vii. 10–12), but here it becomes bear against bear, and a strange nobility emerges: 'One bear will not bite another, and wherefore should one bastard?' (lines 18–20). The other bastard may wish Thersites to the devil, but there is some connection here, however awkward. Thersites' ellipsis at the end of his question, omitting to say 'one bastard bite another' has a subtle effect: he acquires a sense of soleness and integrity that is so lacking in all the others, for he at least knows his own nature.

Elsewhere in Shakespeare, the idea of bears not fighting one another is a more endearing matter of genuine sympathy: Beatrice and Benedick, having been tricked into love, are 'the two bears' who 'will not bite one another when they meet' (*Much Ado about Nothing*, III. ii. 78–9). Though animal imagery like this compromises some element of human dignity, it adds to human flexibility and therefore affirms Pico's idea of humans as the adaptable supplement to God's creation. In *Troilus and Cressida*, however, that flexibility is shown to be mere arbitrariness and incoherence. The play's sourness – even contempt – about humanity is unique in Shakespeare's corpus. The main reason for this is that its pseudo-heroic characters are so insistent on order, dignity and the specialness of their identities.

Macbeth is perhaps the only other play so focussed on human distinction; in this case all that distinction centres on Macbeth himself, who desperately wants to transcend animal nature, but who finds himself pulled further and further into it. Something similar happens to his adversaries: his animality infects all who would challenge him. Lady Macbeth thinks that a 'beast' (I. vii. 47) must have broached the idea of murder with her when he is being (in her view) cowardly; in fact, Macbeth himself has *not* broken 'the enterprise' to her in our hearing. We might infer a missing scene (see Arden 2 notes to these lines), but it might be better to suggest that the idea of murder, being beastly, has broken itself, through the silence of animal spirits and implied connection between the two. In drama of the period, murderous conspirators often share knowledge without us being able to understand rationally how they have communicated with one another. Murderers become connected, become 'the deed's creature'.[34]

Animals rather than rational humans often underpin the events of *Macbeth*, suggesting that deeper processes than the human are at work. Most notably, in the middle of the play, we are given an account of the violation of nature caused by the murder of Duncan: the Old Man says that the darkness of the day is

[34] To use a famous phrase from Middleton and Rowley's *The Changeling* (III. iv. 140). References to Thomas Middleton, *The Collected Works*, ed. Gary Taylor and John Lavagnino (Oxford: Oxford University Press, 2007).

unnatural,
Even like the deed that's done. On Tuesday last,
A falcon, towering in her pride of place,
Was by a mousing owl hawked at, and killed.
ROSSE. And Duncan's horses (a thing most strange and certain),
Beateous and swift, the minions of their race,
Turned wild in nature, broke their stalls, flung out,
Contending 'gainst obedience, as they would make
War with mankind.
OLD MAN. 'Tis said, they eat each other.
ROSSE. They did so—to th' amazement of mine eyes
That looked upon 't. *Enter Macduff.*
Here comes the good Macduff.
How goes the world, sir, now? (III. iv. 10–21)

The deep sense of nature's strangeness (and certainty) is powerfully created here:[35] we are amazed, subject to broken knowledge (wonder), left to ask questions about how the world works, but given no firm sense of causality. Are animals inspired by human deeds or vice versa? The play won't give us a decisive answer.

At the play's very beginning, the weird sisters' familiar animals are invoked, being presented rather as independent causes than as assistants:

1 WITCH. I come, Graymalkin.
2 WITCH. Paddock calls.
(I. i. 8–9)

A cat and a toad, given typifying names, are made into summoners of the play's action. But they are never presented on stage – unlike the Great Cat in Middleton's *The Witch* and the supernatural dog Tom in *The Witch of Edmonton*. The stage presence of an animal is mostly comic (though Tom is rather more ambiguous, as we shall see); yet the mention of animals who do not appear brings something darker and more mysterious into play, implying perhaps that they are part our natures, contained within us as the model of man as epitome suggests. Hence it is that 'the obscure bird' is *Macbeth*'s key figure (II. iii. 59); this refers to the owl, not a symbol of wisdom at this time, but one of *assumed* wisdom or at best arcane, inhuman knowledge, which we saw earlier could be mocked and wondered at if it appeared by day, but whose noise at night is truly terrifying and inhuman, mocking at our knowledge.

35 On the importance of the idea of strangeness in *Macbeth*, see Burrow, *Shakespeare and Classical Antiquity*, p. 191.

The play uses animal imagery to escape from knowledge, as if the Macbeths are keen to do away with their consciousness along with their conscience.[36] Keeping his wife out of the plot to kill Banquo, Macbeth says

> Be innocent of the knowledge, dearest chuck,
> Till thou applaud the deed. Come, seeling night,
> Scarf up the tender eye of pitiful day,
> And with thy bloody and invisible hand
> Cancel and tear to pieces that great bond
> Which keeps me pale! Light thickens, and the crow
> Makes wing to th' rooky wood;
> Good things of day begin to droop and drowse,
> Whiles night's black agents to their preys do rouse.
> Thou marvell'st at my words, but hold thee still:
> Things bad begun make strong themselves by ill.
> (III. ii. 45–55)

The first lines here are addressed to his wife as if in her absence, and reflect a desire to turn to the dark of the wilderness, to non-human unconsciousness and blindness that is affirmed by the apostrophe to night. He wants to separate himself from humanity, from the bonds of human nature, and from the idea of man as a bonding figure at the centre of creation. But then he turns back to his human bond with his wife, a bond he has effectively wished away, and sees that she now regards him as an object of wonder, her knowledge of him broken as he becomes one with the dark forces of nature. He is identified with the murderous crow, the solitary, carnivorous figure that threatens the peaceful rooks.[37]

When the Weird Sisters prophesy that Macbeth will not be defeated till Birnam Wood comes to Dunsinane, he is confident, because he believes that the natural world is fixed and orderly, despite his own breaking of that order. He asks

> Who can impress the forest, bid the tree
> Unfix his earth-bound root? (IV. i. 95–6)

Yet long ago his own identity has become unfixed (his hair is *unfixed* at I. iii. 135, when he first imagines the murder of Duncan). Macbeth presents

36 See Stanley Cavell, *Disowning Knowledge in Seven Plays of Shakespeare*, updated edition (Cambridge: Cambridge University Press, 2003).

37 William Empson, *Seven Types of Ambiguity* (1930; London: Hogarth Press, 1991), p. 19 points out that the power of the image comes from the contrast between the carnivorous, solitary crow and the social, mostly vegetarian rooks. Ted Hughes's *Crow*, his mythic sequence about a solitary, alienated creature, rebelling against God, Nature and femininity, surely derives from these lines. ('His prison is the earth. Clothed in his conviction, / Trying to remember his crimes / / Heavily he flies' – *Collected Poems*, ed. Paul Keegan (London: Faber & Faber, 2003), p. 232).

the natural world as a proper ground and base for action, as a world that is clearer and more forceful/decisive than the pale and uncertain world of human consciousness. Lamenting the escape of Macduff, he reflects

> Time, thou anticipat'st my dread exploits:
> The flighty purpose never is o'ertook
> Unless the deed go with it. From this moment
> The very firstlings of my heart shall be
> The firstlings of my hand. And even now,
> To crown my thoughts with acts, be it thought and done.
> (IV. i. 144–9)

Envy of supposed animal self-identity and simplicity is evident here: the word *firstlings* quietly and poignantly reminds us that Macbeth has no children of his own, that his deeds have replaced biological fertility; yet it also connects his sense of fertility of action with an animal world, one where thought and action can be absolutely identified. Perhaps paradoxically, this is what Macbeth most wants: rather than desiring the crown as mere symbol, he wants a supernatural kind of sovereignty that short-circuits the roundabout business of human thought and representation. He wants his deed to be 'the be-all and the end-all' (I. vii. 5), a desire that goes beyond mere ambition and is the true *hubris* of one who wants to be a transcendent god, to be 'perfect, / Whole as the marble, founded as the rock' (III. iv. 20–1), leaving behind the messy business of being an animal.[38] That he ends up reduced to being a mere 'dead butcher' (V. ix. 35) is an appropriate bringing low, a return into an animal nature that cannot be shuffled off.[39]

Yet even his Nemesis has to be detached from nature in order to destroy this naturally-unnatural opponent. We never see the Macduffs together, but they think of each other through animals. Macduff calls his dead children his 'pretty chickens' (IV. iii. 218), and Lady Macduff, lamenting her husband's absence, reflects that

> He loves us not,
> He wants the natural touch; for the poor wren,
> The most diminutive of birds, will fight,
> Her young ones in the nest, against the owl.
> (IV. ii. 8–11)

[38] Yet animals, as D. H. Lawrence's 'lords of life', can be perfect images of Macbeth's dream; Ted Hughes's 'Hawk Roosting' is a near-perfect articulation of his ambition, having 'no falsifying dream / Between my hooked head and hooked feet'. See *Collected Poems*, pp. 68–9.

[39] As Simon Palfrey argues, 'Macbeth is trying to build a horizon, some kind of founding limit – but, as ever, he cannot quite reach it; or if he does, it ends nothing' – *Shakespeare's Possible Worlds*, p. 323.

Macbeth is an owl, an obscure bird, but Macduff himself lacks the *touch* of nature that makes the whole world kin. Not born of feminine Nature (see Chapter 3), he, like his enemy Macbeth, is an eerily transcendent and supplementary figure.

Animal families

When people are less insistent on their own position as a be-all and end-all, animals can enable unification of the world, making the whole world kin, whether people want that to be so or not. Laurie Shannon's recent study of man and animals shows compellingly how animals were considered part of the political world of the Renaissance period.[40] She makes particularly convincing use of Montaigne in order to critique in advance the post-Cartesian mechanization of animal nature, and demonstrates throughout her study how the mysterious canniness and variety of animals bursts the bubble of human arrogance. Shakespeare's animals are above all mediating figures, and figures who are not quite present, while being omnipresent, shadowy background actors; they are figures of comparison for humans, but they have their own life, and their own comparative relations, and that enables them to connect humans to one another.

Animals, though they don't actually appear on stage, have a vivid presence throughout *As You Like It*. Duke Senior, while thinking about going hunting, says that

> it irks me the poor dappled fools,
> Being native burghers of this desert city,
> Should in their own confines with forkèd heads
> Have their round haunches gored. (II. i. 22–5)

Animals are given citizenship, pitied and patronized simultaneously. The Duke's sentiment, which seems to come from nowhere, prompts the First Lord to describe Jaques' moralizing on the 'spectacle' of a 'hairy fool' of a deer that has been fatally wounded by a hunter (lines 44, 40). Given the pathos of the deer's end, it is hard to see why both men should consider deer to be fools, except in the sense that such fools may be more natural and paradoxically wiser than humans. Jaques' moralizing consists mainly in a complaint that a herd of other deer pass the stricken one without exhibiting compassion, and drawing the exemplary lesson that humans

[40] *The Accommodated Animal*, p. 3 and *passim*. Shannon also makes the valuable point that Shakespeare very rarely uses the word 'animal', preferring the terms 'beast' or 'creature' (pp. 7–9).

tend not to pity the poor; yet Jaques' own pity, useless and over-literary as it is, gives the lie to this very sentiment. He also claims that

> we
> Are mere usurpers, tyrants, and what's worse,
> To fright the animals and to kill them up
> In their assigned and native dwelling-place.
> (lines 60–63)

Jaques, at a basic level, shows how the banishment of the usurped court has forced them to usurp and tyrannize upon others, but in his melancholy, he seems to be speaking more generally, reflecting (like an extreme deep ecologist) that humans are a violation of the natural order (what could be worse than being a tyrant?).[41] Deer themselves present a kind of boundary problem between the natural and the cultivated animal, and the differences between them are the subjects of commonplace jokes;[42] this is probably because they were so carefully husbanded and protected, so that we become aware that their assigned dwelling-place is an aspect of human culture rather than true nativity. There is a sense in which they really are citizens, part of a legal order. Perhaps as a result of thinking about all of this, perhaps as a result of his animal sympathy, Jaques is himself nearly dehumanized, the Duke later saying 'I think he be transformed into a beast, / For I can no where find him like a man' (II. vii. 1–2); this is in the way of a joke, but it demonstrates how thinking about animals challenges our definitions of humanity. Despite notions that beasts are cruel, and despite attempts to privilege human(e) feeling elsewhere, it is precisely sympathy here that seems to make one beastly (or beastliness that makes one sympathetic).

At the beginning of the play, Orlando complains that his brother keeps him in a manner 'that differs not from the stalling of an ox', but also that 'His horses are bred better, for besides that they are fair with their feeding, they are taught their manage and to that end riders dearly hired; but I (his brother) gain nothing under him but growth' (I. i. 10–14).[43] Orlando is treated like a vegetable, with only his soul of growth encouraged, not his animal soul, let alone his rational soul. He is in the wrong part of an animalistic hierarchy. He further asks 'Shall I keep your hogs and eat husks with them? What prodigal portion have I spent, that I should come to such penury?' (lines 36–9) In this phrasing, Orlando alludes to the parable

41 See Shannon, *The Accommodated Animal*, pp. 80–1.

42 E.g. Orsino's punning on hart/ heart at the opening of *Twelfth Night*, and the wordplay about the hunt in *Love's Labour's Lost* (IV. ii. 10–33).

43 See the discussion of Orlando's complaints in Egan, *Green Shakespeare*, pp. 94–5. Egan's reading of *AYL* has many points of contact with my own.

of the prodigal son (who had to sleep in a pigsty): the prodigal son is one who is, at least temporarily, outside the sphere of grace, like an animal. But if Orlando can find his way back to grace, perhaps the animals to whom he is compared can too.

Oliver seems to have an (Erasmian) natural antipathy for his brother: 'my soul (yet I know not why) hates nothing more than he' (lines 165–6), despite his concession of Orlando's natural gentility. Such natural antipathy is of course in another sense *unnatural*, and it takes a natural, animal-mediated process to adjust their relationship. Orlando comes upon Oliver in the forest but does not recognize his ragged brother, who is about to be attacked by a snake which has wound itself around his throat:

> But suddenly
> Seeing Orlando, it unlinked itself,
> And with indented glides did slip away
> Into a bush, under which bush's shade
> A lioness, with udders all drawn dry,
> Lay couching, head on ground, with cat-like watch
> When that the sleeping man should stir; for 'tis
> The royal disposition of that beast
> To prey on nothing that doth seem as dead.
> (IV. iii. 110–18)

Orlando fights and kills the lion – an act which might be considered treason against the king of the beasts;[44] he is driven by, as Oliver says, 'kindness, nobler ever than revenge, / And nature, stronger than his just occasion' (lines 128–9). Confrontations with animals do away with matters of plot and personal history (Orlando's *occasion*), and bring one face to face with the essentials of a relationship. The animals here are both emblems of Orlando and Oliver, and creatures with their own autonomous life, which makes the brothers' conflict seem relatively trivial. As in *As You Like It* as a whole, there is a stripping away of human plots and histories, replacing them with mere configurations or dispositions. The natural pattern trumps the trivia of history.

44 According to Edmund Howe in his continuation of Stow's *Annals* (1631), p. 836, James I at least once baited a lion with mastiffs: the one dog who survived was treated kindly by Prince Henry, who commanded his servant to 'make much of him, saying, hee that had fought with the King of beasts, should neuer after fight with any inferiour creature'. Henry VII, by contrast, after a similar contest, commanded that all mastiffs should be hanged, 'conceauing great disdaine, that an yll fauoured rascall curre should with such violent villany, assault the valiaunt Lyon king of all beasts' – John Caius, *Of English Dogges* (1576), p. 26. The anecdotes subtly tell us something about the royal personages' presumed characters.

Even the apocalyptic world of *King Lear*, though it emphasizes the monstrosity of human conflict, at the same time finds ways to connect people. *King Lear* is Shakespeare's fullest exploration of nature gone wrong. So cataclysmic is the play that mere human agency is not enough to explain it. Lear himself is 'full of changes' and subject to 'unruly waywardness' in his old age, rather as aged nature was supposed to be (I. i. 288, 298). Condemning Cordelia, he says that 'Nature is ashamed / Almost t' acknowledge hers' (lines 212–3), identifying himself in a way with Nature; as he banishes Kent, he says that 'nor our nature, nor our place can bear' his defiance (line 171). In a way, his division of the kingdom and his subsequent rage at the division's failure identify him with a fallen vision of the natural world: he is like Blake's Urizen, a creating deity whose creation is in fact a Fall.[45] His madness is a process in which 'majesty falls to folly' (line 149), with the full implications of the Fall – a Fall which ultimately works itself out in Albany's comment 'Fall, and cease' (V. iii. 265). Its centre is the moment of rage in the storm in which he demands that the thunder 'Crack nature's moulds, all germains spill at once' (III. ii. 8). The creative power of Nature turns destructive as its central figure turns upon himself. Yet the processes of natural creativity and proliferation persist in spite of this central fracture.

The prolific spilling of varied natural beings, though it may often be monstrous, is most often captured in the play's very ambiguous use of animals. France is concerned that Cordelia's offence must be 'monstrous', that 'her offence / Must be of such unnatural degree / That monsters it, or your fore-vouched affection / Fall into taint' (I. i. 217–21); if nature is fallen, it necessarily all becomes monstrous. But this raises a logical problem: if the monstrous is unexceptional, how can we distinguish the monstrous from the normatively natural? Albany (in Q only) argues that 'Humanity must perforce prey on itself / Like monsters of the deep' (IV. ii. 49–50); monstrosity has become necessity. Yet animal comparisons are needed to get him to that thought – Goneril and Regan are 'tigers, not daughters', worse than 'the head-lugged bear' (40, 42). There is a scale of badness (and some goodness) in nature, and the recognition of this helps to avoid the binary thinking that caused the crisis in the first place. Albany says, indeed, that a bear 'would lick' Lear, referring in a peculiar way to the myth that bears licked their offspring into shape: this image is one which fuses and intertwines nature and nurture, suggesting that partial redemption could come from the contemplation of that fusion. If nature (such as Lear's) is

45 See Bate, *Shakespeare and the English Romantic Imagination*, pp. 135–51 for an extensive discussion of Blake's debts to *King Lear*.

bad and wayward, it can only be corrected through a kindness that is also natural.[46]

The play's ambivalence about dogs reflects a similar process of thinking. At the height of his madness, Lear laments that 'The little dogs and all, / Trey, Blanch and Sweetheart, see, they bark at me' (III. vi. 62–3). Edgar may drive off these 'curs' with their poisonous teeth, but Lear's own language shows some potential affection for the dogs, which are little, and whose barking may be misinterpreted, like the speeches of his daughters: it is easy to identify Sweetheart with Cordelia, at least. Later, Lear reminds Gloucester of the sight of a dog barking at a beggar, calling this 'the great image of authority: a dog's obeyed in office' (IV. vi. 158–9). The Quarto here reads 'a dogge, so bade in office', suggesting that a dog is only bad because of its position in life (the compositorial mistake indicates that the line could at least be understood to mean this, and perhaps even that Shakespeare intended to pun on that sense). The beggar here also contributes to the emotional dynamic of Lear's mini-narrative: we see 'the creature run from the cur' (line 157), and there is a suggestion that the dog's power derives from the man's fear, as well as a reminder of the continuity between man's creaturely nature and the artificial role of a dog. Pondering Lear's night on the heath, Cordelia says that 'Mine enemy's dog, / Though he had bit me, should have stood that night / Against my fire' (IV. vii. 35–7): the idea seems to be that such a dog is the lowest of the low, but we may also consider the forgiveness we might owe to a dog whose biting is merely part of its nature, and whose ownership by an enemy is a mere accident. Dogs here become a figure of the lowest common denominator, perhaps even more powerful than the idea of unaccommodated man. As a result, there are more completely positive images of dogs too: the Fool says that 'Truth's a dog', albeit one who is punished while a worse dog 'Lady Brach may stand by the fire and stink' (I. iv. 111–3); it is important, he implies, to distinguish between good dogs and bad.[47] The good and loyal Kent compares himself to 'your father's dog' (II. ii. 136), and though he does so because he is being badly treated, he also reminds us of the virtues of such dogged service. Perhaps most notably, the servant who intervenes to fight Cornwall as he's blinding Gloucester is called a 'dog' (III. vii. 75); though this is an insult, it rebounds, for this man is truly, instinctively good, a credit to dogginess. Looming out of the background, this 'dog' comes to unexpected life in human form, taking instant, instinctive revenge on Cornwall's inhuman (yet exclusively human) cruelty.

[46] See Danby, *Shakespeare's Doctrine of Nature*.
[47] See Shannon, *The Accommodated Animal*, pp. 171–2.

Animal images, then, have a consistent doubleness: insults become compliments when one looks at the world from the right perspective. Images of virtue are also inverted, as when Lear refers to his 'pelican daughters' (III. iv. 75); the pelican, which was supposed to feed its young with its own blood, was a common image for Christ, but here it has been turned around, for their feeding on him is merely cannibalistic, even if it does anticipate Cordelia's Christlike saving of her father. She 'redeems nature from the general curse' (IV. vi. 206): as in Blake's mythology, there may be a hint of gnostic heresy at work here, in which the Son redeems a fallen Father/God.[48] For Gnostics, however, nature is fundamentally fallen, and in need of redemption from an order of grace outside itself.[49] *King Lear's* universe may be fallen, but only relatively so, for it contains some seeds of goodness, however peculiar (even monstrous) they may appear.

Gloucester calls Lear a 'ruined piece of nature' – as Danby points out, this word 'piece' here means masterpiece not fragment.[50] Gloucester thinks that the ruin of such a figure signifies the wearing out of the 'great world' to 'naught' (IV. vi. 134–5). But Gloucester is blind. The fact that one piece (or even masterpiece) of nature, one man is ruined and worn out does not point to the ruin of the whole world, even if it may seem so to do. The emphasis on one man as the centre and epitome of creation leads to too pessimistic and binary a form of thinking. Man can be called a worm or a wolf (e.g. III. vii. 63, IV. i. 33), but there is always more to him. Most powerfully, Lear can lament 'Why should a dog, a horse, a rat have life / And thou no breath at all?' (V. iii. 307–8), but does this mean that there is 'No, no, no life!' (line 304)? Of course it is platitudinous to say that 'life goes on', but the fact that it does is what gives life (and death) poignancy and meaning, even if that meaning is unbearable.

As we saw in the introduction, nature is full of superfluities: if we allow not nature more than nature wants, man's life is cheap as beast's, says Lear.[51] Whereas within the medieval worldview identified by Lewis, everything has its place, Shakespeare's world of nature is more disorderly, weird and wayward, proliferating things that seem to have no purpose.

48 See A. D. Nuttall, *The Alternative Trinity: Gnostic Heresy in Marlowe, Milton, and Blake* (Oxford: Clarendon Press, 1998).

49 Though Blake, I think, would not himself follow this line of thinking: his natural world is fallen, but he does not believe in a transcendent realm beyond it; his Eternity is in this world, in fragmented form. It is possible that Shakespeare may have inspired some of his thinking along these lines.

50 *Shakespeare's Doctrine of Nature*, p. 170. Danby cites Cleopatra calling Antony 'nature's piece 'gainst fancy' (V. ii. 99); see Introduction.

51 See Margreta de Grazia, 'The Ideology of Superfluous Things: *King Lear* as Period Piece', in Margreta de Grazia, Maureen Quilligan and Peter Stallybrass (eds.), *Subject and Object in Renaissance Culture* (Cambridge: Cambridge University Press, 1996), pp. 17–42.

Regan and Goneril try to circumscribe nature, telling Lear that 'nature in you stands on the very verge / Of her confine' (II. iv. 147–8), and Lear responds by saying that 'Age is unnecessary' (line 155). Later, he argues that 'The art of our necessities is strange' (III. ii. 70). What is natural may be in fact unnecessary and peculiar; the idea of what *ought* to be may become unnatural. The naked Edgar, as poor Tom, may be 'the thing itself' (III. iv. 106), a pure animal owing nothing to anyone else or any other animal, but this insight may be misleading; such radical independence is in fact *unnatural* and artificial, the result of Edgar going in disguise after he has become 'nothing' (II. iii. 21 – see Chapter 1, above).

Connections to other animals are not, in the end, 'sophisticated' as Lear claims (III. iv. 106), but natural, even if they are odd. Crab in *Two Gentlemen of Verona* along with the bear in *The Winter's Tale* may be the most memorably incongruous stage animals in Shakespeare, but it's possible that Shakespeare intends the physical stage presence of an animal in *King Lear*. At a moment when he claims that 'Nature's above art' (at least in some respects – IV. vi. 86), Lear catches sight of – and perhaps even picks up – a mouse. He gives it a 'piece of toasted cheese' (line 89). Promethean human art has been needed to toast that cheese, even if it is imaginary. Lear, now dressed in his wild flowers like a nature-god, has come to a nuanced understanding of the interplay between nature, art and necessity, and has arrived at the imaginative and improvisatory knowledge of what will suffice, not from an understanding of the external order of grace but from the sight of a mouse. As Horace put it in *Ars Poetica*, 'parturient montes, nascetur ridiculus mus': 'The mountains are in labour, but what's born is a silly little mouse'.[52] After all this volcanic grandeur, one of the deepest recognitions of connectedness comes in kindness to a mouse: Lear may be the ruined piece/masterpiece of Nature but, from his ruins, he can still bring forth a piece of cheese.

By contrast, Edmund, who proclaims himself a devotee of Nature as divinity, has no such insight or resources. His version of nature is curiously lifeless.[53] Lear begins the play hoping to give his 'largest bounty' 'Where nature doth with merit challenge' (I. i. 52–3). His intended sentiment is that nature and merit should go together, but his phrasing implies a conflict. Edmund, in turn, believes that his fundamental nature is meritorious, but it's not at all clear whether he thinks he is in control of his own nature or if it is fixed. Scornfully sceptical though he is of his father's astrological superstitions, he is wedded to the notion that he has 'More composition,

[52] Horace, *Ars Poetica*, line 139 (my translation).

[53] Kate Soper makes the valuable point that 'what God is to stand up for are rights of inheritance to land which no lusty Nature ever bestowed' – *What Is Nature?*, p. 28.

and fierce quality' because of the circumstances of his conception (I. ii. 12); he may believe that 'I should have been that I am, had the maidenliest star in the firmament twinkled on my bastardizing' (lines 131–3), but he ultimately assents to Edgar's view that 'The dark and vicious place' of his conception cost his father's eyes (V. iii. 173–4). Nature, for him, is merely his own bastard, lustful nature, and despite his confidence, there isn't much vigour or colour in his conception of it: to be natural, for him, is merely to be in opposition to legitimacy (I. ii. 18).[54] Once Nature becomes a simple divinity, it loses its strangeness and life, perhaps because, as C. S. Lewis argues, Nature as divinity can only be a partial picture of nature, made secondary by its opposition to other kinds of being[55] – mere legitimacy, in this case, which is a pallid thing to oppose.

As a result, Edmund's signature speech 'Thou, Nature, art my goddess' (I. ii. 1–22) is very abstract, full of the language of 'law' and 'custom', and even he himself has 'composition' and 'quality' rather than something more vital or animal.[56] When Lear invokes Nature's punishment on Goneril, the effect is much more biological:

> Hear, Nature, hear, dear goddess, hear!
> Suspend thy purpose, if thou didst intend
> To make this creature fruitful.
> Into her womb convey sterility,
> Dry up in her the organs of increase,
> And from her derogate body never spring
> A babe to honour her! If she must teem,
> Create her child of spleen, that it may live
> And be a thwart disnatured torment to her.
> Let it stamp wrinkles in her brow of youth,
> With cadent tears fret channels in her cheeks,
> Turn all her mother's pains and benefits
> To laughter and contempt, that she may feel
> How sharper than a serpent's tooth it is
> To have a thankless child! (I. iv. 275–89)

Even as he invokes sterility, Lear brings things to life: the cognate words *creature*, *increase* and *create* do physical work here, creasing and wrinkling,

[54] Simon Palfrey, *Shakespeare's Possible Worlds*, p. 27, argues that Edmund is 'avidly attuned to his determining "childness", rabidly fixed on life's revenge (against life, on behalf of life).' This reading is strong, but I would dissent from Palfrey's celebration of Edmund: he certainly seems to me to be 'against life' in others, perhaps surprised that it exists; yet he doesn't really act 'on behalf of life', preferring to dwell on his own origins and being unable to move beyond them.

[55] *The Discarded Image*, p. 37.

[56] See Danby, *Shakespeare's Doctrine of Nature*, pp. 44–5; Danby sees more life in Edmund than I do, and he sets up rather a different opposition between Edmund's version of nature and Lear's, but the reading is complementary to mine.

pressing things upon one another, evoking real, physicalized feelings. There is none of this in Edmund, whose repetitions of *base* and *legitimate* merely echo hollowly upon one another. Lear's language *teems*, spills over, and cuts across itself, thwarting his own nature, but Edmund's position as 'Loyal and natural boy' (II. i. 84) is a simple binaristic irony.

Even the ineffective Albany's nature is more vividly characterized: Goneril contrasts him with Edmund, accusing him of 'cowish terror' (IV. ii. 12). This is not just a matter of his supposed cowardice, but of his milkiness: like Macbeth, he is too full of the milk of human–kindness, a 'milk-livered' man (line 50). Goneril's ultimate derision is 'Marry, your manhood, mew!' (line 68 – Quarto only), which also relates him to Macbeth, who lets '"I dare not" wait upon "I would," / Like the poor cat i' the adage' (*Macbeth*, I. vii. 44–5). Though Goneril may prefer the manlier Edmund, the animalistic properties of Albany have more virtue. However compromised and self-thwarting human nature may become as a result of its connection to animality, it has more reality and life than the abstract, pseudo-self-sufficient nature-worship of an Edmund. A touch of animal nature makes the whole world kin, giving the lie to Edmund's claims of self-sufficiency.

Two dogs

The two most striking dogs on the Elizabethan and Jacobean stage illustrate the doubleness of animals, who can both complicate and clarify human relations. As with so many of the animals we've seen in this chapter, the complication is in some way redemptive, the clarification demonic and alienating.

The use of animals to simplify the complexity of human feeling and to supply clarity and force of motive is most fully developed in Rowley, Dekker and Ford's *The Witch of Edmonton*, where the devilish dog Tom helps along a murder. The play's antihero, Frank Thorney, who has bigamously married due to weak filial obedience, finds himself in an intolerably embarrassing tragic double bind, pursued by a clinging wife he doesn't want. In the play's centre, the dog enables him to cut this Gordian knot. The key scene begins with the dog alone on stage, saying:

> Now for an early mischief and a sudden.
> The mind's about it now. One touch from me
> Soon sets the body forward. (III. iii. 1–3)[57]

[57] References to William Rowley, Thomas Dekker and John Ford, *The Witch of Edmonton*, ed. Peter Corbin and Douglas Sedge (Manchester: Manchester University Press, 1999).

The suddenness of action the dog wants to propagate resembles the urgency of action Macbeth desires. Frank is in some ways depersonalized by this: *the* mind is *about* the murder; cognition is rather abstract and wafty, particularly as he will go on to say that he *never thought* of the murder before the dog influenced him. The dog can simplify and embody action, which he does by rubbing up against the young man; yet it's not clear that Frank consciously registers this: he does say 'Thank you for that', but in a rather abstracted way, which may partly refer to what his wife Susan has just said, the words that make him realize he will 'have more trouble' from her, and therefore may as well 'ease all at once' (lines 14–15). External prompts for his deed are hopelessly blurred in his mind, but in the end it doesn't matter, as the deed is done: indeed, he says ''Tis done now, what I ne'er thought on' (line 16) well before he actually commits the murder. The phrase ''Tis done' echoes Macbeth's similar anticipatory language, and shows how a deed's outcome seems to anticipate or pre-empt itself, acting as an Aristotelian final cause. His statement here, that he'd never thought of killing her, rather gives the lie to the dog's statement that the mind was about it before the scene began: the dog seems to know both more and less than the man, and that is the key point about animals on the Renaissance stage, wiser and simpler at the same time than man, they clarify even as they obscure, emblematizing the mystery of humanity and human relations.

Kinship relations are at the core of Shakespeare's most notable scenes with a real animal definitely present – Crab's appearances in *The Two Gentlemen of Verona*. Crab's first scene comes after Launce's parting with his human family. We never meet the rest of Launce's family, but his dog Crab stands in for them all, both pointing up and undermining human feelings about their connections to loved ones. Launce, malapropistically calling himself 'the prodigious son', a phrase that resonates with praises of human dignity such as Pico, tangling these up with the waywardness of fallen humanity represented by the parable of the Prodigal Son. Launce claims that his weeping is a typical fault of his family (his 'kind'), but Crab is less emotional:

> I think Crab my dog be the sourest-natured dog that lives; my mother weeping, my father wailing, my sister crying, our maid howling, our cat wringing her hands, and all our house in a great perplexity, yet did not this cruel-hearted cur shed one tear. He is a stone, a very pibble stone, and has no more pity in him than a dog. A Jew would have wept to have seen our parting; why, my grandam, having no eyes, look you, wept herself blind at my parting. (II. iii. 5–13)

He then proceeds to represent the scene of parting, using his shoes to represent his parents (his mother being the one with 'the worser sole' – line 17), his staff to represent his sister, his hat to represent the maid, and finishing up the mise-en-scene by saying 'I am the dog – no, the dog is himself, and I am the dog – O! the dog is me, and I am myself' (lines 21–3). Launce here wants to define his family's *kind*, their chief characteristics and nature but is unsure whether Crab fits in. The dog is a kind of dangerous supplement. The joke about the cat here is particularly good, but it is not that simple.[58] The cat, wringing her *hands*, does fit in, is humanized (and feminized), but the dog is different. But perhaps that's only because he's leaving with Launce, the one he really loves, perhaps he's just the manliest of them all (and therefore perhaps has the best soul). The idea of an animal as an object of comparison is brought into peculiar and brilliant relief here as a dog is compared to . . . a dog. The belief that animals are somehow simpler and more self-identical than humans is thereby challenged. The family is categorized, as being affectively self-similar, but then it is differentiated, as Launce ridiculously re-presents the scene, muddling himself and his dog on the way, mainly because he wants to show the lack of affect in Crab, who is somehow the point of the whole scene. The use of the staff and the shoes translates the humans into non-human terms, making them wooden (the joke about 'wood [mad] woman' seems to depend on wooden shoes being used – lines 27–8),[59] but that wood has a certain quality of life. Life and the capacity for emotion become relentlessly relative here. Harold Bloom observes that Launce (as a 'person-with-dog') is by far the liveliest character in the play,[60] but it is Crab who undoubtedly steals this scene without speaking. The comedy comes in the way he is made to *refer*: to himself in the other scene, to Launce, and to Launce's whole family. Even as he is most real, he is a metaphorical dog, carrying things to and fro.

The permeability of human and animal categories is developed in Crab's next big scene (IV. iv. 1–39), where he is rebuked for 'play[ing] the cur' with his master by pissing under the Duke's table. Launce's long speech gives a vivid sense of the dog as player, and the speech's subtlety comes in the way Launce turns from addressing the audience to speaking to his dog, whose

[58] John Bradshaw, *Cat Sense: The Feline Enigma Revealed* (London: Allen Lane, 2013), p. xii, comments of such jokes: 'The human mind is perfectly capable of simultaneously holding two apparently incompatible views about animals, without one negating the other. The idea that humans are in some ways like and in others unlike humans is behind the humour of countless cartoons and greetings cards; these simply would not be funny if the two concepts cancelled each other out'.

[59] If Theobald's emendation to F's 'would-woman' is right.

[60] Harold Bloom, *Shakespeare: The Invention of the Human* (New York: Riverhead Books, 1998), pp. 37–8.

thoughts (or rather absence of them) are invoked at the point of address. The dog, who acts as a reminder of the off-stage scene of his disgrace, is not himself reminded of it, being happy where he is, thank you very much. There is something very funny about addressing an animal in the second person, but it's no less queer than addressing the audience or soliloquizing; it is also essential to a proper and polite relationship with animals.[61] Crab has behaved impolitely among a 'company of three or four gentlemen-like dogs'; the sense of class-difference among animals is of course absurd in a way, but reminds us that there are differences between animals, as we've seen in the rest of this chapter, and that human status does tend to translate to their families, including their pets.

The inclusion of animals in a social hierarchy has important affective components. Launce, himself a servant, treats Crab as *his* servant, and is a better master to the dog than Proteus is to him.[62] Launce tells us that he saved Crab from drowning as a puppy, and has been trying to educate him since. Launce clearly takes *responsibility* for Crab in a way that few other Shakespearean characters do for one another: when the Duke wants to hang Crab for pissing under the table, Launce claims that he himself was the pisser, and is whipped out of the room for it. He asks 'How many masters would do this for his servant?' and we might ask how many other characters in all the plays so sacrifice themselves for another.[63] Launce's attempt to get Crab to mimic him ('Did not I bid thee still mark me, and do as I do?') is futile, as Crab steals puddings and pisses against ladies' legs, in a way that his master definitely does not; but the aim to inculcate imitation is a reminder of the translations between man and dog. Launce's inverted tendency to act as a scapegoat for his dog tells us more about his nature than anything. Launce, dealing with his dog, takes away the sins for which he is not responsible, rather like Christ. If Christ's grace is manifested in saving mankind, perhaps mankind has a concomitant duty to save a naughty dog. The fact that Launce has 'more wit' than his dog has enabled Crab to be saved, but of course from some perspectives Crab is a fool to have done so. The scene's comedy relies on Crab not being grateful ('Thou think'st not of this now'). But perhaps man is similarly ungrateful

61 See Haraway, *When Species Meet*, p. 92, on being polite to animals, particularly dogs.

62 Proteus, indeed, has callously told Launce to give Crab as a gift to Silvia. Is it too fanciful to see a parallel with God insisting on Abraham sacrificing Isaac? If it isn't too absurd, the way in which Launce is let out of the sacrifice while still following instructions develops the narrative. In any case the idea of sacrifice and substitution are central to the scene.

63 Desdemona's futile – and possibly self-damning – claim to have killed herself doesn't actually exonerate Othello as she intends.

to Christ, and can only express gratitude by passing on kindness down the natural spectrum.

In a gnomic and resonant passage of Romans, St Paul writes:

> the earnest expectation of the creature waiteth for the manifestation of the sons of God.
>
> For the creature was made subject to vanity, not willingly, but by reason of him who hath subjected *the same* in hope.
>
> Because the creature itself shall also be delivered from the bondage of corruption into the glorious liberty of the children of God.
>
> For we know that the whole creation groaneth and travaileth in pain together until now.
>
> And not only *they*, but ourselves also, which have the firstfruits of the Spirit, even we ourselves groan within ourselves, waiting for the adoption, *to wit*, the redemption of the body. (Romans 8.19–23).

The promised redemption of the human body is bound up here with the hope for redemption of other creatures (which may or may not happen).[64] Perhaps human redemption can only come about when we go down to an animal level, refusing to claim our privileged status.

Animals, then, challenge the human desire to be special, to be the be-all and the end-all, and challenge our attempts to make easy distinctions, forcing humans into a recognition of their own passivity even as human attitudes and ideas do seem, usually involuntarily, to transform the world. They provide a sense of an eerie under-action, going on below and sometimes running beyond the supposedly clear histories of human endeavour. Present or absent, they mediate the complexities of human feeling, but without oversimplifying them. They do so in ways that blur the human belief in clarity of motive and volition. The next chapter will deal with more voluntary human manipulation of Nature, in the arts of diet, medicine and health. But even in those spheres, nature has more mysteries than its manipulators would like to believe.

[64] For a discussion of this passage, see Agamben, *The Open*, pp. 60–2.

CHAPTER 3

Lawful as eating? Food, natural magic and the arts of health

Humanity's most significant way of interacting with the natural world is consuming it – either eating or wearing bits of it. In this way, people transform their environment and allow it to transform them, either as individuals or as social groups, bound together by their common relationship to the natural world.[1] Consumption is the essence of our relationship with the environment, but that consumption can be creative, communal and responsive rather than exploitative. The flipside of an exploitative attitude is a certain disdain for consumption. Hamlet asks himself 'What is a man, / If his chief good and market of his time / Be but to sleep and feed?' (IV. iv. 33–5 – Quarto only); Hamlet answers his own question, and concludes, rather glibly, that such a man would be 'A beast, no more'. He is searching for a higher system of value, and perhaps spotting it in Fortinbras's sense of martial honour (though he's not sure about that really).[2] But his way of framing the question is curious – why would eating be a 'market of his time'? This may be an instance of Hamletian hendiadys,[3] but it also withdraws from a larger question about the *summum bonum*, and suggests that eating and sleeping are forms of culturally motivated transaction: nothing, even the most basic and beastly of activities, is wholly natural;[4] all is part of a temporally motivated and organized art of living, designed to balance and move the humours that make a person who he is. The bodily humours – choler, melancholy, blood and phlegm – were part of a wider scheme which tied bodily health, psychology, the natural elements, and even the planets together in a system of natural harmony. Michael Schoenfeld's now-classic study of bodies and selfhood in Shakespeare's time emphasizes

1 On food as a crucial vector of human relatedness – to the environment, to others, to the divinity – see David B. Goldstein, *Eating and Ethics in Shakespeare's England* (Cambridge: Cambridge University Press, 2013).
2 See Bradshaw, *Shakespeare's Scepticism*, pp. 8–9.
3 Kermode, *Shakespeare's Language* (Harmondsworth: Allen Lane, 2000), pp. 101–2.
4 There may also be a foreshadowing here of Lear's idea that 'man's life is *cheap* as beast's' if we don't allow nature more than nature needs (II. iv. 267, emphasis added).

the 'experiential suppleness' of humoral theory, showing that the human body is experienced as microcosm of the universe, 'interpenetrated' by the humours in complex (and often controversial) ways; this means that though we post-Cartesians may think of physiological language for the emotions as metaphorical, Renaissance writers were much more literal in their usage of such terms.[5] He argues that such language was empowering to the individual, whose control of his own food intake enabled him to have agency over his own emotions.[6] Gail Kern Paster develops some of Schoenfeld's key arguments, showing that the theory of humours enabled individuals to feel strongly interpenetrated and linked with one another and with their environment;[7] if this does not quite involve the modern concept of empathy, it perhaps offers a more visceral imaginative basis for human connectedness than the rather bloodless (not to say cholerless, etc.) and appropriative feeling modern thinkers now often consider central to humanness.[8] Yet this visceral feeling requires the operation of various responsive, interactive arts – arts of cooking, arts of communal eating, and other more magical arts of transformation and connection.

This chapter will explore some of those connections as mediated through food, medicine, and natural magic – these areas may seem to a modern

[5] Michael C. Schoenfeld, *Bodies and Selves in Early Modern England: Physiology and Inwardness in Spenser, Shakespeare, Herbert, and Milton* (Cambridge: Cambridge University Press, 1999), pp. 3, 8.

[6] *Bodies and Selves*, pp. 11, 22–3; in making this case, Schoenfeld offers a powerful counterargument to the abjection of selfhood in New Historicist readings of the Renaissance.

[7] *Humoring the Body*, p. 14: 'In the dynamic reciprocities between self and environment imagined by the psychophysiology of bodily fluids, circumstance engenders humors in the body and humors in the body help to determine circumstance by predisposing the individual subject to a characteristic kind of evaluation and response'.

[8] On empathy, see Simon Baron-Cohen, *The Essential Difference: Men, Women, and the Extreme Male Brain* (London: Allen Lane 2003); Baron-Cohen argues that autism is an extreme form of a 'male' tendency to lack empathy; while he acknowledges that the other extreme (excessive empathy – extreme 'female'-ness) can exist, he does not believe that this would be in any way a pathology: we may, however be reminded of George Eliot's warning that 'If we had a keen vision and feeling of all ordinary human life, it would be like hearing the grass grow and the squirrel's heart beat, and we should die of that roar which lies on the other side of silence. As it is, the quickest of us walk about well wadded with stupidity' – *Middlemarch*, ed. David Carroll (Oxford: Clarendon Press, 1986), p. 189. It is surely significant that Eliot here gives as her example an animal that humans don't *use* and don't treat as vermin, one that seems decorative at best (as grass also is in domestic contexts); that life which stands independent of us still has some relationship to us, but is kept silent and properly mysterious. The last sentence of the paragraph elegantly cuts both ways: the main sense is probably a regret that *even* the most alert ('quickest') of us is wadded with stupidity to a degree, but there may also be a rueful acknowledgement that those most filled with life ('quickest') are so wadded. For a telling protest against the overuse of the concept of empathy, see Thom Gunn, 'Save the word', in *Boss Cupid* (London: Faber, 2000), p. 73: 'Doesn't it make / a rather large claim? Think you can / syphon yourself / into another human[?]'. On the late C20th/ early C21st vogue for empathy (a word invented only in the twentieth century), see Sophie Ratcliffe's *On Sympathy* (Oxford: Oxford University Press, 2008), p. 5; Ratcliffe, like Gunn, thinks sympathy a more useful concept than empathy.

audience decidedly unrelated but were firmly intertwined in the Renaissance, particularly as new Paracelsian ideas created controversy over food.[9] In Dekker's *The Wonder of a Kingdom* (1630), the virtuous and hospitable Gentili tells an apothecary

> I honour their profession,
> What the Creator does, they in part doe,
> For a Phisician's a man-maker too,
> —But honest friend,
> My kitchin is my Doctor, and my Garden,
> Trustie Apothecarie; when they give me pills
> So gently worke they, I'me not choak'd with bills,
> Which are a stronger purge than the disease.
> . . .
> Man was first borne sound, and hee growes ill
> Seldome by course of nature, but by will.
> (IV. ii. 109–16, 129–30)

Medicine is not a separate sphere but is attached to broader regime of food, bodily health, and moral action. That regime is part of an organized attitude to common daily time: an art of living, associated with the roots of the word 'diet', a word which originally means 'course of life, way of living or thinking' (OED diet, *n1*), and which people of Shakespeare's age may have (falsely) etymologically connected with the Latin *dies*, day. Hamlet argues that 'Your worm is your only emperor for diet' (IV. iii. 21), and as such is the ruler of the daily round, the ultimate bringer of health, for the word was also associated with medical regimes. This means that it also becomes associated with the idea of caring for someone, for to share a diet is to share a life, for good or ill.[10]

The difficulties of healthy discrimination between good and bad natural substances are acute, particularly when there is no unitary orthodoxy about what is healthy, and a clear sense that different people, with different humoral complexions, need different foods. This encourages a considerable degree of relativism in the matter of food, particularly in an age when there were major regional variations in food consumption, and when eating habits were constantly evolving: increased trade in the early sixteenth

9 In this and much of what follows, I am indebted to Joan Thirsk's *Food in Early Modern England: Phases, Fads, Fashions 1500–1700* (London: Continuum, 2006).

10 Lady Percy describes the dead Hotspur in terms that anticipate Ophelia's lament for Hamlet: 'He was indeed the glass / Wherein the noble youth did dress themselves / . . . / To seem like him; so that in speech, in gait, / In diet, in affections of delight, / In military rules, humours of blood, / He was the mark and glass, copy and book, / That fashioned others' – *Henry IV Part Two*, II. iii. 21–2, 28–32.

century brought new foodstuffs, but then worse weather in the late Elizabethan period (continuing for much of the seventeenth century)[11] brought about a sense of food crisis, forcing people to rediscover older foods. Food and the natural environment are therefore firmly tied together. If the sixteenth century was a time of social and religious revolution, changes in food consumption were at least as prominent in individuals' daily lives, and provide a vector for thinking about instability of all kinds. Food and the associated arts of health become highly contested, relativistic matters, whose efficacy is a matter of opinion or perspective.

Joan Fitzpatrick argues that 'Food is . . . a dramatist's short hand way of delineating character (the ascetic, Stoic, and glutton) and rank (the hungry poor, feasting aristocrats, and lean soldiers), but in Shakespeare's hands it is exploited in a particularly subtle way, being used to engage with debates about cosmopolitanism, expanding international trade, religion, and philosophy'.[12] Not all of these debates will be addressed in this chapter, though they may be in the background; rather, I want to consider food, medicine and related matters of bodily consumption as vectors for personal transformation. As the key moment of eating in medieval religion – the Eucharist – became at least partly desacralized, some of its communal, sacred, grace-giving properties may have been distributed into other forms of consumption. Fitzpatrick is certainly right that thinking about food had a centripetal effect: it seems to bring almost every aspect of human life to the table.[13] Food is the most direct form of connection between man and nature, and is also the most basic form of cultural art.

Eating is one of the most powerful and (literally) visceral modes in which translation can take place. Hamlet demonstrates to Claudius that 'a king may go a progress through the guts of a beggar' (IV. iii. 30–1); his joke is minatory as well as monitory, but it is also founded on a very particular instance. Polonius, whom he has just killed, is 'At supper', 'Not where he eats, but where 'a is eaten' (lines 17–18). The evening's festivities have gone wrong after Hamlet's play; supper is cancelled and inverted; and the abstract 'something rotten' in the state of Denmark has become concrete, in

11 This was the result of the Little Ice Age: see John F. Richards, *The Unending Frontier: An Environmental History of the Early Modern World* (Berkeley: University of California Press, 2005).

12 Joan Fitzpatrick, *Food in Shakespeare: Early Modern Dietaries and the Plays* (Farnham: Ashgate, 2007), p. 10.

13 See also Estok, *Ecocriticism and Shakespeare*, p. 56, who argues that 'in the representations of illness, we witness a linking of two worlds (the human and the natural), realms that in other discursive areas of the period are increasingly being drawn apart. Illness in the literature of the time is often a process of hybridization of the human and the natural, a process and experience of blurring, rather than a static identity of dis-ease that threatens the firm division between human and nonhuman'.

the form of Polonius's corpse. Polonius has been reduced to being 'the guts' (III. iv. 212), and there is a sense in which the earthly world is merely one of digestion. For all its preoccupation with matters of heaven and hell, *Hamlet* is a play which pulls us back into earthly, digestive reality, full of unweeded gardens and maggots breeding in a dead dog's guts. Hamlet tells Claudius to 'send' someone to find Polonius in heaven, or to search for him himself in hell but brings us back from these metaphysical worlds with perhaps Shakespeare's most shockingly crude joke: 'if indeed you find him not within this month, you shall nose him as you go up the stairs into the lobby' (IV. iii. 35–7). Embodying and therefore refusing to rarefy the sense of smell by the use of 'nose' as a verb, Hamlet also punningly insists that the only kind of *knowing* is bodily, unpleasantly savoury (and takes place in liminal places, for that matter). There are no magical, Eucharistic transubstantiations (a topic he comes back to in his discussion with the gravedigger). Indeed the play's major translation of food comes when we are told that 'the funeral baked meats / Did coldly furnish forth the marriage tables' (I. ii. 180–1); Claudius has attempted to transpose the play's genre and mood, 'With mirth in funeral, and with dirge in marriage' (line 12), but Hamlet insists that this is not really transformative, being merely a matter of 'Thrift' (line 180). In some ways the dietary economy of a play's world determines the nature of its outcome: in *Hamlet*, there are no real translations or purgations – the solid flesh will not melt; but in other plays, food can offer as powerful a mode of transformation as the Eucharist once did. As with Shakespeare's uses of the countryside and of animals, food and the arts of health are more redemptive when they are accepted communally, with responsive, adaptive passivity, and more perilous when people try individualistically to master them. They enable an access of grace – or at least a movement towards grace – when people take them on faith: as with modern notions of faith healing, their efficacy depends on belief.

Interconnected as the various aspects of diet and health are, it is nonetheless possible to make some distinctions as to Shakespeare's use of them. This chapter therefore deals first with the power of healing women, showing how their powers are associated with natural eating, and with their abilities to harness the faith of a community. The next section deals with the communal aspects of hospitality, examining the redemptive powers of group eating. I then move on to a brief discussion of starvation, which Shakespeare represents as the result of individualistic alienation. I conclude with an examination of medicines, poisons and magic, seeing the different effects these have depending on the frame of mind of their users. This cues up the next chapter, in which Prospero's attempts at mastery over nature are grudgingly shuffled off.

Healing women

Helena in *All's Well that Ends Well*, Shakespeare's most medical woman, is constantly associated with food. We saw in the previous chapter that Lear offers a bit of toasted cheese to a (possibly imaginary) mouse; that use of cheese is probably a marker of Lear's poverty as well as his animal sympathies, for cheese was generally thought of as a lower-class dish; Lear has become a lowest-common-denominator, but that may paradoxically make him every inch a king, one who touches the bass-string of humility. Parolles associates Helen with that lowest-common-denominator foodstuff when he complains that her virginity is

> against the rule of nature. To speak on the part of virginity is to accuse your mothers, which is most infallible disobedience. He that hangs himself is a virgin; virginity murders itself, and should be buried in highways out of all sanctified limit, as a desperate offendress against nature. Virginity breeds mites, much like a cheese, consumes itself to the very paring, and so dies with feeding his own stomach. (*All's Well*, I. i. 135–43)

The connections Parolles makes here are of the head-spinning variety: controversies over the value of virginity, suicide, disobedience to parents, the law of nature, and health are all tied together with the rotting, unhealthy cheese.[14] The habits of analogical thinking that once gave a sense of order have now created something eerie and chaotic. Yet Parolles here also reminds us of Hamlet, and Helena of Ophelia: Hamlet, keen to send his unbeloved to a nunnery, tells her father that 'the sun breed[s] maggots in a dead dog' and warns Polonius not to let Ophelia 'walk i' the sun' in case of such conception (*Hamlet*, II. ii. 181–4). In both cases, there is an anxiety about vicious parthenogenesis, a sense that feminine Nature may be dangerously creative without male intervention. Both Hamlet and Parolles, men of words, worry about such self-oriented naturally unnatural conception, and Ophelia dies a virgin suicide, a fate Helena avoids. The difference between comedy – however problematic – and tragedy may simply be that between a cheese and a dead dog.

[14] Parolles is probably just referring to rotten cheese, but it's just possible that he's thinking of cheese deliberately matured with live cheese mites, such as modern Milbenkäse; such cheese, more common in Europe then than now, was particularly disdained in England – see Thirsk, *Food in Early Modern England*, p. 16.

Helena herself is the most notably and professionally magical of Shakespeare's healing heroines, a representative of feminine Nature in its most positively double aspect. The Countess, who later declares herself a mother to Helena in a variety of important senses, describes her in awkwardly complex terms which point to her exceptional qualities:

> I have those hopes of her good that her education promises her dispositions she inherits, which makes fair gifts fairer; for where an unclean mind carries virtuous qualities, there commendations go with pity: they are virtues and traitors too. In her they are the better for her simpleness; she derives her honesty, and achieves her goodness. (I. i. 39–45)

Boiled down, this means that she has inherited good qualities and has preserved them by good behaviour, but despite the claim of 'simpleness' (which may nod to the idea of a herbalist's ingredients, or 'simples'), the Countess's syntax here demonstrates the difficulty of squaring nature with nurture in the case of even a virtuous woman; perhaps the difficulty derives from the Calvinist doctrine that no one can take credit for any grace they have: while we may want to praise such apparently natural virtue, it is not quite hers. This is an issue that seems particularly acute in the case of a woman, for whom virtue is normatively associated with the passive quality of chastity. In addition to this problem, if Helena represents created nature, endowed with some of God's healing grace, she is both superior to the artifice of the social world, but inferior when considered in relation to the divinity. Given that she is presented more often in relation to God than to society, that comparison may seem more urgent; she may be held to higher standards precisely because she is an agent of the divine.

Helena's power comes from her father, 'whose skill was almost as great as his honesty; had it stretch'd so far, would have made nature immortal, and death should have play for lack of work' (lines 18–21). Insistently comparative, this seems like a description of the ultimate father: one who is nearly divine – if not God, the primal father Adam. Even that most (temporarily) perfect of men could not defeat mortality, yet his failure cannot be condemned by humans who are supposedly his descendants, for he is worthy of the fullest filial–patriarchal reverence. Helena's father 'was skilful enough to have liv'd still, if knowledge could be set up against mortality' (lines 30–1), but skill – human art – is not enough: indeed mere *knowledge* is associated with mortality through the tree of knowledge in Eden, which brought death into the world. Despite being a woman, though, Helena *can* defeat mortality. Natural woman as giver of life is in some ways more powerful than masculine art.[15]

The King's illness seems to spread throughout his realm: we are told that the gentry 'are sick', albeit because they lack a martial outlet for 'breathing and exploit' (I. ii. 16–17); later, we are told that 'the younger of our nature, / That surfeit on their ease, will day by day / Come here [to the Italian wars] for physic' (III. i. 16–18), suggesting that bloodlettting is necessary. When they are setting off to war, the lords hope that they will find the king healed on their return, as if their fighting might effect a cure (II. i. 5–10). Yet it's clear that the war is not the cause of the cure: the idea of a connection between King and masculine gentry is too circular, for it's not clear which is the root of the illness. The King has given up on the medical care of male physicians, 'under whose practices he hath persecuted time with hope, and finds no other advantage in the process but only the losing of hope by time' (I. i. 12–15). Their art is mere *practice*, with a sense that they are fooling him, deluding him with false hope: hope is a cardinal virtue, but its false version is all the worse for the high status of its true form. Helena is needed to redeem this into truth. Physicians and soldiers can't cure the king: an external (but still natural) force is required.

As she sets about her father's business, Helena's language describing his medical art is strange and awkward, almost contradictory: she says that his 'prescriptions' were

> Of rare and proved effects, such as his reading
> And manifest experience had collected
> For general sovereignty; and that he willed me
> In heedfull'st reservation to bestow them,
> As notes whose faculties inclusive were
> More than they were in note. (I. iii. 222–7)

These medicines are both rare and proved, both general and to be reserved; they are notes in the sense of being prescriptions but not noted in the sense that they are not famous; they are sovereign in the sense of being supreme panaceas, but also – we may infer – in being particularly applicable to

15 For a fine discussion of the implications of this, particularly of the ways in which Helena subverts male power, see Harry Berger, Jr., *Making Trifles of Terrors: Redistributing Complicities in Shakespeare*, ed. Peter Erickson (Stanford, CA: Stanford University Press, 1997), p. 289; for a similar line of thinking, though with a more negative picture of Helena's power, see Ian McAdam, *Magic and Masculinity in Early Modern English Drama* (Pittsburgh: Duquesne University Press, 2009), pp. 166–78.

the king. Book-learning and experience are tangled up here, as are art and nature, universality and specificity; nature is both a book that is easy to read and a matter of secret knowledge. Helena is 'a poor unlearnèd virgin' (line 240) but can trump the art of schools, even the art of her own father. All this is mere preface, though: she says of her particular remedy for the king, 'There's something in't / More than my father's skill, which was the great'st / Of his profession, that his good receipt / Shall for my legacy be sanctified / By th' luckiest stars in heaven' (lines 242–6). What she may have added, in order to sanctify the legacy she hands on, is her love for Bertram (her 'bright particular star'), but it may also be her own special grace, based on the astrological signs of her birth.

The king, a good Protestant it seems, may believe that 'labouring art can never ransom nature / From her inaidible estate' (II. i. 118–9) but an art that is more natural and less laborious may be effective. Paradoxically, though, a more conspicuously artful language is needed to invoke this natural cure, as the play turns to the longest passage of rhyming couplets in Shakespeare's works (lines 130–210). Helena invokes God as 'He that of greatest works is finisher', and claims to be His 'weakest minister' (lines 136–7); as she makes this modest claim she suggests that God's creation is unfinished, needing her aid to make it complete. She argues against the king's scepticism and claims that he is rejecting 'Inspired merit' (line 148) which comes by 'The greatest Grace lending grace' (line 160). Though she's careful to insist that she's merely the agent of divinity, she does take risks on her own account, saying that if she fails she should be subject to 'Tax of impudence, / A strumpet's boldness, a divulgèd shame' (lines 170–1). It is as if she is provisionally staking her virginity on the effort, using that apparently passive (and, as Parolles said, unnatural) virtue as leverage against the deity. She is even prepared to die, and, as the king says, this shows that she must have either 'Skill infinite, or monstrous desperate' (line 184). She is (in a sense) desperate to earn Bertram as a husband, but the invocation here of monstrosity and infinitude, give her properties that place her outside nature as normatively conceived: she is the unnaturally natural that is needed to redeem nature's failings.

Hearing of Helena's success, Parolles says that it is 'the rarest argument of wonder that hath shot out in our latter times' (II. iii. 7–8). Wonder, as Bacon suggested, is the response of 'broken knowledge', and Lafew agrees that such miraculous events mean that 'we should submit ourselves to an unknown fear' (lines 5–6) rather than 'make trifles of terrors' (lines 3–4). Human presumption is brought down to earth at the very moment a human – 'an earthly actor', as Lafew puts it – performs 'a heavenly effect' (line 24).[16] There is something very strange about such an extraordinary and fearful event taking place in a comedy, yet it is after all an event of renewal. It is possible that Parolles' and Lafew's attitude links to the turn of the century in some way: after many had believed that the world might end in 1600, people had to face a cancelling of apocalyptic hopes and fears, and mutedly greeted the world's continuance/ renewal, recognizing that they were not living in end times but in the middle of things. It is perhaps significant that this muted wonder should be mediated through Parolles, who later accepts 'Simply the thing I am / Shall make me live' (IV. iii. 333–4); people now have to accept the (natural) world on its own terms, without a sense of the promised end to give shape to their lives.

After the cure, the King is 'of as able body as when he numbered thirty' (IV. v. 80–1), but later uses the argument that 'we are old' as a reason for urgency in his plans. His royal *we* here may incidentally bespeak a generalized sense of the antiquity of the world even when redemptive renewal has been accomplished on an individual level. Earlier, the cured King could wonder at Bertram's rejection of Helena in similarly general terms, saying

> Strange is it that our bloods,
> Of colour, weight, and heat, poured all together,
> Would quite confound distinction, yet stands off
> In differences so mighty. If she be
> All that is virtuous – save what thou dislik'st,
> A poor physician's daughter – thou dislik'st
> Of virtue for the name. (II. iii. 118–24)

He goes on to say that Bertram's is 'a dropsied honour' (line 128). There is a kind of general sickness that prevents us recognizing virtue, which is the only meaningfully special or exceptional thing in the world, but which cannot be picked out by the mere skill of a physician examining blood; there is a need to understand true 'difference' rather than mere social 'distinction'. The King makes her status higher, and Bertram significantly calls this act a 'great creation' (line 169); he is referring to the creation of noble status, but the phrase resonates with the idea of great creating Nature. If this allegorically makes the King a god, then Helena is the supplementary natural agency that redeems even God himself, or at least that which completes his creation.

16 Alison Shell, *Shakespeare and Religion*, p. 11, comments that Lafew's discussion of miracles here 'evokes Protestant denigration of Catholic miracle in a way which invests Helena with a saintly aura, but also reminds us that her achievement is explicable in natural terms'.

The King, before being cured, seemed to be willing himself to death, following the example of Bertram's father, whom he cites as saying

> 'Let me not live' –
> This his good melancholy oft began,
> On the catastrophe and heel of pastime,
> When it was out – 'Let me not live,' quoth he,
> 'After my flame lacks oil, to be the snuff
> Of younger spirits, whose apprehensive senses
> All but new things disdain; whose judgements are
> Mere fathers of their garments; whose constancies
> Expire before their fashions.' This he wished.
> I, after him, do after him wish too,
> Since I nor wax nor honey can bring home,
> I quickly were dissolvèd from my hive
> To give some labourers room. (I. ii. 55–67)

Even to ventriloquize the dead friend's death-wish is problematic here, and it could be self-treason, as it involves imagining the death of the king. The friend's 'good melancholy' seems paradoxical to us but refers to the idea that *some* degree of melancholy, as long as it wasn't stagnant, was necessary for humoral balance. There's also a healthy sense that he doesn't want to live too long and wither out the days of his son. In Middleton's *The Phoenix* (1604), the father/king abdicates in favour of youth, and that play celebrates the transition from Elizabeth's to James's rule. If *All's Well* was written around the same time, its portrayal of royal succession is more problematic:[17] the King's son does not appear in they play, and Lafew says that 'your dolphin is not lustier' than the cured King (II. iii. 26); if this refers to the Dauphin, it does rather suggest that the cure has resulted in the King (who feels himself to be thirty again) absorbing his son's youth, and therefore in a sense usurping or displacing him. Nature may abhor a vacuum, but it also doesn't allow there to be two things of the same kind: as Andrew Marvell puts it, 'Nature that hateth emptiness / Allows

[17] Or at least problematic in a different way: see my discussion of *The Phoenix* in *Problem Fathers*, pp. 126–8. *All's Well* remains one of the most difficult Shakespeare plays to date. I am strongly inclined to date it earlier than *Measure for Measure* (whose bed-trick surely derives from that of *All's Well* and its source), and to place it around 1603–4; I am not convinced by arguments for a later date, which seem to hang too much on the use of the name 'Spurio'; See MacD. P. Jackson, 'Spurio and the Date of *All's Well That Ends Well*', *Notes and Queries* 48 (2001), 299; Quentin Skinner, 'A Spurious Dating for *All's Well that Ends Well*,' *Notes and Queries* 60 (2013): 429–34, has convincingly shown that there is no reason to accept the later date, and is inclined to date the play 1604–5. My point, in any case, would be to see it as a play of early Jacobean royal renewal, as well as of post-millennial exhaustion.

of penetration less'.[18] If the King is made young, the young prince must disappear.

Perhaps, then, renewal always comes at a cost. Helena's own purported death tends to suggest this. Thinking her dead, the Countess describes Helena as 'the most virtuous gentlewoman that ever nature had praise for creating. If she had partaken of my flesh, and cost me the dearest groans of a mother, I could not have owed her a more rooted love' (IV. v. 9–12); as often elsewhere in Shakespeare, love is the result of suffering.[19] The roots of love between the Countess and Helena are fascinating, though, lacking the implicit competition that we might see between the King and his son. Fatherhood may be a zero-sum game, but sympathy between women is more creative. As the Countess realizes Helena is in love with Bertram, she says

> Even so it was with me when I was young.
> If ever we are nature's, these are ours. This thorn
> Doth to our rose of youth rightly belong;
> Our blood to us, this to our blood is born.
> It is the show and seal of nature's truth,
> Where love's strong passion is impressed in youth.
> By our remembrances of days foregone,
> Such were our faults, or then we thought them none.
> (I. iii. 128–35)

This moment, and the scene with Helena that follows, constitute perhaps the most fully sympathetic sequence in all of Shakespeare's plays. The use of rhyme here ties the sympathy to the later cure of the King, intimating that the extra 'something' Helena brings to her cure derives in part from the blessing given her by the Countess. The fact that the speech above is not quite a soliloquy, being unusually preceded by an entry for Helena, means that a kind of magical, not quite spoken connection between the two is enabled before their dialogue. That dialogue works itself out through a riddle, with Helena becoming alarmed when the Countess declares herself her mother. Comically tricksy as this is, however, there is an underlying emotional simplicity in the Countess's statement 'You know, Helen, / I am a mother to you' (lines 138–9), for it simply means, 'I love you'. The natural, rooted connection between the two women creates a powerfully sinless circle of forgiveness, even redemption, where faults are none because they are natural; where the pain of the thorn is inflicted on the rose itself,

18 'An Horatian Ode upon Cromwell's Return from Ireland', lines 41–2.

19 Particularly maternal suffering: see *Richard II*, V. ii. 102–10 and *3 Henry VI*, I, i. 220–4.

the thorn is not a symbol of nature's fallenness, but perhaps of Christ's sacrifice. The Countess asks 'What's the matter, / That this distempered messenger of wet, / The many-coloured Iris, rounds thine eye?' (lines 150–2). This is a beautiful moment: only by looking very closely at the girl's eyes growing bigger with tears could she possibly see prismatic division of light in them; Iris is a goddess of divine communication, suggesting that the Countess is a higher goddess ready to give good news; but most importantly, the rainbow is a symbol of divine forgiveness and covenant, which is all the more powerfully conveyed here for being quietly implicit. Like the ideal doctor Helena picks out in her description of her father, the Countess reads her and refers her reading to felt experience. She recognizes that for Helena to think of Bertram as a brother might 'curd' her blood (line 149); this is more than the cliché modern sense of 'blood-curdling': it is felt in the shared humour of blood, which turns to mothers' milk, and which might therefore become cheese if left to stagnate. The Countess sees that Helena must get moving to avoid this, for she *shares* this natural humour.

One may be passively subject to such a humoral problem, but one can also manage to fashion one's own natural destiny through an act of will.[20] Helena's great moment of decision comes before she gets the Countess's blessing, even if that blessing is needed to set her going with full confidence. When Bertram sets off for court, Helena thinks it a pity

> That wishing well had not a body in't,
> Which might be felt, that we, the poorer born,
> Whose baser stars do shut us up in wishes,
> Might with effects of them follow our friends,
> And show what we alone must think, which never
> Returns us thanks. (I. i. 181–6)

This is a wonderful moment of the exercise of the embodied but curiously passive will: she wishes that she could send her will, like a guardian angel, to follow her beloved; yet she is also conscious that her birth, both in terms of status and astrological determinism, lock her into immobility, a mere goodwill that cannot be reciprocated. The tension between active and passive views of the will here chimes with Calvinist views of the will participating in salvation, but not actively so. Her desire for *thanks* is powerful here, for it presses forward into the thanks the King will give her for the cure: he begins their long sequence of rhymed lines by saying 'thanks I give' for her good thoughts of him, insisting that a King ought to

[20] See Schoenfeld, *Bodies and Selves*.

be 'grateful' (II. i. 130, 129). Gratefulness connects, etymologically at least, with the order of grace that will enable her to change her life.

Reciprocity, of various kinds, is central to this. Prompted by the simple goodwill of the otherwise empty Parolles,[21] who says 'Get thee a good husband, and use him as he uses thee' (I. i. 214–5), Helena decides that she can find something in herself to make the best of her world:

> Our remedies oft in ourselves do lie,
> Which we ascribe to heaven; the fated sky
> Gives us free scope; only doth backward pull
> Our slow designs when we ourselves are dull.
> What power is it which mounts my love so high,
> That makes me see, and cannot feed mine eye?
> The mightiest space in fortune nature brings
> To join like likes, and kiss like native things.
> Impossible be strange attempts to those
> That weigh their pains in sense, and do suppose
> What hath been cannot be. Who ever strove
> To show her merit that did miss her love?
> (lines 216–27)

That last question may well prompt some negative answers in our minds, but it doesn't seem to worry Helena. There are some links in this to both Cassius's and Edmund's scepticism about astrological influence, but the tone is different, more open to experience, ready to accept having a wider and freer 'scope' and 'space', and informed by love. She seems to resolve the tension between free will and determinism that was such a problem for both Stoics and Calvinists, accepting that the very fact of determinism gives the conditions for us to work our own good, perhaps even our own salvation. Russ McDonald suggests that the key ethos of the late plays is 'not trying too hard',[22] and in this respect at least Helena resembles the heroines of those romance worlds. She is ready to be *fed*, accepting her natural state as one who receives things from the world as much as she tries to change things from outside. She is prepared to believe that there is more in nature than a stringent philosophy would insist.

21 Lafew describes Parolles as one 'whose villainous saffron would have made all the unbaked and doughy youth of a nation in his colour' (IV. v. 2–4), suggesting that he would have made cowards of them all by making them yellow. Yet, just as it's not at all clear that saffron is a bad thing, it's not clear that Parolles is really villainous: coward he may be, but it was not he who corrupted Bertram. Such saffron figures are often catalysts in Shakespeare – secret ingredients that make things go well. Autolycus, in *The Winter's Tale*, is another.

22 *Shakespeare's Late Style*, p. 148.

Dwelling in possibility a little like Emily Dickinson, she is more prepared to be a king of infinite space than Hamlet, and is happier than the Danish Prince to deal with strange attempts. She loves her 'bright particular star' (line 86) – an arbitrary choice, perhaps, but a *natural* one – and though she initially thinks he is out of her sphere as Polonius tells Ophelia that Hamlet is a prince out of her star, she is more able and prepared than Ophelia to do something about it.[23] Whereas Hamlet 'know[s] not seem', and insists that his outside suit of woe does not match his sorrow, Helena frankly admits that she plays a role to some extent, saying 'I do affect a sorrow indeed, but I have it too' (line 50): it's easy to see this line as meaning that she has a real sorrow for Bertram and an affected one for her father, but that doesn't really fit with her reverence for her father; the apparent disjunction between outward show and inner feeling is more complex in her case than in Hamlet's, entangling romantic love and filial reverence, but allowing each to redeem the other, whereas for Hamlet the feelings destroy one another.

Helena's winning of a husband saves her from woe for her father, but her father's legacy enables her to get going on that. The cure itself, though, is not enough to win Bertram: the cruder and less natural process of the bed-trick is necessary. There is a hint of magical fairy tale stuff in this incident, particularly in the exchange of rings involved. Bertram's ring is his paternal inheritance, whereas Helena's is one given her by the king as a token of thanks and promise of favour: it's clear enough what this means, simply representing the origins of the couple's status, with the exchange representing the unification of those statuses and origins. The rings are rather a simplifying symbol, though, for the sexual exchange is more complicated: after she has slept with Bertram, Helena marvels

O, strange men,
That can such sweet use make of what they hate,
When saucy trusting of the cozened thoughts
Defiles the pitchy night; so lust doth play
With what it loathes for that which is away.
(IV. iv. 21–5)

To say the least, this is an ambivalent reflection on the loss of her much-valued virginity. She knows that Bertram still loathes her, and she sees his actions as defiling – but only defiling to him, I think: she herself is rather

[23] It is possible that the phrase 'bright particular star' refers to the Aristotelian notion that comets were attached to or in pursuit of a particular star – an idea that Bacon describes as long discredited, *New Organon*, p. 157.

gratified, and has enjoyed her sweet use (we might think of the comparable bliss in 'such sweet thunder' (*MND*, IV. i. 118)), even being rather pleased at his saucy trusting, suggesting that the deception has been a spice to her pleasure. Even the last line of this is impersonal: Bertram is replaced by personified lust, and Helena herself is whisked out of the line by the abstraction of herself and Diana into 'what' and 'that'; the line's alliteration on *w* makes it hard to press any really irritated passion into this, and instead creates kiss-shapes on her lips.

The relish of the trick is made acceptable by the fact that it is itself a kind of cure: by abstracting Bertram into lust, she suggests that she is curing that vice. When she first thinks of proposing the bed-trick to Diana, she says that she is going to give the girl 'precepts' (III. v. 100), hinting at a mixture of medical and religious prescription (at this moment Helena is dressed as a pilgrim). She later repeatedly insists that her plan is 'lawful' (III. vii. 30, 45, 46), and it becomes a kind of cure when endorsed by the king, who describes the ring on Bertram's finger thus:

> Plutus himself,
> That knows the tinct and multiplying med'cine,
> Hath not in nature's mystery more science
> Than I have in this ring. (V. iii. 101–4)

It would be enough for him to say that he knows the ring well, but the phrasing here turns it into an embodiment of all the mysterious knowledge of nature that Helena has carried through the play, and that is associated with her virginity and its loss. This has power to create true renewal and increase in this world. To go back to where we started, Helena's virginity is fecund, not yet curdled into cheese: it is paradoxically creative and life-giving, bringing forth something significant from itself. It is also accepting of the fact that she needs outside aids, most notably from the King and the Countess, from Diana, and even a little prompt from the wordily vain Parolles – but she finds the right balance between passivity and activity, and this is the essence of her healing art.[24] Helena makes good use of all the resources she finds in the natural and human world, transforming them for the good; in doing so, she may be Shakespeare's most powerful heroine, a figure whose art and nature (brains and body) are firmly integrated. Perhaps that is why few critics have ever been quite comfortable with her.[25]

[24] Maquerlot, *Shakespeare and the Mannerist Tradition*, p. 151, argues that the play's end 'does its utmost to limit its emotional appeal in order to focus the audience's attention more effectively on the artistry with which it is engineered.' From a certain perspective, this is true, but Helena's emotions are overwhelmingly real.

[25] See Rossiter's discussion of the problem of Helena in *Angel with Horns*, pp. 106–7.

The art deployed in *The Winter's Tale* is even more mysterious, and even more radically renewing. We have seen (see Chapter 1) that Perdita and Paulina both in different ways invoke 'great creating Nature' as central to the play's process of renewal, but a more active medicinal art is also required. Early on Paulina tries to cure Leontes' jealousy with mere words, even if powerful ones:

> These dangerous, unsafe lunes i' th' King, beshrew them!
> He must be told on't, and he shall. The office
> Becomes a woman best. I'll take 't upon me.
> If I prove honey-mouthed, let my tongue blister;
> And never to my red-looked anger be
> The trumpet any more. (II. ii. 28–33)

Vigorous as this declaration is, there may be a problem in having an excessively choleric physician, her red hair being a traditional sign of bad temper. She is able to diagnose the problem, possibly seeing his 'lunes' as a form of dangerous menstruation, but her failure to sugar the pill leads to failure to cure. As if she knows this, she also recognizes at this point that 'the sight o' th' child' and its 'pure innocence' may offer a better chance of cure than her shrewish red rage (lines 38–9).

In the next scene, Paulina's entrance to the King's presence shows an awareness of the danger of fighting choler with choler: when the Servant tries to bar her entrance, she says 'Not so hot, good sir', trying to reduce the temperature of the situation; she claims that

> I come to bring him sleep. 'Tis such as you,
> That creep like shadows by him, and do sigh
> At each his needless heavings, such as you
> Nourish the cause of his awaking. I
> Do come with words as med'cinal as true,
> Honest as either, to purge him of that humour
> That presses him from sleep. (II. iii. 33–9)

The medical language here is complex but orthodox: the humour of his choler keeps rising up, stays on top of him, weighing him down and preventing him from sleeping; pressing to death was a punishment for refusing to give testimony, and here it is an appropriate punishment for one who perversely refuses to see the truth. The sympathetic, imitative, shadowlike movements of his courtiers prevent him throwing this humour off, and indeed feed it. The talk of heavings and nourishment here suggest that Leontes' bed is like one of childbirth, as if he has sympathetically begun to labour like his mistrusted wife. Paulina is the true physician and counsellor, unlike the sycophants who are 'comforting [his] evils' (lines 54–6), because she is able to deliver truth. But she loses her temper, threatening to poke out the eyes of the King's servants, before collecting herself and laying the baby down in front of the King, who thinks that she is 'A mankind witch' (line 68). He's wrong, of course, but such have been the gender reversals that his wrongness is part of a pattern.

Having failed in her attempt to deliver the embodied truth of the child, Paulina will need all her natural witchery to bring the play to a resolution, and in this she must be assisted by the visual arts. The statue of Hermione is supposedly the work of 'that rare Italian master Julio Romano, who, had he himself eternity and could put breath into his work, would beguile Nature of her custom, so perfectly he is her ape' (V. ii. 97–100). There are some similarities in this to the discussion of Helena's father, whose art was also in competition with Nature. Giulio Romano was known as a pornographer, for his illustrations of Aretino, and this fact, along with the idea of Nature having *customers*, may seem to imply that Nature is a bawd whose clients might be distracted by pictures. This seems a little queer, and nearly blasphemous. It is also strangely implied here that all human artists would need in order to create life would be an eternity of effort, but there is also a suggestion that one would need to be in possession of the infinite to bring life into the world: the infinite is the precondition of mortal breath, an idea that anticipates Blake. This invocation of immortal creativity, however conditional/ provisional, seeming weirdly undermined by the idea of the artist as mere *ape*, prepares the way for the revelation of the statue, which is surely Shakespeare's greatest ceremonial moment. The sanctity of this artistic ceremony, though, is partly guaranteed by its very close proximity to blasphemy and idolatry: Paulina's role as host is dubiously close to unlicensed female priesthood; the creation of a human image of this kind may provoke a kind of iconophobia; and the bringing of the transcendent into the earthly may remind us of the problem of the Real Presence in the Eucharist.[26]

With all of this worry floating around, it's not surprising (but it is, precisely, wonderful) that the scene is one of such (ironically) breathless caution. Paulina gives reverence to Leontes as 'sovereign sir', suggesting some of the healing qualities that his status if not his conduct might bring, saying that his visit to her house is 'a surplus of your grace' (V. iii. 2, 7). The King, connected to the order of grace, is a kind of supplement to the natural world, but his participation in the art-ceremony is absolutely

[26] On the issue of idolatry in this scene, see Shell, *Shakespeare and Religion*, p. 18.

necessary: he is not a disinterested, distant consumer. Leontes in turn insists on the 'comfort' she has long been, and compliments her on the 'content' her gallery has brought with its 'many singularities' (lines 1, 11–12); these exceptional artworks are not *lawful*, in the sense that they don't conform to a pattern. They are unnecessary superfluities, but Paulina's presentation of them is *more than* needful courtesy or ceremony, preparing us for the reserved business, the statue that has been kept 'Lonely, apart' (line 18). If the other artworks are like side-chapel saints, we now come to the central salvific figure, the 'dear stone' that is Hermione (line 24), which silently rebukes the King. Art's capacity to provoke emotion, moving others while remaining itself as stone, is invoked here with remarkable power. In Plato's *Phaedrus*, Socrates emphasizes the sterility of painting, saying that 'The offsprings of painting stand there as if they are alive, but if anyone asks them anything, they remain most solemnly silent' (275^{e}). Likewise, Hermione may only be returned to Leontes when she is past childbearing,[27] and her silence to him may reflect the frustrations provoked by art in Plato's reading of it.

So lifelike is this statue that Leontes longs to kiss its hand, but Paulina enjoins patience, a patience which becomes commensurate with Hermione's unmerited suffering, and with the deserved penitential punishment of Leontes (line 46). Paulina even tries to cover up the statue again with a curtain, fearing that continuing to 'gaze' on it will make him fancy it moves (lines 60–1). The dangerously creative power of icons is recognized: Leontes longs for 'The pleasure of that madness' in believing it moves (line 73). Paulina admits that she has 'stirred' his humoral passions, but Leontes thinks 'this affliction has a taste as sweet / As any cordial comfort' (lines 74, 76–7); using the keyword 'comfort', which also has the connotation of physical sustenance (OED comfort *n2*), with which he began the scene, Leontes seems almost to eat the statue as frustration at mere gazing becomes something more nutritive. In the earlier sheep-shearing scene, Camillo said to Perdita, 'I should leave grazing, were I of your flock, / And only live by gazing' (IV. iv. 109–10); these lovely lines' assonation of words of eating and words of looking suggest a tension between those two modes of consumption and connection to the world that the play tries to resolve. Leontes' gazing at the statue is a full resolution of this. We are in the timeless and yet (nearly) satisfied suspension of great art.

[27] See Janet Adelman, *Suffocating Mothers: Fantasies of Maternal Origin in Shakespeare's Plays*, Hamlet *to* The Tempest (London: Routledge, 1992), pp. 235–7.

Perdita and Leontes agree that they could stand looking at the statue for twenty years (their agreeing on that number brings them subtly into alignment – V. iii. 71, 84), and this suspension without suspense then sets up Paulina for her great moment:

> Either forbear,
> Quit presently the chapel, or resolve you
> For more amazement. If you can behold it,
> I'll make the statue move indeed, descend,
> And take you by the hand; but then you'll think
> (Which I protest against) I am assisted
> By wicked powers. (lines 85–91)

This is a callback to the idea of her as a 'mankind witch' we saw earlier, but it also has a weirdly satisfying conditionality.[28] There is much virtue indeed in this *if*: it requires the waking of 'faith' to engage with this, which some *might* think 'unlawful business' (lines 95–6).[29] This is what theatre is to anti-theatrical campaigners, it is what art is to iconoclasts, natural magic to sceptics. All such must depart. But if we can behold it, if we can believe it, it will happen.

Paulina ties language and sight together when she pronounces that we *see* her 'spell is lawful' (line 105): her words are lawful in that they are not profane, not out of the canon, but also in the sense that they conform to nature's laws. They work: as we may say, the proof of the pudding is in the eating. When Leontes, still perhaps entranced by the vision of what Paulina calls Hermione's holy action (i.e. motion), has one more cause for wonder, in touching her and finding her warm. Here again the conditional is invoked in his response, as he says 'If this be magic, let it be an art / Lawful as eating' (lines 110–1). With regal authority, he licenses magic – as monarchs licensed theatre, and as they gave laws about eating, such as instituting fish days.[30] Yet there's obviously more to these wonderfully resonant lines: all of *this* (the deictic gesture is wonderfully particular, wonderfully general) is part of nature, part of the complex system of mutual dependencies and shared pleasure that had been sealed up by the jealous tyrant's infection.[31]

28 See Barton, *Essays, Mainly Shakespearean*, pp. 180–1, on the 'desperate artistic honesty' of this awakening of faith: we are challenged to consider what kind of faith we need here.

29 On the need for faith to bridge the personal, stylistic and formal gaps of the play, see McDonald, *Shakespeare's Late Style*, p. 104.

30 See A. L. Rowse, *The Expansion of Elizabethan England* (London: Macmillan, 1995), p. 326.

31 See Rabkin, *Shakespeare and the Problem of Meaning*, p. 139.

The flow of life resumes, through communal, collaborative art, through an art that is Nature's, natural and open as eating can be.[32]

Hospitality

Eating is a communal matter, creating and dividing social groups. In Chapter 1, I considered local, rural hospitality as a way of embedding humans in the natural world. Here, I want to show that food-based hospitality has healing and possibly redemptive powers. The healing power of natural, shared eating is emphasized when it goes wrong. Timon of Athens's hospitality is a complex matter, involving friendship, reciprocity and generosity as well as folly, but it centres around food, which becomes particularly prominent when the system of sharing breaks down. When Lucullus denies aid to Timon, the steward Flavius responds with a remarkably vivid sense of outrage at this embodiment of ingratitude:

> This slave
> Unto [this hour] has my lord's meat in him;
> Why should it thrive and turn to nutriment,
> When he is turned to poison?
> O, may diseases only work upon 't!
> And when he's sick to death, let not that part of nature
> Which my lord paid for be of any power
> To expel sickness, but prolong his hour! (III. i. 56–63)

There are some odd reversals in this: when we hear *he* is turned to poison, we might expect a desire that the food poison Lucullus, and it does anticipate the poisonous rage to which Timon will turn, but it is Lucullus who is poisonous, and therefore unable to digest healthful food. Flavius wills the revoking of any salvific efficacy Timon's almost Eucharistic flesh might have (the use of the word 'lord' and the idea of paying together invoke the idea of Christ's redemption). To refer to a meal as a 'part of nature' suggests a remarkably holistic understanding of hospitality as a sharing of a common natural world, even if the economic context pushes against that sense of commonality.[33]

Timon's caustically satirical feast at the end of Act Three may seem like a simple complaint at the emptiness of his supposed friends, but it also constitutes a grim lament against the failures of a broader commonality.

32 Fitzpatrick, *Food in Shakespeare*, pp. 68–79 takes a rather different, but perhaps complementary line on the role of food in *The Winter's Tale*, arguing that Leontes' jealousy is a medical problem (based on sympathetic pregnancy) and that the vegetarian feast in Bohemia is a crucial curative.

33 See Fitzpatrick, *Food in Shakespeare*, pp. 113–5 on the cannibalistic language of *Timon*.

Timon introduces the feast by saying 'your diet shall be in all places alike' (III. vi. 66–7), suggesting that at least part of his point is a desire for equality, for a world which would therefore not require loans and gifts. Having given a general set of curses on social-hospitable relations, he concludes his preface to the banquet: 'For these my present friends, as they are to me nothing, so in nothing bless them and to nothing are they welcome' (lines 82–4). But the nothing he gives them is in fact something: it is water. Telling his guests to lap at it like dogs obviously points the insult in a way that is typical of this play, but the fact remains that there is something essential there, something that cannot be wished away. As dogs, they are lowest common denominators, as we saw in the last chapter. Even if the water is lukewarm, water is the most crucial element of any diet, as the Greeks felt it important to emphasize (*ariston men hudor* – water is best).[34] However, he uses the water as a form of purgative, washing his face in it to remove their 'flatteries' and 'villainy' from his countenance before flinging it back in their faces (lines 91–3); this is an odd gesture, one which does not heal him and which is intended to curse them, as he says 'Of man and beast the infinite malady / Crust you quite o'er!' (lines 98–9). Though he calls his gestures 'physic' (line 100), this is obviously ironic, and in no way – either positive or negative – efficacious. Timon's gestures are as futile and empty as modern homeopathic medicine. Indeed, it seems that all he does at this point is throw the empty dishes at his guests,[35] who scurry off, none the wiser as to the reasons for his actions. The Second Lord simply says that 'Lord Timon's mad', and the Third Lord agrees, saying, 'I feel 't upon my bones' (line 119); the latter statement may imply some intuitive understanding, or may reflect the fact that Timon's curse has got to him, but the general sentiment is one of bafflement rather than healing. As we saw in Chapter 1, a stranger engagement with the natural world is necessary to prevent the whole play from feeling empty.

For different reasons, there is a similar feeling of emptiness in *Love's Labour's Lost*. In *Love's Labour's Lost*, the young lords believe that their plan to sequester themselves for the sake of study is a 'fast':

> The mind shall banquet, though the body pine;
> Fat paunches have lean pates; and dainty bits
> Make rich the ribs, but bankrupt quite the wits.
> (I. i. 24–7)

34 Pindar, 1st Olympian, line 1.

35 See Arden 3 ed., note to line 99 SD: he may also throw stones and cloaks, though the latter would flap around the stage rather feebly.

Longaville here insists that the needs of the mind and body are in competition, and the play allows the body to win out when the young men fall in love with the visiting ladies. The initial framing of the men's vows, though, emphasizes moderation in eating at least as much as the restraint of sexual appetite. Berowne protests against the plan that they will have one fast day a week, and only one meal a day besides (as well as only three hours' sleep a night); he considers the rules 'barren tasks, too hard to keep' (line 47), and that 'every man with his affects is born, / Not by might mastered, but by special grace' (lines 151–2). He seems to be introducing a Protestant mode of thinking against the King's imposition of a Catholic scheme of good works. Like Luther, whose crucial insight was that man could not obey the Law, he believes that the effort they've committed themselves to is futile. Like Calvin, he insists that man must accept his utter powerlessness, and rely on God's grace. However (like a good Erastian), he also accepts that he will have to conform, outwardly, to the rules imposed, at least until the King's own desires bring about a reformation. The play's plot validates Berowne's protestant scepticism, and that may also invalidate Longaville's sense that the body and mind are in fundamental competition.

The idea that intellectual pursuits are an alternative to food is burlesqued later in the play when Nathaniel explains Dull's stupidity:

> Sir, he hath never fed of the dainties that are bred in a book;
> He hath not eat paper, as it were; he hath not drunk ink;
> his intellect is not replenished; he is only an
> animal, only sensible in the duller parts;
> And such barren plants are set before us, that we thankful should be—
> Which we of taste and feeling are—for those parts
> that do fructify in us more than he. (IV. ii. 24–9)

Like Plato in *Phaedo*, he makes distinctions between different kinds of animals' sensory capacities, but the ideas here are presented as fundamentally absurd. The passage follows on from a tediously pedantic series of puns about deer, where again the issue is the making of distinctions between different animals. The attempt to map ideas about education onto more a more naturalized schema tends to collapse just as Nathaniel's verse speaking collapses. Within this mode of thinking, 'taste and feeling' are required to understand texts, with the result that there is a blurring between intellectual and bodily capacities. There is also a sense that books are mere 'barren plants', which provide food only for some, and only in a limited way. A more literal feeding is also necessary for health.

The young lords think that their love is a disease; but Berowne is sceptical of Dumaine's sense that his beloved is a 'fever' in his blood, saying that 'incision / Would let her out in saucers' (IV. iii. 95–6); the medical discourse is treated as ludicrous, for simpler modes of thinking and living can bring about health. Berowne demands of his forsworn colleagues 'Say, can you fast? Your stomachs are too young, / And abstinence engenders maladies' (lines 290–1); like the doctors who attend *All's Well*'s King, they are 'barren practisers' (line 322), uselessly trying to impose medical and other schematic arts onto aspects of life that are freer and less rule-bound. Love, he explains

> Lives not alone immurèd in the brain,
> But with the motion of all elements,
> Courses as swift as thought in every power,
> And gives to every power a double power,
> Above their functions and their offices.
> (lines 325–9)

Whereas the play's initial premise offered a zero-sum competition between body and mind, Berowne's idea of love, which is clearly connected to his idea of grace,[36] allows each to augment the other. The proverbial 'swift as thought' simile ties the mind to the elements of the body, creating a doubling of human capacities beyond mere function and officious duty. Here is the true fruition, beyond the barrenness of enclosed intellectuality.

The play is 'a great feast of languages' (V. i. 36–7),[37] but its characters must fall to and eat in a more literal – though not literary – sense. Berowne asks for 'one sweet word' with his mistress (actually the Princess rather than Rosaline), and she mockingly lists 'Honey, and milk, and sugar: there is three'; not to be outdone, he gives the more elaborate (and intoxicating) 'Metheglin, wort, and malmsey' (V. ii. 230–3). The play's gesturing at food and drink, without supplying them, evokes the sense that words themselves are vectors of hunger and thirst, yearning for their more solid meanings. Rosaline complains that the men's wits are 'gross gross, fat fat' (line 268), suggesting that she assents to Longaville's earlier connection of wit and thinness. Her doubling of the (in any case synonymous) words nonetheless suggests a certain desire or at least relish for the fatness involved, a sense of pleasure in the unnecessary and excessive, which also associates itself with Berowne's belief in love's provision of 'double power'.

36 He concludes with the sentiment 'charity itself fulfils the law' (line 338).

37 See the fine discussion of this in Barber, *Shakespeare's Festive Comedy*, pp. 112–3; Barber is, I think, too sanguine about the satisfactions of merely verbal wit.

After the ladies have bested their wits, Boyet worries that the lords will not be able to 'digest this harsh indignity' (line 289). The verbal linking of dignity and digestion here reflects the play's more general weighing of natural and cultural values. The young men have had to suffer a comical purge after their linguistic feast, but the terms of this are not quite as simply digestive as they would be in later humours comedy. Berowne promises to abandon 'Taffeta phrases, silken terms precise' for 'russet yeas and honest kersey noes' (lines 406, 413), proposing a change of clothes rather than a change of diet. Clothes are generally used as an image of artifice in Shakespeare, but here a distinction is made between artificial and natural clothing; indeed, clothing and diet do go together to some extent in the period, as sumptuary laws applied to both.[38] Between the phrases about clothing, Berowne does reintroduce digestive language, in more viscerally unpleasant terms than elsewhere in the play, saying that the 'summer flies' of 'Figures pedantical' 'Have blown me full of maggot ostentation' (lines 408–9). Like Hamlet's dead dog, he has started to breed, but in a fetid, verminous, empty way. From this point on, the play's discourse of disease becomes more intense. Berowne admits that he himself is still 'sick' and sees the marks of love as a 'plague' on his colleagues (lines 417, 421).

The young men will need further purgation, in terms that are similar to but more serious than the terms of their initial oaths: the Princess enjoins them to go

> To some forlorn and naked hermitage,
> Remote from all the pleasures of the world,
> There stay until the twelve celestial signs
> Have brought about the annual reckoning.
> If this austere insociable life
> Change not your offer made in heat of blood;
> If frosts and fasts, hard lodging and thin weeds
> Nip not the gaudy blossoms of your love
> But that it bear this trial, and last love;
> Then at the expiration of the year,
> Come challenge me. (lines 795–805)

Again, clothing and food are tied together (along with lodging): they are part of a whole daily way of life, which is one of the meanings of the word diet. Berowne, meanwhile, is sent off to 'Visit the speechless sick, and still converse / With groaning wretches' (lines 851–2). If the King's task

38 Wilfrid Hooper, 'The Tudor Sumptuary Laws', *The English Historical Review*, Vol. 30, No. 119 (Jul., 1915): 433–449, p. 435. These laws, in addition to regulating apparel, regulated the number of dishes that could be served at a meal.

is merely penitential, Berowne, who was most sceptical at the beginning about man's ability to do good, is sent to do active good works in order to cure his disease – even though his task in the hospitals will be merely to make the sick laugh. The play, then, does not decide whether good works are ultimately consequential, but they may like laughter make life more bearable. The play is concerned, in its romantic plot, with how to make a 'world-without-end bargain' (line 789), but it also ties this up with its concern about day-to-day living.

Failed or subverted hospitality such as that we encounter in *Timon* or *Love's Labour's Lost* leaves one feeling empty; the rites and ceremonies of drama seem to be unravelled. This reflects some sense that the communal experience of drama is ultimately unsatisfying: we need to go for dinner afterwards. In *The Comedy of Errors*, however, there is a sense of rich satisfaction and natural human sympathy, built round a plot which centres in some ways on dinner. From the start of the play, we are aware that 'dinner-time' is a key temporal marker (I. ii. 11); Dromio of Ephesus, in the first case of mistaken identity, comes to call Antipholus of Syracuse urgently home for a meal, saying

> The capon burns, the pig falls from the spit;
> The clock hath strucken twelve upon the bell:
> My mistress made it one upon my cheek:
> She is so hot, because the meat is cold.
> (lines 44–7)

The play's sense of chaos centres around this meal, which raises temperatures close to madness; the sense of temporal urgency that drives the farcical plot is firmly embodied, the meal being associated with the clock and the blows the servants receive – as Dromio says, 'Methinks your maw, like mine, should be your clock' (line 66). Instinctive appetite should pull people along without conscious clock-watching. The play's much vaunted temporal unity is in large part dependent on a shared sense of when to eat.

The central dinner is, above all, a figure for Antipholus of Ephesus's marriage, Adriana is particularly concerned with her husband's meal, and our first encounter with her shows her impatience that he return to it on time, even though her sister insists that men should be free to spend their time as they wish (II. i. 1–9). She is infuriated that he should dine away from home, saying 'His company must do his minions grace, / Whilst I at home starve for a merry look (lines 87–8). Without her husband, it seems, she cannot eat, whereas he has freedom to eat elsewhere: her hunger becomes a version of her jealousy. Adriana is a strange mixture of impatient shrew and pitiable loyal wife; she laments that he once thought her all that is valuable, and wonders

O, how comes it,
That thou art then estrangèd from thyself?
Thyself I call it, being strange to me,
That, undividable incorporate,
Am better than thy dear self's better part.
(II. ii. 119–23)

This model of absolute identification between husband and wife is as firm and embodied as any in Shakespeare, seeming more like the identification with the friend in the *Sonnets* than any other marital relationship. As a result, Adriana's jealousy seems genuinely moving, not the mere intellectual error of an Othello or a Leontes. She worries that

I am possessed with an adulterate blot;
My blood is mingled with the crime of lust:
For if we two be one, and thou play false,
I do digest the poison of thy flesh,
Being strumpeted by thy contagion.
(lines 140–4)

The sense that she has become sinful because of her husband's sin is powerful, rooted in a sense of infection and digestion that goes beyond mere fear of venereal disease, being based on a real belief that 'man and wife is one flesh' (*Hamlet*, IV. iii. 52).

The irony of this is that she throws these accusations at her husband's brother, Antipholus of Syracuse. But this fact doesn't quite invalidate her feeling: we later discover that Antipholus of Ephesus is indeed engaged in at least a dalliance with a courtesan; and, after all, the twin brother *is* in a sense identified with her husband, and she is in danger of being unwittingly an adulteress with him. Her insistence that Antipholus of Syracuse dine with her may have euphemistic connotations, for they will 'dine above' in privacy (line 207). Of course, Luciana's presence prevents this being a fully sexual encounter, but this only complicates matters, as another form of putative adultery emerges when Antipholus of Syracuse falls for Luciana (who is the one who offers the final, decisive invitation to dinner – line 219). Dining with someone of the opposite sex may, in fact, be as intimate a matter as sex: when couples divorced in the period, they divorced *a foro et a lecto*, from bed and board, as if the two were equally important; in many traditional cultures, for a wife to eat with another man is a worse infidelity than the sexual.[39]

All this is accentuated, of course, when the true husband is barred from entry to the house, an incident that is as humiliating to him as any cuckolding could be, not least because he has brought friends to dinner. Indeed, Antipholus of Ephesus is planning to use this dinner for the sake of his male friendship circle rather than as a moment of marital intimacy, his key purpose being to cheer up Balthazar, to remove his melancholy with food and hospitality. There is something decidedly ceremonious about this, a fact that is emphasized by the turn to rhyme:

> ANTIPHOLUS E. Y' are sad, Signior Balthazar, pray God our cheer
> May answer my good will and your good welcome here.
> BALTHAZAR. I hold your dainties cheap, sir, and your welcome dear.
> ANTIPHOLUS E. O, Signior Balthazar, either at flesh or fish,
> A table full of welcome makes scarce one dainty dish.
> BALTHAZAR. Good meat, sir, is common; that every churl affords.
> ANTIPHOLUS E. And welcome more common, for that's nothing but words.
> BALTHAZAR. Small cheer and great welcome makes a merry feast.
> ANTIPHOLUS E. Ay, to a niggardly host and more sparing guest:
> But though my cates be mean, take them in good part;
> Better cheer may you have, but not with better heart. (III. i. 19–29)

The repeated emphasis here on goodwill and heart, on cheer, merriment and welcome, underpinned by self-deprecation, collectively insist on the emotive qualities of hospitality and its ability to cure melancholy. Yet all this warmth is ironically turned into 'nothing but words' when they are denied entrance to the house. Dromio of Ephesus highlights the humiliation that this causes when he says 'Your cake here is warm within: you stand here in the cold. / It would make a man mad as a buck to be so bought and sold' (lines 71–2). The sudden lowering of temperature is associated with imagery of a cuckold's horns and of prostitution: if the wife is whoring herself, and if man and wife are one flesh, it is the man's flesh that is being bought and sold. Balthazar tries to make the best of this, and (successfully) encourages Antipholus of Ephesus to depart and avoid 'slander' (line 105), but the damage is done, and a degree of madness becomes inevitable, driving the rest of the play.

39 Richard Wrangham, *Catching Fire: How Cooking Made Us Human* (London: Profile Books, 2009). Even now, English law considers sharing of food rather than sharing a bed as the definition of cohabitation (I'm grateful to one of Cambridge University Press's anonymous readers for this point).

Antipholus of Ephesus does cool himself down a little by going off for dinner elsewhere. At this dinner, we are told that he offers the courtesan a chain (in revenge for Adriana's treatment of him – IV. iii. 68–70). We don't see any of the play's dinners: the privacy involved accentuates the sense that dinner is a form of significant intimacy.[40] The courtesan then accosts Antipholus of Syracuse and offers to 'mend our dinner' (line 59), suggesting that there has been something unsatisfying about her dinner with his brother, or hinting at the insatiable nature of a courtesan. Antipholus of Syracuse runs off from her, thinking her a 'sorceress' (line 66), accepting Dromio's innuendo-laden warning that 'he must have a long spoon that must eat with the devil' (line 64). This taps into the larger sense that Ephesus is a place of witches, conjurors and magicians (I. ii. 97–102, II. ii. 188–92, III. ii. 156, IV. iii. 11), but the play's true magic comes from other sources.

Dr Pinch, brought in to deal with Antipholus of Ephesus's supposed malady, is a representative 'conjuror' (IV. iv. 47), but his powers are dismissed in the end: he is

> A mere anatomy, a mountebank,
> A threadbare juggler and a fortune-teller,
> A needy, hollow-eyed, sharp-looking wretch,
> A living dead man. (V. i. 239–42)

Dr Pinch is a kind of zombie, with no connection to life or nature. Of course, in one sense, Antipholus is not mad, and all of Pinch's pulse-feeling and diagnosis of paleness is in vain; but there is a sense in which he is suffering from some condition, and this needs to be resolved by the life-giving power of women and the recovery of the natural family.

Adriana describes an existing condition in her husband:

> This week he hath been heavy, sour, sad,
> And much different from the man he was;
> But till this afternoon his passion
> Ne'er brake into extremity of rage.
> (lines 45–8)

We can understand how the errors of the day have led to various passions and extremities, but there is no assignable cause for a week-long problem with Antipholus of Ephesus's health and temper. This may suggest that he has naturally, intuitively anticipated the events of today, through natural

40 See Burrow, *Shakespeare and Classical Antiquity*, pp. 150–1, on the power of Shakespeare's evocation of the marriage, whose off-stage, domestic space is never fully intruded on.

sympathy with the sufferings of the rest of his family. The Abbess, however, diagnoses the condition differently, arguing that his illness was caused by 'The venom clamours of a jealous woman' which 'Poisons more deadly than a mad dog's tooth' (lines 69–70) and that

> Thou say'st his meat was sauced with thy upbraidings:
> Unquiet meals make ill digestions,
> Thereof the raging fire of fever bred,
> And what's a fever but a fit of madness?
>
> (lines 73–6)

Perhaps because she is naturally though unwittingly connected to her son, the Abbess here takes his side against his wife, who is unnaturally related to him, giving him excessive, saucy food; and it does seem that Antipholus may have had a better dinner with the courtesan (whom he thanks for her 'cheer' – line 393).[41] But the fact that there is no real madness rather invalidates her diagnosis: there's a sense that both women are confabulating, looking for causes where there is none. The women then compete over who is to treat the madness, the Abbess insisting that she has 'wholesome syrups, drugs and holy prayers' which can cure him (line 104), and Adriana claiming that it is her 'office' to 'Diet his sickness' (line 99). Whoever is in the right, it is clear that such cures are women's business.

Neither needs, of course, to provide a cure. The madness is shown to be collective, a function of holistic familial circumstances rather than a matter of one individual's humoral problems. The Duke says 'I think you all have drunk of Circe's cup' (line 271); *all* have become beastly-mad in the process of the play, like Odysseus's crew turned to swine. Once the confusions have been unravelled, there is a recognition that all have been subject to a kind of madness, but that madness has brought them all together, like a herd of undifferentiated animals. The Abbess refers to the events of the play as 'this sympathizèd one day's error' (line 398). Though each of them has had very different experiences, a collectivity of cheer has emerged, each having some natural feeling for the others' experience, which will be resolved in 'a gossips' feast' (line 406).[42]

[41] Richard C. McCoy, *Faith in Shakespeare*, pp. 49–50, shows how the play's curative properties come through an emphasis on daily life, emphasizing the importance of the 'recreation' that is Antipholus's due (p. 78), and seeing this as enabling a form of secular redemption; interestingly, though McCoy does not make this link explicit, he makes a similar point about 'recreation' in *The Winter's Tale* (p. 123).

[42] As Richard Strier, *The Unrepentant Renaissance: From Petrarch to Shakespeare to Milton* (Chicago: The University of Chicago Press, 2011), p. 185 points out, a gossips' feast was 'the secular aftermath of a baptism', a sacred but not ecclesiastical celebration. Strier's whole chapter on *Comedy* gives a fascinating and acute account of the play's sanctification of the bourgeois family.

Such feasting is the prototypical instance of a comedic ending, though usually taking place beyond the play's end: at the end of *Bartholomew Fair*, Justice Overdo invites the other characters to supper, where Cokes plans to have 'the rest of the play at home' (V. vi. 95).[43] Drama in the sixteenth century was deeply tied up with meals: early court plays were 'interludes' between courses of a banquet, and court performances continued to be performed during or after lavish dinners. There is a sense in which a play is merely an appetiser or *amuse bouche*, preparing or refreshing its consumers for more substantial fare.

Starvation

If plays are meant to keep us hungry, even to work up a hunger, this may result in there being something strangely unreal when drama tries to represent starvation, which was all too real a problem in the climate crisis of the late sixteenth and early seventeenth centuries; but there are other reasons for the strangeness of staging starvation. Though starvation might be the most grimly *natural* form of death, Shakespeare always treats it as culturally mediated, a marker of social isolation or banishment. The one character in Shakespeare whom starvation really does help to kill is Jack Cade in *Henry VI Part 2*. He begins his final scene with the lament

> Fie on ambitions! fie on myself, that have a sword, and yet am ready to famish! These five days have I hid me in these woods and durst not peep out, for all the country is laid for me; but now am I so hungry that, if I might have a lease of life for a thousand years, I could stay no longer. Wherefore, on a brick wall have I climbed into this garden, to see if I can eat grass, or pick a sallet another while, which is not amiss to cool a man's stomach this hot weather. And I think this word 'sallet' was born to do me good; for many a time, but for a sallet, my brain-pan had been cleft with a brown bill; and many a time, when I have been dry and bravely marching, it hath served me instead of a quart pot to drink in; and now the word 'sallet' must serve me to feed on. [*He lies down picking of herbs and eating them.*] (IV. x. 1–15).

Clearly this moment is meant to be one of poetic justice against the ambitious rebel who has taken up arms against his supposed betters, but there is a little more to it. He has invaded Iden's 'quiet walks', 'This small inheritance my father left me', which Iden considers 'worth a monarchy' (lines 17–19). Cade appears to believe that he could have gone on living

[43] References to *The Cambridge Edition of the Works of Ben Jonson*, ed. David Bevington, Martin Butler and Ian Donaldson, 7 vols. (Cambridge: Cambridge University Press, 2012).

in the woods ('for a thousand years'), which are conceived as a world beyond the nation-state whose enmity he has incurred, even if he would have remained hungry: there's a sense that his hunger has *tempted* him into unnecessary danger; starvation (need) is differentiated from hunger (greed), and Cade seems guilty of the latter. The sin for which he is punished in this scene is therefore the theft of the herbs, the violation of Iden's property. The joke about 'sallets' involves a pun on *salad* and *sallet* in the sense of the headpiece of a helmet (see Arden 3 note): in the past, as a leader of rebels, Cade has inappropriately worn a helmet and drunk beer from it; now his eating salads, which we might think driven by mere necessity, is treated as a similar gesture of indecorous overreaching. It seems to be the act of an overheated man, whose rebellious temper needs cooling off, rather than that of a man on his last legs.

Cade threatens Iden, vainly believing that he has the strength to beat the landowner despite not having eaten meat for five days (lines 38–40). Iden says that he will not fight a 'poor famished man' (line 44), at least not at 'odds',[44] but he does fight him one-to-one, and easily defeats him. Cade claims that 'Famine and no other hath slain me' (line 60) and that he is 'vanquished by famine, not by valour' (line 75). We may be inclined to agree with him, and to think Iden's victory dishonourable, but that does not add to his dignity: we are meant to side with the landowner rather than the vagabond, for starvation is something fearful and dangerous rather than genuinely pitiful here. The scene seems to suggest that Cade has chosen his own starvation, and that Cade could in any case have survived if he had stayed outside the human realm, so that his intrusion is a yielding to temptation that is justly punished.[45] Iden, the Edenic possessor of perfect property, sees Cade's response to him as 'saucy' (line 36), and the phrase may imply that the theft of food is an unnecessary self-indulgence, an appropriation of luxury rather than substance, sauce rather than meat. The play represents and partly approves a highly conservative fiction: that some of the poor both deserve their condition of starvation, and for that matter aren't really starving anyway.[46] As with Marie Antoinette, and Menenius

[44] It's debatable whether Iden does have 'five men' with him (line 40) – Q's stage direction does have them enter, but their absence in F may imply that they are figments of Cade's imagination, the claim of the presence being a mark of his Falstaffian bravado.

[45] See the astute discussion of this scene in Maus, *Being and Having in Shakespeare*, pp. 106–10.

[46] For other aspects of Shakespeare's ambivalence towards Cade, see William C. Carroll, *Fat King, Lean Beggar: Representations of Poverty in the Age of Shakespeare* (Ithaca: Cornell University Press, 1996), pp. 138–40; Carroll also points out that F gives Iden a wall to his garden rather than hedges (as in Q), thereby avoiding any sense that the landowner is an unjust encloser of commons. See also Estok, *Ecocriticism and Shakespeare*, p. 53.

in *Coriolanus*, we are encouraged to disbelieve in the reality of starvation. Such starvation cannot be relieved, and is outside the dietary economy of the nation. Wild and civilized starvation are distinguished.

However, if starvation can be courteously relieved, and properly mediated, it does become an object of pity. Both *As You Like It* and *Cymbeline* give us scenes of the relief of famine that embody a virtuous human sympathy. Orlando's demand for food from the exiled courtiers is at first blush as violent and indecorous as Cade's theft, but there are subtle and decisive differences: Orlando is asking for nourishment not for himself, but for the loyal retainer Adam; he intrudes on a place that isn't anyone's particular property, the forest being a kind of commons even if the legitimate court has made its home there; finally, of course, Orlando is a gentleman, and if he is rough and discourteous in his approach, there is still a sense in which he's entitled by his status to ask for hospitality.[47] To a modern audience, these will seem pettifogging distinctions, but they mattered in Shakespeare's time, and Shakespeare sets up the scene of Orlando's demand with real care for these matters. On the point of his expulsion from his brother's house, Orlando has worried that he might have to 'go and beg my food . . . / Or with a base and boisterous sword enforce / A thievish living on the common road' (II. iii. 31–3); his concern here for the danger of indignity or crime shows a scruple of honour that wouldn't enter into Jack Cade's head. His humility is emphasized by being prepared to take money from Adam and his acceptance that he will have to seek 'some settled low content' (line 68). We might think that Cade's desire for herbs is a desire for something similar, but that rebel came to it through ambition. Orlando clearly owes something to Adam for his help, so that when Adam is dying of starvation (II. vi. 1–3), he is *obliged* to turn discourteous, which therefore becomes a higher form of courtesy. Adam's name, finally, adds a sense of primal obligation: he represents the condition of humanity in general, as well as the tradition of patriarchal loyalty. As a result, the obtaining of food is seen here as the most basic of needs rather than as a mark of social indecorum.

Just before Orlando enters, Duke Senior has been engaged in an exchange with Jaques that also prepares the way for a positive reception. The Duke has rebuked Jaques for trying to tax vices when he has been 'a libertine' himself (II. vii. 65), and Jaques has rather feebly tried to justify himself, saying that his satire would be harmless, 'like a wild goose', 'Unclaimed of any man' if there were no one guilty of vice (lines 85–7). This notion

[47] See Fitzpatrick, *Food in Shakespeare*, p. 64.

of freedom is oddly suggestive, even if not directly relevant to Orlando's situation; it perhaps sets up the idea of wild food, which is no one's property. Orlando enters wildly, with sword drawn, and insists that no one eat the food in front of them. There's a touch of madness in Orlando at this point, which might remind us of his name's source (Ariosto's *Orlando Furioso*). Yet there's also a degree of farce, for when Orlando demands 'Forbear, and eat no more', Jaques replies 'Why, I have eat none yet' (lines 88–9), presumably because he's been waffling on, so that he hasn't got round to starting his dinner, leaving his food as unclaimed as his satire; for good measure, he calls Orlando a 'cock' (line 90). The Duke points out that none of this is 'good manners' (line 92), and this piques Orlando into admitting his error in that respect: he knows his situation has lost him the habit of 'smooth civility; yet I am inland bred / And know some nurture' (lines 96–7) even if this recognition doesn't prevent him from continuing to insist that none eat until his 'affairs are answered' (line 99).[48] What makes this urgency more forgivable is that *he* is starving (line 104); until now, we have assumed that it was only Adam in that lamentable condition: the fact that Orlando concealed his own starvation from his servant is a further point to his credit. Once he recognizes that the court is a gentle place, rather than a savage one, he recovers his manners, and all goes well. He describes himself as a doe looking after a fawn (line 128), and this animal image paradoxically highlights his gentility. From roughness, we find the deepest form of courtesy, as is characteristic of this play, and of the pastoral mode in general. Jaques, trying on the role of satirist, may have considered himself as one who could 'Cleanse the foul body of th' infected world' (line 60), but more basic kindness achieves this.

If Adam's starvation represents the way in which natural man can prompt and even demand kindness, a still higher form of kindness emerges in *Cymbeline*'s use of the idea of starvation. Imogen here is even more hardy in her hunger than Orlando: she knows that she 'should be sick', but is helped from this by her (rather stoic) 'resolution' (III. vi. 3–4). Even though she thinks of Posthumus as false here, the mere thought of him is enough to make her hunger go away, when before she was 'at point to sink for food' (lines 15–17). She reflects that 'famine, / Ere clean it o'erthrow nature, makes it valiant' (lines 19–20), words that redound back onto Orlando's rough courage. At the same time, the idea that moral strength can allay or

48 As Barber, *Shakespeare's Festive Comedy*, p. 254, points out, it's out of character for Orlando, and has no origin in his source: Shakespeare is making a point. Barber argues that that point is to remind us again of the difference between liberty and banishment; that seems right, but I think there's a little more to it; the boundary between the natural and the courteous, the wild and the tame, is fragile.

even prevent starvation reflects badly on Jack Cade, whose hunger may be construed as weakness. In all cases, though, there is the strange sense that hunger is the necessary consequence of moving outside the social world, as if no food can possibly be acquired in such exile. Food is taken to be a social rather than a natural thing; outside the community, it seems, one cannot eat. Imogen later refuses to make a fuss about her illness (like Orlando), saying that she is 'not well; / But not so citizen a wanton as / To seem to die ere sick' (IV. ii. 7–9); only middle-class citizens would make a fuss in such circumstances, she suggests, yet her confused word-order delicately points at her real suffering. Attitudes to food are tied up with class: as she is a princess, she – according to pastoral convention – is more like a country-dweller than a citizen, with simpler needs, and higher knowledge of nature. Yet, despite her claims of strength, she does *die* of this sickness/starvation, or so we may believe (see IV. ii. 194 SD and Martin Butler's Cambridge edition note to these lines). As we will see, her illness is a puzzle, possibly caused by a potion, but also caused by her alienation from the land and its edible produce. This is perhaps because her royal status has been withdrawn by her going into exile. She has become a kind of nothing, as Coriolanus is when he leaves Rome. Self-banished like Coriolanus, she believes in a world elsewhere, that there are 'livers out of England', but because she has not left England (or at least, not quite), she cannot be nourished. But this is not enough of an explanation for her condition. Starvation is merely the negative side of diet. More actively dangerous substances are needed to be fatal. If Cade dies not only as a result of starvation, but also as a result of eating Iden's salad, Imogen's apparent death also needs to be doubly motivated, by the potion she has been given as well as her starvation.

Medicine and natural magic

This takes us on to specifically prepared medicines or 'physic' (whose very name derives from the Greek word for nature). If starvation is at least as much a social as a natural matter, a similar balance needs to be found in our thinking about the most privileged of transformative substances – medicines and potions, which cannot always be crisply distinguished from ordinary foodstuffs, and whose properties are not essential but have moral and social dimensions. Just before she goes into the cave, Imogen says that she will 'taste of' the drug Pisanio gave her (line 38), and she presumably does so while she is inside. That drug is a classic instance of a reversible, ambiguous substance, both poison and cure, one which changes its force and meaning on each occasion it is transmitted during the play.[49] We know – or may think we know – that the potion is harmless, but the different ways in which it is discussed may have an effect on its meaning and effect. In any case, Imogen is genuinely sick from starvation *before* she takes it, and we can't be sure that the potion will help with that sickness. Perhaps it does so because she believes that it will. The Queen initially requests it from Cornelius, claiming that she wants to 'amplify [her] judgment' about medicines (I. v. 17) by trying out poisons and experimenting with cures; she says that she has been tutored in medicine by Cornelius, and that the King has requested her 'confections' (line 15).[50] She insists that Cornelius can have no objection to giving her poisons 'Unless thou think'st me devilish' (line 16). Cornelius, however, does 'know her spirit' (line 34), and doesn't trust her with anything so dangerous, giving her instead a box containing a drug that will only cause 'show of death' (line 40), producing a temporary stupefaction. The Queen then pretends to drop the box in front of Pisanio, claiming that

> It is a thing I made, which hath the King
> Five times redeemed from death. I do not know
> What is more cordial. (lines 62–4)

This supposedly casual gift to Pisanio is presented as a sort of bribe, yet it is also intended to do away with him: the ambiguity of the Queen's attempt to corrupt Pisanio is nicely captured in the doubt about the drug's meaning. Its fictional attachment to the King's life makes it a particularly special or sovereign kind of medicine, and in some senses the Queen's lie about it may actually make it redemptive rather than harmful.

The play's discourse of medicine adds further layers of complication to the box of ambiguous medicine, which makes the box – otherwise rather a farcical object of exchange – into a more richly symbolic object. Cloten claims that Imogen is mad to reject him, and that he won't leave her in such a dangerous state – to which Imogen responds that 'Fools cure not mad folks' (II. iii. 101).[51] Whatever may ail her, only her husband can provide the cure: later, she receives a letter from him, praying to the gods

[49] This is clearly like Derrida's *pharmakon*: see Jacques Derrida, 'Plato's Pharmacy', in *Dessimination*, trans. Barbara Johnson (1981; London: Bloomsbury, 2004).

[50] Geoffrey Hill argues that the Queen 'is a practioner of Bacon's "degenerate Naturall Magicke"' – 'Some Observations on *Cymbeline*', in *Collected Critical Writings*, ed. Kenneth Haynes (Oxford: Oxford University Press, 2008), p. 67. It is interesting to note that Queen Anne had been supplied with a 'Cordial' by Sir Walter Ralegh, despite the fact that her husband King James had imprisoned Ralegh in the tower for treason; see Raleigh Trevelyan, *Sir Walter Raleigh* (London: Allen Lane, 2002), p. 415.

[51] Compare Feste's jocular attempts to cure Malvolio's madness, and Berowne's task of making the sick laugh. Folly is, however ambiguously, curative.

Let what is here contained relish of love,
Of my lord's health, of his content—yet not
That we two are asunder; let that grieve him:
Some griefs are med'cinable, that is one of them,
For it doth physic love—of his content,
All but in that! (III. ii. 30–5)

The switchback of feeling here parallels the reversibility of the drug: to cure her own grief, she wants Posthumus to be healthy and content, though she limits that content with a wish that he is grieved at their parting, for such a shared grief is itself a cure for grief, improving mutual love. But the letter turns out to be ambiguous itself: it purports to request a reunion but is in fact part of a plot by the jealous Posthumus to have Imogen killed.

Yet this plot, like that of the Queen, is reversed, for Pisanio, whom Posthumus has suborned for the murder, is ultimately more loyal to Imogen than to her husband. Once he has made the decision to tell her of the plot, Imogen tells him 'Thou art all the comfort / The gods will diet me with' (III. iv. 179–80); the word comfort here, as so often, points to situations in which an individual is somehow good for another's health. The idea of diet looks forward to Imogen's later starvation, and connects physical and psychological health with the idea of food. It also seems to prompt Pisanio to remember the box of medicine given him by the Queen, which he describes thus:

Here is a box, I had it from the Queen,
What's in 't is precious. If you are sick at sea,
Or stomach-qualmed at land, a dram of this
Will drive away distemper. (lines 188–91)

This isn't exactly what the Queen said about it, but that shift suggests the way medicinal objects can be remotivated as they pass through various people's hands: the situation of handover, and the intentions of the parties involved seem to affect the qualities of a medicine. Its alleged curative properties come to be *true*, saving Imogen from starvation.[52]

Imogen accordingly takes it at a moment when she thinks of the idea of the sea. She has seen the courtesy of supposed wilderness dwellers, and reflects

[52] It is typical of tragicomedy that two wrongs end up making a right, or that two harmfully-intended actions bring about health: for instance, in Webster's *The Devil's Law Case* (pub. 1623), Romelio stabs Contarino, intending to kill him, but in doing so cures him of a wound he had received in an earlier duel.

Our courtiers say all's savage but at court.
Experience, O, thou disprov'st report!
Th' imperious seas breeds monsters; for the dish,
Poor tributary rivers as sweet fish.
I am sick still, heart-sick. Pisanio,
I'll now taste of thy drug. (IV. ii. 33–8)

Her decision to take the drug is based on the association of ideas rather than on rational grounds. Her metaphor for the paradoxical goodness of the little rather than the great is not all that convincing (doesn't the sea produce fish just as edible as the rivers, even if it also has whales in it?), and seems to serve only to remind her of the idea of sea-sickness with which Pisanio recommended the drug. Her continued sickness is also not given a specific cause here: now that the cave-dwellers have fed her, starvation may not be the reason. (Imogen is too good a wife to blame her treatment by her husband, but we might take that as a factor too). There is a sense, then, that her illness is a larger mystery, both over- and under-determined. When Belarius first sees her, he says 'But that it eats our victuals, I should think / Here were a fairy' (III. vi. 40–1).[53] Perhaps he speaks truer than he knows: perhaps she has become a fairy or other form of spirit, incapable of human nourishment in her husband's absence and as a result of her self-banishment from her father's court. If so, the dreamlike cure and naturalized grounding we saw in Chapter 1 is all the more necessary. Her name (in its traditional version) may mean 'one who is born from the depths', and she is perhaps Shakespeare's most startlingly *reborn* figure, in that she comes more fully to *life* than Hermione; it is surely significant that the historical Cymbeline's reign coincided with the life of Christ.[54] Her rebirth as 'fruit' (V. v. 263 – see Chapter 1, above) redeems all of Shakespeare's lost, suicidal young women: Ophelia, Desdemona and Juliet. She is, in Belarius's terms, 'an angel! or if not, / An earthly paragon', and he even announces her entrance in terms that would be appropriate for the birth of Christ: 'Behold divineness / No elder than a boy' (III. vi. 42–4). The risk-taking involved in her taking the drug is crucial to her redemptive possibilities: it is a kind of suicide, in the sense that Russian roulette is, a giving up of the will not so much

53 John Kerrigan, *Archipelagic English: Literature, History and Politics 1603–1707* (Oxford: Oxford University Press, 2008), pp. 137–8 shows that this belief is an aspect of the Welshness of Belarius and the Princes, and helps to ground them as robustly unsophisticated correctives to the corrupt modernity of Cymbeline's court, with its political intrigues and medical experimentation.

54 On Imogen/Innogen's name, see *Cymbeline*, ed. Martin Butler (Cambridge: Cambridge University Press, 2005), p. 77. On preserving Imogen as the name (as I think, on balance, we should), see John Pitcher, 'Names in *Cymbeline*', *Essays in Criticism* 43 (1993): 1–16.

to chance, in her case, but to nature, and the ambiguities and belief-based efficacies of medical art.

The transmission of an ambiguous medicine is also central to *Romeo and Juliet*, where it is the vector that brings about the play's tragic outcome. When we first encounter Friar Lawrence, he is picking herbs, and though these are not specifically the basis for the potion he gives Juliet, his description sets a keynote for the play's use of such substances. He comes 'Now ere the sun advance his burning eye, / The day to cheer and night's dank dew to dry', to pick 'baleful weeds and precious-juicèd flowers' (II. iii. 5–6, 8), insisting on grasping the right moment, and recognizing the mixed character of what Nature provides. He knows that

> The earth that's nature's mother is her tomb;
> What is her burying grave, that is her womb;
> And from her womb children of divers kind
> We sucking on her natural bosom find:
> Many for many virtues excellent,
> None but for some, and yet all different.
> (lines 9–14)

This acceptance of diversity and relativism is a keynote of Shakespeare's understanding of nature's properties. Yet there is also a faithful sense that 'mickle is the powerful grace that lies / In plants, herbs, stones, and their true qualities, / For naught so vile that on the earth doth live / But to the earth some special good doth give' (lines 15–18). Grace seems to emerge as a result of earthly diversity. Yet even that which is inherently good can be made bad if it is 'strained from that fair use' and 'Virtue itself turns vice, being misapplied' (lines 19, 21). This passage encapsulates much of the double attitude to nature that we have seen throughout this study. The order of grace is – or at least can be – part of the order of nature, whose rudeness can be harmful when misapplied, and can therefore lead to tragedy, but which also has special powers for the good when properly deployed or taken in the right way. Earth is both the source of life and the cause of death; it is, startlingly, 'nature's mother', as the substance is given priority over the abstraction. As in a course of *diet*, good timing is necessary to make things right, just as Friar Lawrence needs to pick his medicines at exactly the right time: the ambiguous, crepuscular moment of dawn is the play's key moment, its *kairos*, the moment which if correctly seized can lead on to victory.[55] Romeo and Juliet will die at a similar moment, through a failure of timing as well as a failure to use nature's virtues properly.

[55] A. D. Nuttall argues that 'in *Romeo and Juliet* causation seems to be supernaturally threatened. It is a firm law of drama and story that predictions are fulfilled. In *Romeo and Juliet* the predictions are left in suspension, strangely at odds with the event', and goes on to suggest that the play's visions

Romeo tells Friar Lawrence that his and Juliet's 'remedies / Within thy help and holy physic lies' (lines 51–2), and it is as much his natural wisdom as his spiritual advice that they need. Later, he warns Romeo that

> These violent delights have violent ends,
> And in their triumph die, like fire and powder,
> Which as they kiss consume. The sweetest honey
> Is loathsome in his own deliciousness,
> And in the taste confounds the appetite.
> (II. vi. 9–13)

The Friar's *exempla* here are pretty feeble, for the gunpowder image is quite exciting, and the idea that honey puts you off your dinner is nannyish, but his emphasis on the dangers of feeding fits with the Friar's role as a dietary advisor: throughout, he is preoccupied with Romeo's *temper*, the heat of his passion as humorally conceived (e.g. II. iii. 29, III. iii. 115). His job is to resolve the circumstantial problems that have altered Romeo's temper, and for this, he needs to use his medical skill.

He uses this skill, however, not on Romeo but on Juliet, whom he gives the potion, in order to cause her apparent death. His idea is prompted by Juliet expressing suicidal thoughts, and he responds that if she has 'the strength of will to slay thyself', she will be able to 'undertake / A thing like death', so he promises her the 'remedy' of the potion (IV. i. 73–4, 76). He gives a lengthy and vivid description of the potion's effects (lines 94–106), which emphasizes the daring and strength of will she will need in order to undergo the ordeal, suggesting that the drug is not enough on its own but requires the exercise of human strength to make the plan work. As she's about to take the potion, she describes the 'faint cold fear [which] thrills through my veins, / That almost freezes up the heat of life' (IV. iii. 15–16), and expresses distrust of the Friar (lines 24–6). Perhaps her weakness, her unbelief, is the problem, perhaps her temper is not up to the ordeal, but the problem, in a way, may be that she, rather than Romeo, has to be the one who suffers.[56] There's a horrible irony as she lies in a death-like state, for all around her (IV. iv) preparations for a wedding feast go on. It's as if she's being cooked for her proposed husband Paris even as she's being chilled for Romeo.

Romeo and Juliet is a play that could be a comedy, but which switches to tragedy through the influence of sickness and medicine, and of belief

seem to be taking place in an 'almost-but-not-quite-parallel universe' – *Shakespeare the Thinker* (New Haven: Yale University Press, 2007), p. 118.

[56] Ramie Targoff, *Posthumous Love: Eros and the Afterlife in Renaissance England* (Chicago: University of Chicago Press, 2014), p. 121 argues that Juliet's imagination in some ways causes her death.

and claims about them. The play's turning point is clearly the death of Mercutio, and as he receives his death wound he exclaims 'A plague a' both houses', repeating the sentiment a further two times, seemingly to make the curse more effective (III. i. 91, 99–100, 106). Plague, indeed, is the primary reason for the Friar's plan going wrong: his messenger to Romeo, Friar John, is prevented from leaving Verona because of the town officers' fear that he has been infected with plague (V. ii. 5–16); the collocation of *fear* and *infection* here infect the play with tragedy.[57] Plague, whose causes were not understood, and which was often considered an environmental issue,[58] is also something that human will and emotion can bring into play.

Romeo, in turn, uses medicine to bring about his own doom. Having heard of Juliet's death, he turns to an apothecary, from whom he demands poison. That apothecary is, significantly, described as poor and thin: 'Meagre were his looks, / Sharp misery had worn him to the bones' (V. i. 40–1). In practical terms, this poverty and starvation means that the apothecary is open to corruption by Romeo, willing for the sake of money to hand over dangerous poison (he says 'My poverty, but not my will, consents' – line 75); but in imaginative terms, his thinness makes him a figure of Romeo's desperation and devotion to death. Turning to his help makes tragedy inevitable: it's as if Romeo hands his own life over to this will-less individual, saying 'Farewell! Buy food, and get thyself in flesh' (line 84); contemptuous as this gesture is, Romeo seems to be passing over his own flesh and capacity for growth to this man.

It's often noted that Romeo (at least early in the play, when he's in love with Rosaline) is addicted to Petrarchan paradox (e.g. I. i. 174–82, 188–94), but though he mostly abandons such language, more visceral medical versions of such paradoxes dominate the play's denouement. Romeo calls his poison 'cordial and not poison' (V. i. 85), perhaps the most pointed statement of the doubleness and reversibility of medical substances. When he takes the poison at Juliet's grave, he emphasizes the flavour of that poison, calling it 'bitter conduct' and 'unsavoury guide' (V. iii. 116). He blesses the 'true apothecary' at this point because 'thy drugs are quick' (lines 119–20). The irony here is powerful: Romeo means that he's pleased he doesn't have to suffer long and thinks that he's being taken quickly to Juliet, but the other connotations are more horrible, for his haste is a reason for tragedy (Juliet's about to wake up), and there's also the sense that 'quick'

[57] On the interwoven motif of the plague in the play, see Jonathan Bate, *Soul of the Age: The Life, Mind and World of William Shakespeare* (London: Viking, 2008), p. 13.

[58] See Ernest B. Gilman, *Plague Writing in Early Modern England* (Chicago: University of Chicago Press, 2009), p. 13.

means *alive*, again stressing the doubleness of the poison.[59] When Juliet finds Romeo dead, she wants to take some of his poison but is annoyed that he's been greedy with it:

> O, churl, drunk all, and left no friendly drop
> To help me after? I will kiss thy lips.
> Haply some poison yet doth hang on them,
> To make me die with a restorative.
> (V. iii. 163–6)

This horrible moment brings together all the doubleness of the play's use of potions but is ineffective. As Romeo has died with womanly poison, Juliet will have to die in manly wise by stabbing herself. The play's inversions are complete, because the doubleness of nature has not been well handled. Aristotle argues that tragedy involves the medical purgation of pity and fear, but here fear has prevented proper medical intervention: its key medicinal figure Friar Lawrence has become one 'that trembles, sighs and weeps' (line 184); he claims to be 'the greatest' but is in the end 'able to do least' (line 223).[60] The rude will of fate has defeated grace. There is no transcendence of the natural condition.[61]

Macbeth's natural magicians are much eerier and lowlier, but much more capable than Friar Lawrence, partly because they attempt only to prophesy, not to influence the plot directly. The Weird Sisters, aka. the 'weyard' (Folio spelling), or wayward sisters, represent both fate,[62] and everything that is unaccountable and abnormal in nature, and the play represents Shakespeare's most powerful conflict between the good and ill forces of the natural world. Charles Lamb described the Weird Sisters as 'foul anomalies',[63] which is wonderfully apt: the word 'foul' hints punningly at their avian qualities, able to hover through the air, being natural but at the same time not of this earth; and they are anomalous in the key sense

59 For a valuable commentary on this scene, see Brian Cummings, *Mortal Thoughts: Religion, Secularity and Identity in Shakespeare and Early Modern Culture* (Oxford: Oxford University Press, 2013), pp. 183–4.

60 Kastan, *A Will to Believe*, p. 52, argues that 'the tragedy is at least in part a function of the Friar's failure to act as a friar, in ministering to Romeo's heart instead of his soul'; yet I would suggest that the problem is his inability to bring grace into the natural world.

61 Targoff, *Posthumous Love*, chapter 4 shows how Shakespeare systematically removes any sense of an afterlife from his play's sources.

62 On the nature of the Weird Sisters, see the penetrating discussion in Anthony Harris, *Night's Black Agents: Witchcraft and Magic in Seventeenth-Century English Drama* (Manchester: Manchester University Press, 1980). At p. 34, in particular, he shows how the ambiguity of the Sisters is prompted by ambiguity about them in Shakespeare's source, Holinshed's chronicles.

63 Cit. Harris, *Night's Black Agents*, p. 186.

that they don't obey the normative rules of the natural universe but are still part of it.

This makes the Weird/Wayward Sisters highly questionable figures, natural, supernatural and unnatural at the same time: are they like the imaginary dagger which, according to Macbeth 'marshall'st me the way that I was going' (II. i. 42), as if they were mere signposts to the inevitable end? When they disappear from their first meeting with Macbeth, Banquo says of them,

> The earth hath bubbles, as the water has,
> And these are of them. Whither are they vanished?
> (I. iii. 79–80)

Being bubbles, intrusions of one element into another, they are exceptions to nature's basic, simple rules, the kinds of secondary phenomena that Aristotle argued philosophers should not concern themselves with, and which Bacon described as 'vast and strange swellings' in sea, earth or sky; though these 'exuberancies and irregularities' are ultimately tied down, they are objects of wonder.[64] But that does not make them unnatural or supernatural (the elements of the play which make them decisively supernatural seem to be Middleton's).[65] Yet they are able to provoke Macbeth to think that 'nothing is, but what is not' (lines 141–2); it is the human mind that can create new nothings, new forms of destructive chaos.

In their most witchy mode, the sisters prepare a grim meal, containing snake, newt, frog, bat, dog, witches' mummy, a Jew's liver and a baby's finger, among other delights (IV. i. 1–38).[66] This is only the most notable example of problematic foodstuffs in the play. When Macbeth and Banquo receive the initial prophecy, the latter wonders whether they have 'eaten on the insane root / That takes the reason prisoner' (I. iii. 84–5); this probably refers to hemlock, and the suggestion that the events of the play have been prompted by natural substances resonates throughout. A sense of natural growth accompanies this, Macbeth wondering if the weird sisters can 'look into the seeds of time' (line 58) to see what will grow there; in the next scene, Duncan tries to promote healthier growth in Macbeth, saying 'I have begun to plant thee, and will labour / To make thee full of growing' (I. iv. 28–9),[67] but the process of the play encourages the bad seeds to grow

64 *The Works of Francis Bacon*, VI: 413.
65 See Middleton, *Collected Works*, ed. Taylor and Lavagnino, for an edition of *Macbeth* indicating Middleton's probable changes to the text.
66 See Fitzpatrick, *Food in Shakespeare*, pp. 47–9 on the possible medical effects of this concoction/brew.
67 Scott, *Shakespeare's Nature*, pp. 129–34 demonstrates the ways in which the play's protagonists cut themselves off from natural impulses.

out, and much of this has to do with the failure to provide proper food and hospitality.

Murdering Duncan is clearly a major social faux pas. Macbeth recognizes that as Duncan's 'host' as well as kinsman (I. vii. 14), killing him is a particularly grim violation. This resonates with classical myths, in which failures of hospitality are principal causes of tragedy. Duncan's own language points to this as a central issue: he says of Macbeth that 'he is full so valiant, / And in his commendations I am fed; / It is a banquet to me' (I. iv. 54–6). The sense that Macbeth's primary duty is to feed his king is very strong here. When Lady Macbeth then says that her husband's nature is 'too full o' th' milk of human kindness' (I. v. 17), she suggests that he is naturally one who converts blood into something nourishing; when she goes on to exchange her 'milk for gall' (line 48), she subverts this nourishment and sets up the violation of food-based hospitality and natural connection between people.[68] Her ironic statement of hospitality 'He that's coming / Must be provided for' (lines 66–7), and her welcome to Duncan have a 'double' quality (I. vi. 15), in which equivocation and poisonous reversibility replace the 'double trust' Macbeth believes in (I. vii. 12).

The murder's natural resonances are stronger than that of any other deed in Shakespeare. In this case, 'Nature seems dead' (II. i. 50), the source of life is about to be cut off.[69] The doubleness of Nature is nowhere eerier and more powerful. Referring to Duncan's serving-men, Lady Macbeth says 'death and nature do contend about them' (II. ii. 7), and the vector for this change is the drugged wine she has given them. This wine is a mysteriously double substance, for 'That which hath made them drunk hath made me bold; / What hath quenched them hath given me fire' (lines 1–2); her periphrastic description here adds to the mystery of the substance, which is reinforced a little later by the Porter's discussion of the equivocal nature of alcohol (II. iii. 25–36). She and the wine have become embodiments of nature turned against itself (for the animal effects of this, see Chapter 2, above). The rest of the play will be an attempt to provide physic for this.

After the failure of hospitality to Duncan, the play's central banquet is an attempt to return to normal hospitality, but it is obviously rather spoiled by the appearance of a ghost. Banquo is the 'chief guest', whose Lady Macbeth describes in extravagant terms:

68 Harris, *Night's Black Agents*, p. 52, points out that Lady Macbeth's self-unsexing doesn't make her masculine; rather, it transforms her into a sexless creature, as demonic (and indeed angelic) spirits were supposed to be.

69 See MacFaul, *Problem Fathers*, p. 133.

If he had been forgotten,
It had been as a gap in our great feast,
And all-thing unbecoming.
(III. i. 11–13)

The word 'gap' here may remind us of the possibility of a 'gap in nature' that admiration for Cleopatra might have produced were it not that nature abhors 'vacancy' (*Antony and Cleopatra*, II. ii. 218, 216) – the idea of a violation of fundamental natural rules is projected onto this banquet, and Banquo's ghost comes to fill the gap, as an unbecoming, inappropriate 'all-thing'.[70] At the banquet itself, Lady Macbeth says that 'the sauce to meat is ceremony, / Meeting were bare without it (III. iv. 35–6); her feeble pun on meeting/ meat may remind us of all that's unmeet and unnatural about this event – and all that's supplementary, all that is a saucy intrusion, and perhaps even of the absence of Duncan, who was the 'very source' of his sons' blood (II. iii. 98). Wishing, disingenuously, that Banquo were at the feast, Macbeth tries to ceremonialize by the use of a toast, saying 'To all, and him, we thirst, / And all to all' (III. iv. 90–1); this sense of deep need resonates with Lady Macbeth's earlier sense of a gap, and the very thirst seems to invoke the real presence of Banquo, whose ghost enters at this moment. Yet when he sees the ghost, Macbeth is seen to have 'displaced the mirth, broke the good meeting, / With most admired disorder' (lines 108–9); he, rather than the ghost that no one else can see, is the cause of disorder and the destruction of hospitable happiness. At the end of the scene, he admits that he has 'Strange things' in his head (line 138), being able to see more than the conventional order of nature.

Yet no medicinal effort on his part can be effective. He tells Lady Macbeth's doctor to

Throw physic to the dogs, I'll none of it.
Come, put mine armour on; give me my staff.
Seyton, send out. Doctor, the thanes fly from me.—
Come, sir, dispatch.—If thou couldst, doctor, cast
The water of my land, find her disease,
And purge it to a sound and pristine health,
I would applaud thee to the very echo,

[70] There are some weird and telling parallels between the plays, which were probably written in the same year: Macbeth parallels his own relationship with Banquo to that between Mark Antony and Caesar (III. i. 54–6); the consequence of Cleopatra's famous appearance on the barge is that Antony is left sitting alone in the marketplace (II. ii. 215), an odd inversion of the excess of company at Macbeth's banquet, where he has nowhere to sit as a result of the ghost's appearance. In both cases the effect of the naturally unnatural violation of the order of things is the displacement of masculine authority.

That should applaud again.—Pull 't off, I say.—
What rhubarb, cyme, or what purgative drug,
Would scour these English hence? (V. iii. 47–56)

It's significant that he's so distracted while pondering purgation here. He, unlike the English King who can cure scrofula with his mere touch of 'strange virtue' (IV. iii. 156), has no such regal power to heal. Cathness intends to 'Meet . . . the med'cine of the sickly weal' (V. ii. 27), the paradox of the last phrase resonating with the returning pun on *meet/meat* here. The cure is bound to be bloody rather than meet. Malcolm wants to 'make us med'cines of our great revenge' (IV. iii. 214), but he cannot be the purgative figure. Instead, Macduff, the unnatural man, one who is 'not of woman born', must be the healer. Of course, this just means that he was born by Caesarian section, but the riddle has more imaginative implications: the operation would almost certainly have killed his mother (if she weren't already dying), and it detaches him from womanly nature insofar as the mother's birth canal metonymically constitutes 'woman'.[71] Perhaps as a result, he (according to his wife) 'wants the natural touch' (IV. ii. 9); Rosse insists that Macduff 'best knows / The fits o' th' season' (lines 16–17), but there is a sense in which this knowledge comes at a cost. Temporally informed and structured, such knowledge exists in 'times when we are traitors / And do not know ourselves' (lines 18–19). Macduff calls himself 'naught' (IV. iii. 225), and though this mainly means that he is bad (naughty) for having left his wife and children to die, it also implies that he is a radical *nothing*, something out of the order of nature that can heal the gap created by the murders. Such nothings – which thankfully cancel each other out – are the true violations of nature, invoked purely by the mind, they are like the Cartesian ego, trying to transcend its embodiment.[72] This is Shakespeare's zero-point, the end of tragedy: the be-all and the end-all of masculine ambition.[73] Graham Bradshaw argues that '*Macbeth* terrifies, not by denying the existence of "order" in some dogmatically sceptical

[71] Janet Adelman, *Suffocating Mothers*, p. 161, argues that the function of Caesarian birth in *Macbeth* is to detach human generation from mothers, creating a fantasy of male 'self-birth'. Katherine Park, *Secrets of Women: Gender, Generation, and the Origins of Human Dissection* (New York: Zone Books, 2006), p. 154 argues that those born by Caesarian section were treated as particularly special people, free of supposed feminine weakness.

[72] Rossiter, *Angel with Horns*, pp. 218–9: 'Macbeth becomes the embodiment of everything antagonistic and self-directed; and yet he is made the symbol of the utter emptiness of mere antagonism and self-assertion.' This surely applies to Macduff, too.

[73] Rossiter, *Angel with Horns*, p. 211, finely discusses 'Macbeth's *impulsion* (rather than his decision, as an ambitious man would feel it) to assert *his* pattern on the world: to make Macbeth Scotland. Instead, he finds he has made Scotland Macbeth: his damned soul has infected a whole country, even the whole universe'.

or nihilistic way, but by making its reality so alarmingly uncertain'.[74] Nothing is, but what is not, in the world of *Macbeth*: the mind creates its own phantasms, its own version of reality, jumps over life, radically detaches us from the source of being. The usurping King, who wants to be everything, the be-all and the end-all, can't even sit down to a meal. From this point on, the healing powers of feminine romance and more accepting wise passivity must supervene. Macbeth (and his antagonist) try to purge the natural world by escaping it, jumping the life to come, but we must return to the bank and school of time. There is no purgation possible in *Macbeth*, no art that will suffice. *The Tempest*, as we will see in the final chapter, offers a tentative, troubled version of such a sufficient art.

[74] *Shakespeare's Scepticism*, p. 224.

CHAPTER 4

The Tempest

Shakespeare's last single-authored play ties together many of this book's themes: its location, Prospero's mysterious island, is a strangely liminal space, and one that enables transformations and redemptions of a limited sort; the island's one native, Caliban, is a figure of animality who challenges our notions of what it is to be human; Prospero's magical art, meanwhile, weirdly balances between natural feeling and transcendence, a balance that is focalized through his attitude to eating on the island and its penitential meanings. The island, a naturally-unnatural environment, is a place where human feelings and thoughts can change the world and be changed by it.

The qualities of the isle

Alison Shell argues that Prospero's island is a 'heterocosm: a discrete imaginative world custom-built for a particular play, where cosmology is symbiotically related to narrative and structure'.[1] The island is not just a heterocosm in the sense that it is other to the normal world, but in the deeper sense that it is radically other to *itself*: it is both a purgatory and a paradise, a place of the highest redemptive art and a home of the most fallen nature. As David Norbrook argues, 'The magic island of Shakespeare's play is at once an instance and an allegory of the players' project of opening up new spaces for discourse. It is a place where no name, no discourse, is entirely natural; language and nature are neither simply conflated nor simply opposed to one another'.[2] It is also a space of wonder, with all the ambivalence about that emotion that characterizes Shakespeare's attitude to the natural world.

1 *Shakespeare and Religion*, p. 13.
2 David Norbrook, '"What Care These Roarers for the Name of King": Language and Utopia in *The Tempest*', in Kiernan Ryan (ed.), *Shakespeare: The Last Plays* (Harlow: Longman, 1999), p. 251 (essay originally published in 1992).

On arrival at the island, Gonzalo attempts some consolation for the nobles' shipwrecked state and sense of loss, saying that their sorrow 'Is common', shared by sailors' wives and others, and that their preservation is a 'miracle' (II. i. 4, 6). The state of mind represented by the island is both a lowest common denominator and a wonder; as such, it resembles the golden but quotidian world of pastoral literature. As in pastoral, Gonzalo attempts to read that nature and draw lessons from it about mankind and civilization, creating an easily mocked but seductive vision of the island as a potential utopia.[3] Were he in charge (though there is 'No sovereignty'), 'All things in common nature should produce / Without sweat or endeavour' (lines 157, 160–1); it is hard to see how this would be effected, unless he had some magic like Prospero's. His communist idea, moreover, is intriguingly phrased, with the word 'common' seeming as much to qualify 'nature' as to be part of the phrase 'all things in common'; as with the suffering he earlier described, the state of the natural world is common. His idea is as much consolatory as practical, but it sets a tone for the play, in which the island represents a shared but multiplex experience.

Yet that sharing is not so obvious from the first. As with the 'sympathizèd' experience of *The Comedy of Errors*, the characters of this play are having a common experience of this strange environment from different perspectives.[4] Adrian sees the island as being 'of subtle, tender and delicate temperance', and Gonzalo sees 'everything advantageous to life' there, but Antonio scoffs at these comments, seeing the air as 'rotten' and the absence of 'means to live' (lines 42–3, 50, 48, 51). It's possible that Gonzalo and Adrian are making the best of things, flattering their king's hopes, while Antonio is being earthily realistic or cynical; yet we can also read the former pair more positively, seeing them as having the kind of awoken faith *The Winter's Tale*'s Paulina enjoins. If so, their faith may really make the place better, and this clearly relates to them being better men than the treacherous Antonio, who may be experiencing a radically different island. On the basis of faith and moral character, then, the island may be a different thing to different men. Certainly, each group of shipwrecked characters has a different experience, cut off from the others: Ferdinand has his love suit with Miranda, Stephano and Trinculo their drunken rampage, and

[3] On the absurdity of his utopian impulses, see Scott, *Shakespeare's Nature*, p. 203.

[4] See the excellent commentary on this passage in A. D. Nuttall, Two Concepts of Allegory: A Study of Shakespeare's *The Tempest* and the Logic of Allegorical Expression (New Haven: Yale University Press, 2007), p. 142. See also See David Norbrook's discussion of this sequence in 'What Care These Roarers', pp. 255–6; Norbrook shows how Shakespeare uses Montaigne here in order to complicate the nature of utopian discourse, which is always embedded in the political situation of its speaker.

the king and courtiers their purgatorial experience. The fact of the good Gonzalo being with those who are to be punished makes the differential more radical in that case (and as his goodness involves loyalty to the bad means that even the good must share a bit of punishment). Sebastian says of Gonzalo 'I think he will carry this island home in his pocket and give it his son for an apple' (lines 91–2), and this wonderful comment packs in a lot.[5] The island is somehow portable, a potential gift, but it is also double-edged, reminding us of the fatal apple of Eden and the apple of discord. Like a duck-rabbit,[6] or like Queen Elizabeth's communion, the essential transformation is a matter of what we take it *for*.

The island's transformations, like the translations in *As You Like It*, are 'rich and strange' (I. ii. 402); they are not simple moral patterns. Antonio and Sebastian are made for a while even worse than they once were, and there seems to be something strangely involuntary in the emergence of their treason. Alonso is made sleepy by the 'quality o' th' climate' (II. i. 200), but Antonio and Sebastian are not. Sebastian describes himself as 'standing water' and Antonio says he'll 'teach [him] how to flow' (lines 221–2). Here we see the activation of humours for which the characters don't exactly have responsibility. Alonso's sleepiness, which connects to Sebastian's sense of 'Hereditary sloth' (line 223), is perhaps as much a cause of treason as anything in the plotters themselves;[7] this makes the incident a replay of Antonio's treason against Prospero, where 'an evil nature' 'Awaked' and *grew*, as almost a natural result of Prospero being a 'stranger' to his state (I. ii. 93, 113, 76). Treason is strangely other: it is so unaccountable that individual responsibility seems to be compromised in it. Its re-enactment on the island makes a kind of sense of it, but still an alienated sense. The initial retelling of Antonio's treason exists in a mysterious past, a 'dark backward and abysm of time' that is radically separate from the play's own action (line 50). At the play's end, when Prospero forgives Antonio and Sebastian, he seems to say that their 'inward pinches . . . are most strong' for the treason against Alonso (V. i. 77); the effect of this parenthetical, aside phrasing is to suggest that his pivotal, performative utterance of forgiveness is forgiveness for the treason not against himself but against the other legitimate ruler. Forgiveness, like the treason that prompted it, becomes radically displaced. Perhaps only things that have happened on the island can be settled on the

5 See Palfrey, *Late Shakespeare*, p. 142.

6 See Ludwig Wittgenstein, *Philosophical Investigations*, ed. P. M. S. Hacker and Joachim Schulte, trans. G. E. M. Anscombe, 4th edition (Oxford: Blackwell, 2009), p. 204. The image is one which can be read either as a duck or a rabbit (but not both at the same time).

7 Compare the sleepiness of the betrayed lion in Spenser's *Mother Hubberd's Tale*.

island: things in the abysm of time that is the *real* world cannot be properly handled here.[8]

Ferdinand sees the island as a 'paradise', and he wants to 'live here ever' (IV. i. 124, 122). As he is the future King of Naples, this will not be possible, but he does gain from the island, at least in an optative sense, a blessing of 'Earth's increase' (line 110). The source of this blessing, though, is problematic: it is possible that Ceres speaks the key lines, but the Folio text actually attributes them to Juno, even though they end 'Ceres' blessing so is on you' (line 117). Ceres herself seems rather coy, wondering why she's been summoned to 'this short-grassed green' (line 83), and being more concerned about her feud with Venus than about the ceremonies going forth in her name. Her final role in the masque is to whisper mysteriously with Juno (line 124 SD), making us doubtful as to what her real message is, and implying that there is more to her than can be represented. The blessing, however curiously mediated, is very firmly located in the particular (but strangely indefinite) location of the island, Ceres being summoned by Iris to *sport* 'Here on this grass-plot, in this very place' (lines 73–4).[9] Ceres is called *away* from her proper business, her 'rich leas / Of wheat, rye, barley, fetches, oats, and pease' (lines 60–1), to come and engage in decidedly impractical play in the masque on the island.

Whatever the nature of the blessing that Ferdinand gets, he does definitely get Miranda, and for him at least there's a powerfully metonymical connection between place and person. Miranda is the one who remembers little but life on the island, and for whom the outsiders constitute a 'brave new world' (V. i. 183). She is also the embodiment of the redemptive qualities of the island. From the first, she is full of sympathy for the sufferings of others – not just the shipwrecked (I. ii. 3–6, 27), but also for her father and for her younger self (lines 132–5). Prospero sees her as having saved him, calling her a 'cherubin',[10] 'Infusèd with a fortitude from heaven' (lines 152, 154). Being outside the order of the normal world, she might almost be an unfallen, salvific figure. She denies being a 'wonder' (despite her name – line 428), but there is something extraordinary about her, radically connected to both the order of nature and to that of grace.

With the peculiar diminutive phrasing of affection, Prospero calls Miranda 'Poor worm' (III. i. 31). Yet a few moments later Ferdinand says

8 As Nuttall argues, this is an aspect of the play's sense of coming into meaning; it is 'pre-allegorical', in his terms – *Two Concepts of Allegory*, p. 159.

9 Kristen Poole, *Supernatural Environments*, pp. 203–9, shows how specific and measured, yet spatially peculiar, this place is, emphasizing how mankind tends to get tangled in nature here, even while trying to get some distant, Archimedean purchase on the world.

10 Shakespeare tends to use this, incorrectly, as a singular form.

that she is 'So perfect and so peerless, [. . .] created / Of every creature's best' (lines 47–8). Though this depends on difference of perspective – the familiarity of a father and the wonder of a new suitor – the competition of these terms sets up the doubleness of Miranda, wholly part of the world but wholly transcendent. In this, she resembles Pico's vision of what humanity might be. It is perhaps for this reason that she is so often put into the separated position of spectator, as sympathetic witness of the shipwreck, as pitying audience to Prospero's backstory, and as notably silent spectator of the masque of Ceres (IV. i). Her silence in the play's final sequence then becomes more accountable: after she has celebrated the bravery of the new world, Prospero cuts her off with ''Tis new to thee' (V. i. 184), and she does not speak again. Prospero's tone here may be cynically world-weary, throwing cold water on her enthusiasm. But it may also be deeply regretful, for as she is thrown into the real world, she like the island may melt into a kind of non-existence. At this moment her subjective wonder is at its height, but that can only diminish in future; similarly, her objectively wonderful position as an innocent, trailing clouds of grace, must inevitably vanish.

As a heterocosm, the island is necessarily precarious and provisional, like Miranda's virginity. It is not worth the less for that, but its value and its precariousness are tightly tied together. Alonso's jostled senses come to a deep sense of wonder at the play's denouement when he says 'These are not natural events, they strengthen / From strange to stranger' (lines 227–8). There is fear here, but also a growing sense of the coherence of this world's strangeness.[11] It is 'as strange a maze as e'er men trod' (line 242); this sense of *amazement* is founded on the inability to stand above and survey things, and it is more acute in Alonso's case for the belief that a king *ought* to have such an overseeing position. Like John Donne, the King is 'involved in mankind',[12] walking on the ground and getting confused as a result. Alonso is reminded of his humanity, and of the wonder that is associated with humans' broken knowledge. Temporarily at least, Prospero, with his magic, and Miranda, representing possibly unfallen nature (that which should be wondered at), may have a position that stands outside humanity, but none can hold it for long.

[11] Compare Hippolyta's sense of the strange consistency ('constancy') of the lovers' story in *A Midsummer Night's Dream* (V. i. 26). See Nuttall, *Shakespeare the Thinker*, pp. 122–5 on this.

[12] *Devotions Upon Emergent Occasions*, in John Donne, *Selected Prose*, ed. Evelyn Simpson, Helen Gardner and Timothy Healy (Oxford: Clarendon Press, 1967), p. 101.

Caliban's humanity

If Miranda is one key embodiment of the qualities of the island, Caliban is a less perfect but in some ways more proper possessor of them. As the island's only native, he has a deeper connection to the place than anyone, knowing where to find food and drink for Prospero and Miranda (I. ii. 339). He also seems to read the island's alterity best, telling Stephano and Trinculo

> Be not afeard, the isle is full of noises,
> Sounds, and sweet airs, that give delight and hurt not.
> Sometimes a thousand twangling instruments
> Will hum about mine ears; and sometimes voices,
> That if I then had waked after long sleep,
> Will make me sleep again, and then in dreaming,
> The clouds methought would open, and show riches
> Ready to drop upon me, that when I waked
> I cried to dream again. (III. ii. 135–43)

The power of these lines depends to a considerable extent on their provisionality (note the use of *if*, and *methought*). Caliban's dreaminess is like Alonso's amazement, mingling fear and wonder. His ability to *hear* is crucial, and may suggest an unfallen aspect to his character, for it was thought that the ability to hear the music of the spheres was something lost in the Fall of man. The riches ready to fall on him may represent the possibility of grace, but they also suggest something uncomfortably looming, or at least tantalizing. The sadness with which these lines end embodies the sadness of being a conscious human, woken into language by Prospero's teaching. Yet the insult added to this injury is the doubt that Caliban is human at all.

Prospero's first reference to Caliban is as a 'freckled whelp' whom Sycorax 'did litter here' (I. ii. 282–3). We saw in Chapter 2 that animal insults are common in the period, often a way of thinking about the lowest common denominator of life, and the reference here may seem the emotional inverse of Prospero's affectionately calling Miranda a worm. But Prospero emphasizes Caliban's inhumanity more literally by saying that he is 'not honoured with / A human shape' (lines 283–4). This is central to the problem of defining Caliban: if he is not human, why does Prospero need to *say* that he lacks a human shape? If he is human, why does he lack such honour? There's also an implication in the concept of *honour* that human shape is a kind of supplement, an unnecessary gift; but if so, its lack could hardly be the basis for an insult. Possibly, as Prospero is talking here to Ariel, he is pointing up the contrast between his servants: Ariel, the spirit, *is* honoured with such shape, while not being human; Caliban, who *may* be human, lacks that defining feature. As a result, he challenges our sense of what it is to be human.[13]

Prospero admits that 'we cannot miss' Caliban (line 311) – i.e. that he and Miranda can't do without his services. Clearly, Ariel and the spirits cannot minister to their material needs. Or is this a fiction? Could it be that Prospero uses Caliban's apparent services to mask the help he gets from spirits he'd rather conceal from his daughter? When Ferdinand takes on Caliban's fuel-gathering duties, the service seems more nominal and ceremonial than necessary, and it may be that Caliban's service was of a similar character. If there's doubt about Caliban's nature, there's also room for doubt about whether he is needed. But that is a question we may ask about humans in general: are we necessary to nature? or are we an honourable, but basically decorative and ill-defined supplement?

Prospero further contrasts Caliban with Ariel in addressing the former as 'thou earth' (line 314), whereas Ariel is clearly associated with higher elements. If Caliban is earth, though, he is human, in the radical sense.[14] While Prospero may insist that the devil himself was Caliban's father (line 320), there's no way to know this (paternity being notoriously uncertain). Caliban's notorious and gleeful desire to 'people' the isle with Calibans shows that he has a fundamentally biological nature (and that he considers himself a person – line 351). Prospero's way of putting the matter is striking: he says 'thou didst seek to violate / The honour of my child' (lines 347–8). This leaves some doubt about whether it was an attempted rape or merely clumsy courtship, but the main point is that emphasis on *honour* again, a concept that is surely socially constructed and irrelevant to Caliban. Caliban's response – 'O ho, O ho, would't had been done' (line 349) – mocks the idea of honour, but also in its passive construction suggests the absence of rational motive or active will in his desires. Motive, like honour, is part of a social structure and world that is fundamentally alien to the island. Caliban, oriented wholly to the earth of his birth, is only interested in filling it up, inhabiting it as fully as possible, not in constructing narratives (or utopias) that supervene upon that land. By contrast, as Antony Harris points out, in order for his theurgic powers to work properly, Prospero needs to be particularly chaste, imposing chastity on Ferdinand and Miranda as

[13] See Palfrey, *Late Shakespeare*, p. 156.

[14] See Harrison, *Forests*, p. 7.

well as on Caliban.[15] But that may also make him more inhuman than Caliban.

Miranda thinks that Ferdinand – in contrast to Caliban – must be a 'spirit' (line 412), and she needs Prospero's reassurance that he's human: 'I might call him / A thing divine, for nothing natural / I ever saw so noble' (lines 418–20). As with Alonso's later sense of strangeness of the play's events, the idea of the unnatural is invoked to express positive wonder, as a reflection of broken knowledge. An aristocratic human, from the innocent, unknowing perspective of Miranda, looks even stranger than Caliban.

Caliban's radical association with the natural world of the island can be seen even in his curses and punishments:

> All the infections that the sun sucks up
> From bogs, fens, flats, on Prosper fall, and make him
> By inch-meal a disease! His spirits hear me,
> And yet I needs must curse. But they'll nor pinch,
> Fright me with urchin-shows, pitch me i' th' mire,
> Nor lead me, like a fire-brand in the dark
> Out of my way, unless he bid 'em; but
> For every trifle are they set upon me,
> Sometime like apes that mow and chatter at me,
> And after bite me; then like hedgehogs which
> Lie tumbling in my barefoot way, and mount
> Their pricks at my footfall; sometime am I
> All wound with adders, who with cloven tongues
> Do hiss me into madness. (II. ii. 1–14)

He is deeply embedded in this world, but not able to gain any transcendent perspective on it. His barefoot connection with the land is only painful: the hedgehogs that prick his feet remind us of the serpent that is to bruise fallen man's heel; the adders' double tongues suggest that the doubleness of language alienates fallen man from a paradise that might have been his own. Like the courtiers later, he is bewildered and amazed by his progress through the island. Yet he also feels enough of a connection to the earth that he can invoke its harmful qualities on Prospero, however unsuccessfully (in this, he resembles Richard II – see Chapter 1, above).

The cursing, however, does seem to effect a separation from his master, and the emergence of a new relation. As this scene goes on, he encounters Trinculo and Stephano, the former of whom thinks him a 'strange fish' (line 27). Immediately, Trinculo thinks of how Caliban might be exploited:

[15] Harris, *Night's Black Agents*, p. 131.

> Were I in England now (as once I was) and had but this fish painted, not a holiday fool there but would give a piece of silver. There would this monster make a man; any strange beast there makes a man. When they will not give a doit to relieve a lame beggar, they will lay out ten to see a dead Indian. (lines 27–32)

The last part of this comment shows that Trinculo does basically admit Caliban's humanity, albeit humanity of an alien kind. The highly ironic notion that this monster might 'make a man' has the main sense that it would make him rich, but also suggests that such a troublingly semi-human figure is a paradoxical means to fashion full humanity. This is the inverse of Jack Cade's sense that animal products such as parchment and seals might undo a man (see Chapter 2, above), but in different ways both Trinculo and Cade see the boundaries of man and animal as threatening humanity's privileges. Trinculo's rather out-of-character social criticism reminds the audience that a fascination with alien humanity can distract us from seeing the blurred or maimed humanity of poor and wounded men closer to home. If exotic people trouble our categories of humanity and consequent fellow-feeling, that is merely a sign that all social difference can have a similar effect.

Stephano rather than Trinculo becomes Caliban's new king and master, because he has 'celestial liquor' to give him (line 117). He suggests that Caliban needs this drink in order to have the capacity to speak, saying 'Here is that which will give language to you, cat' (lines 82–3); this is based (as the Arden 3 editors point out) on the wittily proverbial praise of ale that 'would make a cat speak'. Yet Stephano has already heard Caliban speak, and has commented 'Where the devil should he learn our language' (lines 66–7). The casual invocation of the devil here may imply a fear that such speech (like the serpent's in Eden) comes from the devil, and that it is better to rationalize it away by attributing it to strong drink. Yet drink itself is associated with the demonic: Cassio in *Othello* laments that he has been assailed by 'the devil drunkenness', and that 'men should put an enemy in their mouths to steal away their brains' (II. iii. 296, 290–1).[16] Like speech, drink is a marker of human separation from nature. In fact, though, it was Prospero who notoriously taught Caliban language: as this is so, we might see the parallels between Prospero and Stephano, seeing them both as devilish figures who effect a fall in Caliban, alienating him from the natural world. Caliban says that Prospero 'keep[s]' the island 'from' him (I. ii. 343–4), phrasing that implies an illegitimate feudal tenure, but also

[16] The word 'enemy' here refers to the etymology of Satan's name.

that Prospero has caused a separation between Caliban and nature, has forced his fall. Caliban's sexual desire for Miranda can be seen as unfallen desire, like his unfallen possession of the land. Prospero has interrupted both connections.

Caliban, then, embodies a double attitude to man in the state of nature: he reflects a common fantasy of perfect connection to nature and to one's own self (like Macbeth's), at the same time as he is condemned for savagery. Yet there is no way back from his fallenness, however much it may be externally imposed. He can't simply return to nature, so he needs to 'be wise hereafter / And seek for grace' (V. i. 295–6). *Hereafter* suggests a moment of *metanoia*, a changing of the mind necessary for repentance; whether it will be successful is very much in doubt, but he is *prepared* for grace, even if grace must ultimately come unsought. *Here*after, however, also suggests a spatial as much as a temporal shift of ground: his search for grace will take place away from the island. Acknowledged as belonging (in whatever sense) to Prospero, even if he is still a 'thing of darkness' (lines 275–6), Caliban is surely to be taken from his island. If he is not to be made a 'marketable' commodity as Antonio (like Trinculo) thinks he can be (line 266), Caliban must cling to Prospero. Whatever is to happen to him, though, it is clear that he must be, like Bottom, *translated*: carried across the sea, transported into grace or exchanged for money.

Prospero's art

Prospero's powers are, above all, transformative, but they are not able to carry him across the sea. He's been able to do all sorts of things on the island,[17] but he hasn't been able to escape it, a point highlighted when he asks the audience to release him and waft him across the sea with their approval and applause (Epilogue 5–12). This is a sign, perhaps, that his material relationship to the island is rather alienated, even while he has transcendent powers that seem in part to depend on it. As we've seen, he seems to have needed Caliban's help in obtaining fuel and sustenance.

His material alienation from the environment is in some sense re-enacted in the banquet scene. Prospero invisibly presides over the delivery of the banquet, brought on by '*several strange shapes*' and accompanied by '*strange music*' (III. iii. 19 SD). Estrangement is obviously the keynote here. Seeing this, the usually sardonic Sebastian says

[17] Including, as Egan points out, deforesting it – *Green Shakespeare*, pp. 155–6.

Now I will believe
That there are unicorns; that in Arabia
There is one tree, the phoenix' throne, one phoenix
At this hour reigning there. (lines 21–4)

It may be that what he really means is that he'll no more believe in what he's now seeing than in the existence of those mythical creatures. But his examples are suggestive: both the unicorn (who supposedly missed the boat at Noah's flood) and the phoenix (image of the perpetual identity of royalty) are in some ways transcendent beings, not quite afflicted by human fallenness. As such, they are rather unnatural (of course, if they don't exist they're doubly so), but some of their transcendent glamour here accrues to the invisible Prospero, for good or ill.

Sebastian, casting aside doubts and wonder as to the nature of those who provided the feast, falls onto the material side: with a hint of a pun, he says 'No matter, since / They have left their viands behind; for we have stomachs' (lines 40–1); Alonso, initially reluctant, is persuaded to 'stand to, and feed, / Although my last, no matter, since I feel / The best is past' (lines 49–51). This repetition of 'no matter', ironically materialistic as it is, has a further irony in that it seems to cast the matter of the food away, and seems to prompt the moment when Ariel enters as a harpy and makes the banquet vanish. Sarah Beckwith brilliantly connects the removal of the banquet to the theology of the Eucharist, showing how controversies over its meaning were tied up with questions of the subjective states of those who received the Lord's Supper, particularly whether they were in a state of charity with one another.[18] The implication of all this may be that the courtiers should be thinking about other matters (their guilt) before the matter of food, and clearly the main point of the scene is the setup of Prospero's penitential punishment on Antonio, Sebastian and Alonso, but we may wonder if he does have the capacity to provide them with real food.

Caliban, responding early on in the play to Prospero's threats of torture, rather gnomically says 'I must eat my dinner' (I. ii. 330). Whether he is merely prompted by Prospero having just mentioned honey, thinking of feeding himself up before his sufferings, or merely expressing a general and distractible (and solitary) appetitiveness as part of his character, Caliban seems to be the only person in the play who eats: it is appropriate, as he is the truest inhabitant of the island. Other characters are less able to eat, perhaps because to do so would prevent them from leaving the island.[19] At

[18] *Shakespeare and the Grammar of Forgiveness*, pp. 150–7.
[19] One thinks of the myth of Proserpine.

the play's end, Prospero says that his story is 'Not a relation for a breakfast' (V. i. 164), presumably because it's a long story more fit to accompany a longer meal; the penitential fast that the courtiers have undergone, though, is implied in the word *breakfast,* it being a necessary meal after fasting for religious reasons (such as to receive communion), rather than a ceremonial meal at which talk would be appropriate. Prospero later invites them to his cell to hear his story (lines 301–5), but does not mention whether he will provide a meal (indeed his mention of 'waste' may suggest not). Sustenance is somehow not part of his narrative of magic and forgiveness. Prospero accounts for Alonso's bewilderment by saying 'You do yet taste / Some subtleties o' the isle' (lines 123–4), suggesting that the weirder experiences of the island are gustatory, and must be purged for full understanding to emerge. At the end of the banquet scene Gonzalo says that Antonio, Sebastian and Alonso experience their guilt as being 'like poison' (III. iii. 105). Prospero's medicine for this guilt is not material, and this is partly because Antonio denies the materiality of his conscience, which is like a melting candy rather than a recalcitrant chilblain (II. i. 277–81). By starving the villains, Prospero has effected an embodiment of their consciences, but he has done so by immaterial means.

Ariel's relationship to material nature is as ambiguous as that of his master. When he was subject to Sycorax, he was 'a spirit too delicate / To act her earthy and abhorred commands' (I. ii. 272–3), which perhaps implies that he refused (or was incapable of responding to) her sexual advances. For this rejection of her natural self, he was given the cruelly appropriate punishment of being confined in a tree (wood being the basic form of matter according to some ancient Greek thought). Yet Ariel experiences his gratitude for freedom in natural terms: as Prospero says, he 'think[s] it much to tread the ooze / Of the salt deep, / To run upon the sharp wind of the north, / To do me business in the veins o' th' earth / When it is baked with frost' (lines 252–6). Such experience of the innards of nature seems to depend on his relationship to Prospero. His good opinion of the experience, what he *thinks* of it, may also depend on his relationship to his master and other humans, for he may appreciate his freedom all the more for the servitude to which it is bound.

More generally, there seems to be some transfer or translation of capacities between Prospero and Ariel. If Prospero gets something of Ariel's transcendent capacities, it is Ariel's sense that he would pity the nobles 'were I human' that seems to prompt Prospero's human pity (V. i. 20 – the line is beautifully shared). When Prospero invokes the elves, etc. that have aided his magic, he calls them 'weak masters' (line 41), indicating the ambiguity of the relationship involved (and reminding us of the inversion of power in *Doctor Faustus*), but also pointing to his own fundamental weakness (restated in the Epilogue, lines 2–3). When Prospero says 'The rarer action is / In virtue than in vengeance' (V. i. 27–8), the sense is clear enough, but the diction is peculiar.[20] The *rarity* of virtue may faintly echo Ariel's name, and surely points to the idea of the transcendent, the rarefied properties of the air; but this is paradoxical as the word *virtue* is more firmly tied to his identity as a *man* (Latin: *vir*) than as one who rises above humanity. Through this mixture of human and superhuman, natural and supernatural, Prospero gets in some ways the best of both worlds.

Yet it's hard to feel entirely comfortable about his forgiveness, and perhaps that's another reason that the word virtue replaces it. Addressing Antonio, Prospero calls him 'most wicked sir, whom to call brother / Would even infect my mouth' (lines 130–1). There's still something poisonous in oral experience of whatever kind. Perhaps due to his sense of the limitations of words, then, Prospero forgives Alonso in a bodily way, by embracing him. This is one of Shakespeare's most insistent recognition scenes, Prospero declaring himself thus:

> Behold, sir King,
> The wrongèd Duke of Milan, Prospero.
> For more assurance that a living prince
> Does now speak to thee, I embrace thy body.
> (lines 106–9)

The embrace is not just a form of welcome but involves a bodily transfer or translation of power, as Prospero takes on his true identity. Seemingly as a matter of course – or force majeure – Alonso resigns the dukedom of Milan, cutting Antonio out of the loop. Prospero goes on to address Antonio and Sebastian in animalistically diminishing terms as a 'brace of lords' (line 126), but it's not at all clear that he embraces either of them, for there's no need to take a regal body from them. Indeed, the word 'brace' may point up the absence of a fraternal embrace, suggesting that their conspiratorial bracing of each other will have to do. Antonio may be his 'Flesh and blood' (line 74), but the connection between them will not be renaturalized. Rather, his recognition of Alonso, like his acknowledgement of Caliban, is a *self*-recognition, a provisional acceptance, however grudging, of his own humanity.

20 Beckwith, *Shakespeare and the Grammar of Forgiveness*, pp. 149, 165 gives a fine discussion of the nature of Prospero's release effected by his forgiveness, and of Prospero's need to become fully human to do so, but does not press on the problematic use of the word 'virtue'.

Prospero's connections to others, then, are precarious and apt to be self-involved. And his connection to his art and his island are similarly tenuous. He knows that his art is 'vanity' (IV. i. 41), empty and insubstantial. Such a position makes him also believe that the natural world itself is an 'insubstantial pageant', 'such stuff / As dreams are made on' (lines 155–7). His magic garments are 'trumpery' (line 186), but his gown is also a metonym for his art (I. ii. 25). His position as magical artist makes him devalue the material world completely. He can never be in a position of wonder, amazement and entanglement as the other characters are. Though Caliban ends up in a pond full of horse-piss (and we may wonder where the horses came from to provide this),[21] he, like all the lower characters in the world, is more *in* the world, for good or ill, than Prospero can be.[22]

Prospero must leave this island, this place of distance and detachment, in order to become human again, and in order to die. When he returns to Milan, Prospero promises, 'Every third thought shall be my grave' (V. i. 312). Whether or not this implies that he will die soon (and I'm inclined to think it does), it casts mortality as the great narrative end of the play.[23] It also connects Prospero back to his fundamentally human nature, which he has nearly lost.[24] Ariel, on his first entrance, addresses Prospero in double terms, firstly as 'great master', the transcendent organizer of the play-world, but secondly, more punningly as 'grave sir', as if reminding him that he is mortal (I. ii. 189). The grave's a fine and private place, but none I think, do there embrace, as Andrew Marvell would have it: Prospero, thinking monastically of his grave, embracing Alonso only to get back the undying, regal part of himself, and probably not embracing the brother whom he's forgiving (or virtue-ing), is perhaps the loneliest character in all literature. For Thomas Hobbes, writing a generation after Shakespeare, the life of man in a state of nature was solitary, poor, nasty, brutish and short; for Shakespeare, the truest solitude comes when one tries to stand, like Prospero and Macbeth, outside nature.

21 Prospero uses his garments as a 'stale' or decoy to entrap Caliban, and it may be that this *word* evokes the material stale of horse-piss (IV. i. 187, 199).

22 Poole, *Supernatural Environments*, pp. 208–9 sees Prospero as embodying providence and the others' entanglement in nature as threatening; her point is well made, but that is to see only one side of the matter.

23 Rather than as something Prospero can reverse by waking the sleepers from graves. For a good discussion of the problems involved here, see Harris, *Night's Black Agents*, p. 135.

24 Beckwith, *Shakespeare and the Grammar of Forgiveness*, p. 171, eloquently discusses the sense of disappointment the play's end provokes, arguing that this has to do with the disappointment of returning to a radically human state, with no external guarantor.

Prospero asks the audience's 'indulgence' to set him free from 'this bare island' (Epilogue. 20, 8). The deliberate appeal to abandoned and disparaged Catholic means of being 'pardoned' from one's sins (line 19) teases the audience to think about different possibilities as to how the supernatural world works. Thinking makes things so, but it has to be collaborative thinking, between characters, between characters and the audience, and between man and the natural world. In accepting this need for collaboration, Prospero becomes abject: having been the most masterly of characters, he is now laid low, his humility reconnecting him to his humanity and his position on the earth (*humus*). As we have seen throughout this study, for humans to have any hope for salvation, of whatever kind, they must accept their relationship to the natural world, acknowledging their human particularities, such as language, and the awareness of mortality, both of which necessarily alienate them from nature, but without claiming the sole mastery that they may think their alienation entails.

Bibliography

Adelman, Janet, *Suffocating Mothers: Fantasies of Maternal Origin in Shakespeare's Plays,* Hamlet *to* The Tempest (London: Routledge, 1992)

Agamben, Giorgio, *The Open: Man and Animal*, trans. Kevin Attell (Stanford: Stanford University Press, 2004)

Bacon, Francis, *The Advancement of Learning*, ed. Michael Kiernan, in *The Oxford Francis Bacon* (Oxford: Clarendon Press, 2000)

The New Organon, trans. Michael Silverthorne, ed. Lisa Jardine (Cambridge: Cambridge University Press, 2000)

The Works of Francis Bacon, ed. J. Spedding, R.L. Ellis, and D.D. Heath, 7 vols. (London: Longman's, 1857–74)

Barber, C.L., *Shakespeare's Festive Comedy: A Study of Dramatic Form and its Relation to Social Custom* (1959; Princeton: Princeton University Press, 2012)

Barbour, Reid, *English Stoics and Epicureans: Ancient Legacies in Early Stuart Culture* (Amherst: University of Massachusetts Press, 1998)

Barkan, Leonard, *Nature's Work of Art: The Human Body as Image of the World* (New Haven: Yale University Press, 1975)

Barnes, Jonathan (ed.), *The Complete Works of Aristotle: The Revised Oxford Translation*, 2 vols. (Princeton: Princeton University Press, 1984)

Baron-Cohen, Simon *The Essential Difference: Men, Women, and the Extreme Male Brain* (London: Allen Lane 2003)

Barton, Anne, *Essays, Mainly Shakespearean* (Cambridge: Cambridge University Press, 1994)

Bate, Jonathan, '"Hide thy life": The Key to Shakespeare', *Times Higher Education Supplement*, 6 August 2009

(ed.), *The Romantics on Shakespeare*, (London: Penguin, 1992)

Shakespeare and the English Romantic Imagination, 2nd edition (Oxford: Clarendon Press, 1989)

The Song of the Earth (London: Picador, 2000)

Soul of the Age: The Life, Mind and World of William Shakespeare (London: Viking, 2008)

Beckwith, Sarah, *Shakespeare and the Grammar of Forgiveness* (Ithaca: Cornell University Press, 2011)

Berger, Harry Jr., *Making Trifles of Terrors: Redistributing Complicities in Shakespeare*, ed. Peter Erickson (Stanford, CA: Stanford University Press, 1997)

Second World and Green World: Studies in Renaissance Fiction-Making (Berkeley: University of California Press, 1988)
Harold Bloom (ed.), *Hamlet: Bloom's Shakespeare through the Ages* (New York: Infobase Publishing, 2008)
Shakespeare: The Invention of the Human (New York: Riverhead Books, 1998)
Boehrer, Bruce, *Environmental Degradation in Jacobean Drama* (Cambridge: Cambridge University Press, 2013)
Shakespeare among the Animals: Nature and Society in the Drama of Early Modern England (New York: Palgrave, 2002)
Borlik, Todd A., *Ecocriticism and Early Modern English Literature: Green Pastures* (New York: Routledge, 2011)
Bouwsma, William J., *John Calvin: A Sixteenth-Century Portrait* (New York: Oxford University Press, 1988)
Bradshaw, Graham, *Shakespeare's Scepticism* (Brighton: Harvester, 1987)
Bradshaw, John, *Cat Sense: The Feline Enigma Revealed* (London: Allen Lane, 2013)
The Dramatic Works of Richard Brome, 3 vols. (London: John Pearson, 1873)
Bruno, Giordano, *Cause, Principle and Unity; And Essays on Magic*, ed. and trans. Robert de Lucca and Richard J. Blackwell (Cambridge: Cambridge University Press, 1998)
Bryson, Bill, *Shakespeare: The World as a Stage* (London: Harper Perennial, 2008)
The Works of Thomas Campion, ed. Walter R. Davis (New York: Norton, 1970)
Burrow, Colin, *Shakepeare and Classical Antiquity* (Oxford: Oxford University Press, 2013)
Caius, John, *Of English Dogges* (London, 1576)
Carroll, William C., *Fat King, Lean Beggar: Representations of Poverty in the Age of Shakespeare* (Ithaca: Cornell University Press, 1996)
Cassirer Ernst, Kristeller, Paul Oscar and Randall, John Herman Jr. (eds), *The Renaissance Philosophy of Man* (Chicago: The University of Chicago Press, 1948)
Cavell, Stanley, *Disowning Knowledge in Seven Plays of Shakespeare*, updated edition (Cambridge: Cambridge University Press, 2003)
Coates, Peter, *Nature: Western Attitudes since Ancient Times* (Cambridge: Polity, 1998)
Collingwood, R. G., *The Idea of Nature* (London: Oxford University Press, 1945)
Collinson, Patrick, 'The Monarchical Republic of Queen Elizabeth I', in *Elizabethan Essays* (London: HambledonPress, 1994), pp. 31–57
Cooper, Helen, *Pastoral: Mediaeval into Renaissance* (Ipswich: D. S. Brewer, 1977)
Shakespeare and the Medieval World (London: Bloomsbury, 2010)
Copenhaver, Brian P., and Schmitt, Charles B., *Renaissance Philosophy* (Oxford: Oxford University Press, 1992)
Cormack, Bradin, *A Power to Do Justice: Jurisdiction, English Literature, and the Rise of the Common Law, 1509–1625* (Chicago: The University of Chicago Press, 2007)
Cummings, Brian, *Mortal Thoughts: Religion, Secularity and Identity in Shakespeare and Early Modern Culture* (Oxford: Oxford University Press, 2013)

Danby, John F., *Shakespeare's Doctrine of Nature: A Study of King Lear* (London: Faber and Faber, 1949)

Davis, Philip, *Shakespeare Thinking* (London: Continuum, 2007)

Debus, Allen G., *Man and Nature in the Renaissance* (Cambridge: Cambridge University Press, 1978)

de Grazia, Margreta, 'The Ideology of Superfluous Things: King Lear as Period Piece', in Margreta de Grazia, Maureen Quilligan and Peter Stallybrass (eds.), *Subject and Object in Renaissance Culture* (Cambridge: Cambridge University Press, 1996)

The Dramatic Works of Thomas Dekker, ed. Fredson Bowers, 4 vols. (Cambridge: Cambridge University Press, 1953–61)

Derrida, Jacques, *The Animal that I Therefore Am*, ed. Marie-Louise Mallet, trans. David Wills (New York: Fordham University Press, 2008)

The Beast & the Sovereign, 2 vols., ed. Michel Lisse, Marie-Louise Mallet and Ginette Michaud, trans. Geoffrey Bennington (Chicago: University of Chicago Press, 2009–11)

Of Grammatology, trans. Gayatri Spivak (Baltimore: Johns Hopkins University Press, 1976)

'Plato's Pharmacy', in *Dessimination*, trans. Barbara Johnson (1981; London: Bloomsbury, 2004)

Donaldson, Ian, *Ben Jonson: A Life* (Oxford: Oxford University Press, 2011)

The Poems of John Donne, ed. Robin Robbins, 2 vols. (Harlow: Longman, 2008)

Selected Prose, ed. Evelyn Simpson, Helen Gardner and Timothy Healy (Oxford: Clarendon Press, 1967)

The Sermons of John Donne, ed. George R. Potter and Evelyn Simpson, 10 vols. (Berkeley: University of California Press, 1953–62)

Egan, Gabriel, *Green Shakespeare: From Ecopolitics to Ecocriticism* (Abingdon: Routledge, 2006)

Eliot, George, *Middlemarch*, ed. David Carroll (Oxford: Clarendon Press, 1986)

Eliot, T. S., 'Shakespeare and the Stoicism of Seneca', in *Selected Essays*, 3rd ed. (London: Faber and Faber, 1951)

Elizabeth I, *Collected Works*, ed. Leah S. Marcus, Janel Mueller, and Mary Beth Rose (Chicago: The University of Chicago Press, 2000)

Empson, William, *Seven Types of Ambiguity* (1930; London: Hogarth Press, 1991)

The Colloquies of Erasmus, trans. Craig R. Thompson (Chicago: University of Chicago Press, 1965)

Estok, Simon C., *Ecocriticism and Shakespeare: Reading Ecophobia* (New York: Palgrave Macmillan, 2011)

Ficino, Marsilio, *Commentary on Plato's Symposium on Love*, trans. Sears Jayne (Woodstock, CT: Spring Publications, 1985)

Platonic Theology, trans. Michael J. B. Allen with John Warden, ed. James Hankins with William Bowen, 6 vols. (Cambridge, MA: Harvard University Press, 2001–)

Fitzpatrick, Joan, *Food in Shakespeare: Early Modern Dietaries and the Plays* (Farnham: Ashgate, 2007)

Fletcher, Angus, *Time, Space, and Motion in the Age of Shakespeare* (Cambridge, MA: Harvard University Press, 2007)

Ford, John, *'Tis Pity She's a Whore and Other Plays*, ed. Marion Lomax (Oxford: Oxford University Press, 1995)

Foucault, Michel, *The Order of Things: An Archaeology of the Human Sciences* (London: Tavistock Publications, 1970)

Fowler, Alastair, *Renaissance Realism: Narrative Images in Literature and Art* (Oxford: Oxford University Press, 2003)

Frye, Northrop, *Anatomy of Criticism: Four Essays* (1957; Princeton: Princeton University Press, 2000)

Fudge, Erica, *Brutal Reasoning: Animals, Rationality, and Humanity in Early Modern England* (Ithaca: Cornell University Press, 2006)

Stephen Gaukroger, *The Emergence of a Scientific Culture: Science and the Shaping of Modernity 1210–1685* (Oxford: Oxford University Press, 2006)

Gilman, Ernest B., *Plague Writing in Early Modern England* (Chicago: University of Chicago Press, 2009)

Goldstein, David B., *Eating and Ethics in Shakespeare's England* (Cambridge: Cambridge University Press, 2013)

The Poetical Works of Gray and Collins, ed. Austin Lane Poole (London: Oxford University Press, 1919)

Greenblatt, Stephen, *Shakespeare's Freedom* (Chicago: The University of Chicago Press, 2010)

Will in the World: How Shakespeare Became Shakespeare (London: Jonathan Cape, 2004)

Gunn, Thom, *Boss Cupid* (London: Faber, 2000)

Haraway, Donna, *When Species Meet* (Minneapolis: University of Minnesota Press, 2007)

Harris, Anthony, *Night's Black Agents: Witchcraft and Magic in Seventeenth-Century English Drama* (Manchester: Manchester University Press, 1980)

Harris, Victor, *All Coherence Gone: A Study of the Seventeenth-Century Controversy over Disorder and Decay in the Universe* (London: Frank Cass, 1949)

Harrison, Robert Pogue, *The Dominion of the Dead* (Chicago: The University of Chicago Press, 2003)

Forests: The Shadow of Civilization (Chicago: The University of Chicago Press, 1992)

Haydn, Hiram, *The Counter-Renaissance* (1950; New York: Grove Press, 1960)

The English Poems of George Herbert, ed. Helen Wilcox (Cambridge: Cambridge University Press, 2007)

Hill, Geoffrey, 'Some Observations on Cymbeline', in *Collected Critical Writings*, ed. Kenneth Haynes (Oxford: Oxford University Press, 2008)

Höfele, Andreas, *Stage, Stake and Scaffold: Humans and Animals in Shakespeare's Theatre* (Oxford: Oxford University Press, 2011)

Hooker, Richard, *Of the Laws of Ecclesiastical Polity: Preface, Book I, Book VIII*, ed. Arthur Stephen McGrade (Cambridge: Cambridge University Press, 1989)

Hooper, Wilfrid, 'The Tudor Sumptuary Laws', *The English Historical Review*, Vol. 30, No. 119 (Jul., 1915): 433–449

Hoskins, W. G., *The Making of the English Landscape* (1955; Toller Fratrum: Little Toller Books, 2013)

'The Rebuilding of Rural England, 1570–1640', *Past and Present* 4 (1953), 44–59

Hughes, Ted, *Collected Poems*, ed. Paul Keegan (London: Faber & Faber, 2003)

Jackson, Ken, and Marotti, Arthur F., 'The Turn to Religion in Early Modern English Studies', *Criticism* 46 (2004): 167–90

Jackson, MacD. P., 'Spurio and the Date of All's Well That Ends Well', *Notes and Queries* 48 (2001), 299

Johnson on Shakespeare, ed. Walter Raleigh (London: Oxford University Press, 1908)

The Cambridge Edition of the Works of Ben Jonson, ed. David Bevington, Martin Butler and Ian Donaldson, 7 vols. (Cambridge: Cambridge University Press, 2012)

Kantorowicz, E. H., *The King's Two Bodies: A Study in Mediaeval Political Theology* (Princeton: Princeton University Press, 1957)

Kastan, David Scott, *A Will to Believe: Shakespeare and Religion* (Oxford: Oxford University Press, 2014)

Kendall, R. T., *Calvin and English Calvinism to 1649* (Oxford: Oxford University Press, 1979)

Kermode, Frank, *Shakespeare's Language* (London: Allen Lane, 2000)

Kerrigan, John, *Archipelagic English: Literature, History and Politics 1603–1707* (Oxford: Oxford University Press, 2008)

Kerrigan, William, and Braden, Gordon, *The Idea of the Renaissance* (Baltimore: Johns Hopkins University Press, 1989)

Krieger, Elliot, *A Marxist Study of Shakespeare's Comedies* (London: Macmillan, 1979)

Lane, Belden C., 'Spirituality as the Performance of Desire: Calvin on the World as the Theatre of God's Glory', *Spiritus* 1 (2001): 1–30

Latour, Bruno, *We Have Never Been Modern*, trans. Catherine Porter (Cambridge, MA: Harvard University Press, 1993)

Lewis, C. S., *The Discarded Image: An Introduction to Medieval and Renaissance Literature* (Cambridge: Cambridge University Press, 1964)

Studies in Words, 2nd edition (Cambridge: Cambridge University Press, 1967)

Lovejoy, A. O., *The Great Chain of Being* (Cambridge, MA: Harvard University Press, 1964)

Mabey, Richard, *Nature Cure* (London: Chatto and Windus, 2005)

MacFaul, Tom, *Male Friendship in Shakespeare and his Contemporaries* (Cambridge: Cambridge University Press, 2007)

Poetry and Paternity in Renaissance England: Sidney, Spenser, Shakespeare, Donne and Jonson (Cambridge: Cambridge University Press 2010)

Problem Fathers in Shakespeare and Renaissance Drama (Cambridge: Cambridge University Press, 2012)

Maquerlot, Jean-Pierre, *Shakespeare and the Mannerist Tradition: A Reading of Five Problem Plays* (Cambridge: Cambridge University Press, 1995)
Marlowe, Christopher, *Doctor Faustus: A- and B-Texts (1604, 1616)*, ed. David Bevington and Eric Rasmussen (Manchester: Manchester University Press, 1993)
Maus, Katherine Eisaman, *Being and Having in Shakespeare* (Oxford: Oxford University Press, 2013)
McAdam, Ian, *Magic and Masculinity in Early Modern English Drama* (Pittsburgh: Duquesne University Press, 2009)
McCabe, Richard A., *Incest, Drama and Nature's Law, 1550–1700* (Cambridge: Cambridge University Press, 1993)
McCoy, Richard C., *Faith in Shakespeare* (Oxford: Oxford University Press, 2013)
McDonald, Russ, *Shakespeare's Late Style* (Cambridge: Cambridge University Press, 2006)
McRae, Andrew, *God Speed the Plough: The Representation of Agrarian England, 1500–1660* (Cambridge: Cambridge University Press, 1996)
McCulloch, Diarmaid, *The Reformation* (London: Viking, 2004)
MacIntyre, Alasdair, *Dependent Rational Animals: Why Human Beings Need the Virtues* (London: Duckworth, 1999)
'Epistemological Crises, Dramatic Narrative and the Philosophy of Science', in *The Tasks of Philosophy: Selected Essays Volume 1* (Cambridge: Cambridge University Press, 2006)
McKibben, Bill, *Eaarth: Making a Life on a Tough New Planet* (New York: St Martin's Press, 2010)
Middleton, Thomas, *The Collected Works*, ed. Gary Taylor and John Lavagnino (Oxford: Oxford University Press, 2007)
Midgley, Mary, *Are You an Illusion?* (Durham: Acumen, 2014)
(ed.) *Earthy Realism: The Meaning of Gaia*, ed. Mary Midgley (Exeter: Societas, 2007)
Milton, John, *The Complete Shorter Poems*, ed. John Carey, 2nd edition (London: Longman, 1997)
Paradise Lost, ed. Alastair Fowler, 2nd edition (London: Longman, 1997)
Morton, Timothy, *The Ecological Thought* (Cambridge, MA: Harvard University Press, 2010)
Ecology without Nature: Rethinking Environmental Aesthetics (Cambridge, MA: Harvard University Press, 2009)
Norbrook, David, '"What Care These Roarers for the Name of King": Language and Utopia in The Tempest', in Kiernan Ryan (ed.), *Shakespeare: The Last Plays* (Harlow: Longman, 1999)
Nuttall, A. D., *The Alternative Trinity: Gnostic Heresy in Marlowe, Milton, and Blake* (Oxford: Clarendon Press, 1998)
Shakespeare the Thinker (New Haven: Yale University Press, 2007)
Two Concepts of Allegory: A Study of Shakespeare's The Tempest and the Logic of Allegorical Expression (1967; New Haven: Yale University Press, 2007)

Orlin, Lena Cowen, *Locating Privacy in Tudor London* (Oxford: Oxford University Press, 2007)

Palfrey, Simon, *Late Shakespeare: A New World of Words* (Oxford: Oxford University Press, 1997)

Poor Tom: Living "King Lear" (Chicago: University of Chicago Press, 2014)

and Stern, Tiffany, *Shakespeare in Parts* (Oxford: Oxford University Press, 2007)

Shakespeare's Possible Worlds (Cambridge: Cambridge University Press, 2014)

Panofsky, Erwin, *Studies in Iconology: Humanistic Themes in the Art of the Renaissance* (New York: Oxford University Press, 1939)

Park, Katherine, *Secrets of Women: Gender, Generation, and the Origins of Human Dissection* (New York: Zone Books, 2006)

Parker, Geoffrey, *Global Crisis: War, Climate Change and Catastrophe in the Seventeenth Century* (New Haven: Yale University Press, 2013)

Paster, Gail Kern, *Humoring the Body: Emotions and the Shakespearean Stage* (Chicago: University of Chicago Press, 2004)

Pitcher, John, 'Names in Cymbeline', *Essays in Criticism* 43 (1993): 1–16

Plato, *The Complete Works*, ed. John M. Cooper (Indianapolis: Hackett Publishing, 1997)

Poole, Kristen, *Supernatural Environments in Shakespeare's England: Spaces of Demonism, Divinity and Drama* (Cambridge: Cambridge University Press, 2011)

Rabkin, Norman, *Shakespeare and the Problem of Meaning* (Chicago: The University of Chicago Press, 1981)

Ratcliffe, Sophie, *On Sympathy* (Oxford: Oxford University Press, 2008)

Richards, John F., *The Unending Frontier: An Environmental History of the Early Modern World* (Berkeley: University of California Press, 2005)

Roberts, Jeanne Addison, *The Shakespearean Wild: Geography, Genus, and Gender* (Lincoln, NE: University of Nebraska Press, 1991)

Robinson, Marilynne, *Gilead* (London: Virago, 2005)

Rossiter, A. P., *Angel with Horns: Fifteen Lectures on Shakespeare* (1961; Harlow: Longman, 1989)

Rowley, William, Dekker, Thomas, and Ford, John, *The Witch of Edmonton*, ed. Peter Corbin and Douglas Sedge (Manchester: Manchester University Press, 1999)

Rowse, A. L., *The Expansion of Elizabethan England* (London: Macmillan, 1995)

Sagar, Keith, *Literature and the Crime against Nature: From Homer to Hughes* (London: Chaucer Press, 2005)

Sanders, Wilbur, *The Winter's Tale* (Boston: Twayne, 1987)

Schoenfeld, Michael C., *Bodies and Selves in Early Modern England: Physiology and Inwardness in Spenser, Shakespeare, Herbert, and Milton* (Cambridge: Cambridge University Press, 1999)

Scott, Charlotte, *Shakespeare's Nature: From Cultivation to Culture* (Oxford: Oxford University Press, 2014)

John Sellars, *Stoicism* (Durham: Acumen, 2006)

Shannon, Laurie, *The Accommodated Animal: Cosmopolity in Shakespearean Locales* (Chicago: The University of Chicago Press, 2013)
Shell, Alison, *Shakespeare and Religion* (London: Methuen, 2010)
Shipman, Pat, *The Animal Connection: A New Perspective on What Makes Us Human* (London: Norton, 2011)
Sidney, Sir Philip, *An Apology for Poetry, or The Defence of Poesy*, ed. Geoffrey Shepherd (Manchester: Manchester University Press, 1965)
Skinner, Quentin, 'A Spurious Dating for All's Well that Ends Well,' *Notes and Queries* 60 (2013): 429–34
Soper, Kate, *What is Nature?: Culture, Politics and the Non-Human* (Oxford: Blackwell, 1995)
Spenser, Edmund, *The Faerie Queene*, ed. A. C. Hamilton, text ed. Hiroshi Yamashita and Toshiyuki Suzuki (Harlow: Longman, 2001).
Spurgeon, Caroline, *Shakespeare's Imagery and What It Tells Us* (Cambridge: Cambridge University Press, 1935)
Strier, Richard, *The Unrepentant Renaissance: From Petrarch to Shakespeare to Milton* (Chicago: The University of Chicago Press, 2011)
Targoff, Ramie, *Posthumous Love: Eros and the Afterlife in Renaissance England* (Chicago: University of Chicago Press, 2014)
Tawney, R. H., *Religion and the Rise of Capitalism: A Historical Study* (London: John Murray, 1926)
Tayler, Edward William, *Nature and Art in Renaissance Literature* (New York: Columbia University Press, 1964)
Telesio, Bernadino, *La Natura Secondo i suoi Princìpi*, ed. R. Bondì (Milan: Bompiani, 2009)
Thirsk, Joan, *Food in Early Modern England: Phases, Fads, Fashions 1500–1700* (London: Continuum, 2006)
Thomas, Keith, *Man and the Natural World: Changing Attitudes in England 1500–1800* (London: Allen Lane, 1983)
Tillyard, E.M.W., *The Elizabethan World Picture* (London: Chatto & Windus, 1943)
Trevelyan, Raleigh, *Sir Walter Raleigh* (London: Allen Lane, 2002)
Tromly, Fred B., *Fathers and Sons in Shakespeare: The Debt Never Promised* (Toronto: University of Toronto Press, 2010)
van Wyck Smith, M., 'John Donne's Metempsychosis', *RES* 24 (1973)
Walsham, Alexandra, *The Reformation of the Landscape: Religion, Identity, and Memory in Early Modern Britain and Ireland* (Oxford: Oxford University Press, 2011)
Wilders, John, *The Lost Garden: Shakespeare's History Plays* (London: Macmillan, 1978)
Williams, Raymond, *The Country and the City* (London: Chatto & Windus, 1973)
Keywords: A Vocabulary of Culture and Society, revised ed. (London: Flamingo, 1983)
Williams, Wes, *Monsters and their Meaning in Early Modern Culture: Mighty Magic* (Oxford: Oxford University Press, 2011)

Willis, Deborah, *Malevolent Nurture: Witch-Hunting and Maternal Power in Early Modern England* (Ithaca: Cornell University Press, 1995)
Wittgenstein, Ludwig, *Philosophical Investigations*, ed. P. M. S. Hacker and Joachim Schulte, trans. G. E. M. Anscombe, 4th edition (Oxford: Blackwell, 2009)
Wordsworth, William, *The Major Works*, ed. Stephen Gill, revised edition (Oxford: Oxford University Press, 2000)
Wrangham, Richard, *Catching Fire: How Cooking Made Us Human* (London: Profile Books, 2009)
Wyatt, Sir Thomas, *The Complete Poems*, ed. Ronald A. Rebholz (Harmondsworth: Penguin, 1978)

Index

Lightning Source UK Ltd.
Milton Keynes UK
UKHW020621170119
335706UK00010B/182/P

9 781107 543577